the EUROPEAN BUSINESS handbook 2002

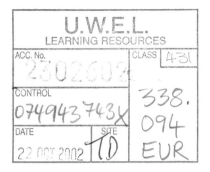

the
EUROPEAN
BUSINESS handbook
2002

CONSULTANT EDITOR: **ADAM JOLLY**

Published by
 Kogan Page

Recommended by

RECOMMENDED BY
INSTITUTE OF DIRECTORS

EULER
TRADE INDEMNITY

ROYAL &
SUNALLIANCE

jobcentreplus

THE WALL STREET JOURNAL EUROPE.   HILL & KNOWLTON

First edition published in 1993

This (ninth) edition published in 2002

Kogan Page Ltd
120 Pentonville Road
London N1 9JN
www.kogan-page.co.uk

© Kogan Page 2002

British Library Cataloguing in Publication Data

A CIP record for this book is available from the British Library.

ISBN 0 7494 3743 X

Typeset by JS Typesetting, Wellingborough, Northants.
Printed and bound in Great Britain by Thanet Press Ltd, Margate, Kent.

Currently owed £387,000!
He's more concerned about Tim's adding up.

"Whatever the **matter**, **grey** is the best choice"

Making the right choice is critical.

As one of the UK's leading commercial insurance companies, we set world-class standards in providing innovative professional and financial risk solutions.

All designed to thoroughly safeguard you and your company's financial stability now and in the future.

All built on a deep and thorough knowledge of business insurance.

To make the right choice with confidence, visit **www.profin.uk.royalsun.com** to discover Management Assurance – our essential portfolio of management insurance protection – safe in the knowledge that you've made a wise decision.

Pick our brains.

MEMBER

General Insurance
STANDARDS COUNCIL

ROYAL &
SUNALLIANCE

CONTENTS

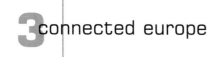
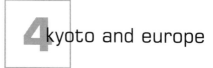

6 selling in europe

7 sources of funding

energy for the future

- **Competitive Prices**
  Clearly presented competitive prices

- **Service**
  Key Account Management and services

- **Coverage**
  National group with generation and supply resources

- **Contract Management & Billing**
  A fully integrated customer management system

- **Energy Supply**
  Electricity and gas for single sites and groups

- **Innovation**
  Contracts matched to your needs

Scottish Hydro-Electric

SOUTHERN
ELECTRIC

SWALEC

☰ Scottish and Southern Energy

Call our National Sales Office on

08457 210 220

or Fax us on

01256 304 269

Alex McWhirter, head of business enterprise at Yorkshire's regional development agency, explains how its £25m fund is going to work.

8 selecting a location

9 buying and selling european companies

10 the european company

We always take care of other people's money. Only this time our money is taking care of other people.

Milbury Community is a leading provider of health and community care for people with learning disabilities and other dependency needs. A full review by Duke Street Capital revealed a dedicated organisation with an excellent reputation and a first rate team of management and staff. However, we diagnosed that a lack of capital was hampering growth and immediately arranged further finance. This will enable Milbury to expand its residential homes across the country and continue to provide a positive lifestyle for more than 1000 people.

duke street capital

OUR CAPITAL. YOUR GAIN

Dukes Court, 32 Duke Street St James's, London SW1Y 6DF Tel: +44(0)20 7451 6600 Fax: +44 (0)20 7451 6601 mail@dukestreetcapital.com www.dukestreetcapital.com

Duke Street Capital III Limited, Duke Street Capital IV Limited and Duke Street Capital V Limited are regulated by FSA.

Jobcentre Plus is the new face of the public employment service in Britain. It is a new service committed to helping you fill your vacancies quickly and with the right people.

The Jobcentre Plus national network offers employers tailored recruitment solutions, using the latest call centre and internet technology. With over 1000 Jobcentres and Jobcentre Plus offices, we can find the right people when you need them.

For further information or to place a vacancy, contact Employer Direct on

0845 601 2001

A textphone service is available for people with speech or hearing impairments on
0845 601 2002

www.jobcentreplus.gov.uk

jobcentreplus

 *JobCentre*

Part of the Department for Work and Pensions

"Jobcentre Plus is the new face of the public employment service in Britain. It is a new service committed to helping you fill your vacancies quickly and with the right people.

In meeting these challenges, we will draw on the experiences and successes of the New Deals and other programmes to develop a service with greater flexibility, more use of personal advisers and a focus on the needs of both employers and individuals."

**Leigh Lewis,
Chief Executive, Jobcentre Plus**

In March 2000, the Prime Minister, Tony Blair announced the most ambitious reform of the welfare state since it began. The aim was to bring central government's employment and benefits agendas together to provide a more integrated service for jobseekers and employers.

Jobcentre Plus is all set to build on the technological improvements of the last few years, and the ongoing development of New Deal schemes. The aim is to put the needs of employers at the heart of the new service. Jobcentre Plus is already up and running in some 50 offices across the country. From April 2002, the other Jobcentres and social security offices will become part of the Jobcentre Plus network. Over the next few years there will be a rolling programme to convert offices to deliver the new enhanced service across the country. However, many of the improvements aimed at employers that are described below are already in place.

A personal, professional service

The improved vacancy-taking system is complemented by the introduction of two new local roles to give you the in-depth local knowledge you need to find the right people quickly.

- Local Account Managers are experts in the local labour market and in understanding employers' recruitment needs. They work with key local employers to agree a level of service, such as determining the need for tailored recruitment packages. They also work closely with Jobcentre Plus advisers to give them a greater understanding of your needs so we can better match the jobseekers we see with your requirements.

- Vacancy Service Managers are your personal named contact. Based locally in Jobcentre Plus offices, their aim is to ensure that all your vacancies are filled as swiftly and effectively as possible.

We are committed to building better relationships with you to help us understand your specific needs, and provide you with high quality and individually tailored support.

The way forward

Over the past year, we have also launched the new Employer Direct service. This new telephone service provides employers with a national service through a network of customer service centres. With dedicated customer service advisers and longer opening hours, we have made it easier for you to give us details of the posts you want to fill. All this is accessible by calling a single national number – **0845 601 2001**.

As well as modernising how we interact with employers, Jobcentre Plus will also bring you access to a much wider range of potential recruits, not just people claiming Jobseeker's Allowance. We will be using the latest technology to help you choose the right people in the shortest time.

At the heart of these developments is the internet based job bank which won the prestigious e-Business Website of the Year award for 2001. Now every

Jobcentre and Jobcentre Plus office will have access to every vacancy held across Britain, as well as to jobseekers and employers across Europe.

In early 2001 all these vacancies went online, becoming accessible to jobseekers 24 hours a day on the internet through the job bank. With around 350,000 jobs this is one of the world's largest internet recruitment facilities. The job bank also holds details of over 500,000 learning opportunities and 600 career profiles. Jobseekers will be able to search the job bank from anywhere with internet access; from home, from cyber-cafes, from public libraries and technology centres.

In addition, Jobpoints – public access touch screen kiosks – have replaced traditional vacancy display boards in Jobcentres. As with the internet, the Jobpoint will guide the user through a simple search process to produce a manageable selection of vacancies which match their specific needs and print out the vacancy details. The Jobpoint project was also recognised at the Computing 2001 Awards for Excellence by scooping the award for Most Innovative e-Business Project of the Year. Through Jobpoints, your jobs are already accessible in locations outside Jobcentre Plus offices, such as local supermarkets. Plans are underway to extend this access over the coming months.

The European angle

Improvements have also changed the way that other existing services are delivered, for example the European Employment Services (EURES) network.

The EURES network is a system that exists to support labour mobility between all European and Economic Area (EEA) member states, by exchanging vacancies, applications for work and information on living and working conditions. Although EURES has been operational for a number of years, by linking it to the job bank we have made European vacancies accessible to many more jobseekers and employers. Jobseekers from the EEA visit the site to view international vacancies, of which there is an average stock of around 25,000 along with information on living and working conditions.

The EURES internet site will soon offer a complete package comprising job vacancies, CV database, information on living and working conditions, information on skills surpluses and skills shortages by country and by region.

UK employers seeking to recruit from elsewhere in Europe should notify their vacancies to Employer Direct, who can arrange for vacancy details to be shown on the EURES system.

All this means that your jobs will be seen by many more people than ever before. So whether you want to fill one or one thousand vacancies, the new Jobcentre Plus business aims to offer you the service you need to find the right person for your organisation.

Our recruitment professionals will ensure you get the best attention. They will make sure that you will receive an individual service and that your recruitment process runs smoothly and efficiently. Our Jobcentre Plus teams are experts in the local labour market and understand the needs of your business.

In addition to all of these innovations, we have launched the Employers' Charter detailing the levels of service you can expect from Jobcentre Plus. This will be the basis of our unique central government business-to-business measurement as Jobcentre Plus goes forward.

If you have any queries about Jobcentre Plus and how we can meet your recruitment needs, contact Employer Direct on **0845 601 2001** or speak to your Local Account Manager or Vacancy Service Manager.

Safety Management in the European Community

As you, more than likely, already know, much of Britain's health and safety law has originated in Europe in recent years. Any proposals from the European Commission, agreed by the Member States, have to be implemented into UK domestic law and most of it is based on the principle of 'risk assessment'.

The technical application of 'risk management' is theoretically the same throughout the Community, in that, regardless of the size or nature of the organisation, the Board (or other 'guiding mind') is legally responsible for setting policy; organising and training the workforce; planning and implementation; measuring and reviewing performance and under normal circumstances arranging for the systems to be independently audited, on a regular basis.

Most of you will already be accustomed to the general principles of:

- Appointing 'Competent' health and safety assistance
- Risk assessment
- Risk reduction
- Risk monitoring
- Providing appropriate 'Information, Instruction, Training and Supervision'
- Health surveillance
- Worker consultation and liaison with other interested parties
- Setting up emergency procedures

but you may not be aware of how these principles are developed, worked and enforced in the rest of the Community, or the fact that the Commission has established a European Safety Agency, based in Bilbao, Spain, to "encourage improvements in the working environment by providing Community bodies, the Member States and those involved in safety and health at work with technical, scientific and economic information of use in the field of safety and health at work".

A recent information project, entitled "The State of Occupational Safety and Health (OSH) in the European Union (EU) – Pilot Study" has drawn on data supplied by each of the 'Focal Points (i.e. in the UK the Health and Safety Commission and its operating arm, the Executive – HSC/E)' to provide an overview of the state of play and the need for the development of additional preventive actions to control emerging risks. In short, the principle risks are those arising from:

- Noise and/or vibration
- Repetitive movement
- Strenuous working posture/handling of heavy loads and/or chemicals
- Adverse psycho-social working conditions (e.g. high speed or monotonous work, workplace violence and stress etc.)

The most frequently identified sectors at risk were firstly, by far, construction, followed by metal fabrication, agriculture, healthcare and food and beverage manufacture, in that order. These emerging risks and the sectors highlighted are being given priority treatment, as part of the ongoing work programme of the Agency, with the additional allocation of a 5 million euro SME accident prevention programme. The enlargement process must surely affect these findings and will, no doubt, highlight the comparatively poor state of safety and health in the candidate countries, although preparatory work is already underway to develop tripartite Focal Points, implement national strategy frameworks and train labour inspectors to raise standards.

The 'problem' is that national provisions for health and safety demonstrate a considerable gap between countries, particularly between those with a history of such provision and those beginning to install the infrastructures needed. Some of Europe has highly bureaucratic and decentralised structures, with legislation and regulation emanating from regional or federal legislatures. Further, some countries, like Germany, are classified as having 'dual' systems, reflecting shared responsibilities for implementing legislation between regional trade supervisory bodies and technical inspectorates of professional insurance associations. In those organisations with a works council or statutorily elected employees' representative body, legally guaranteed participation in safety and health in the workplace exists, together with a place on the occupational safety and health committee. The 'competent' safety 'experts' are also certified to legally required standards.

By comparison, the United Kingdom structures emanate from a centralised and integrated but more voluntaristic system. This means that a functional (i.e. goal-setting) as opposed to prescriptive (i.e. detailed technical specification) approach is adopted, leading to a higher level of 'ownership' at corporate level. There are (currently) no statutory works councils and there is no legally required level of training for the 'competent person(s)', which the employer has a duty to appoint. Although European Directives aim to harmonise the technical standards in safety and health, national models and identities clearly remain.

For instance, in Spain, the National Insurance (NI) system is utilised for the stage one implementation of safety 'projects', the equivalent of a combined Initial Status (or gap) Review, 'generic' Risk Assessment and the training of a nominated 'co-ordinator' from within the organisations' workforce. All employers are able to nominate a 'Mutua' to pay their additional NI contributions, which are, in turn, used to pay compensation to the victims of occupational accidents, or their dependants. The 'Mutuas' are generally industry specific, although the final choice lies with the contributing organisation, providing the initial 'project(s)' in accordance with a statutory scale of charges relating to the risk level and size of organisation, in terms of number of employees. The only persons certified, by the Regional Government, to undertake these projects are first-degree holders who have undertaken a 600-hour post-graduate safety 'experts' course, with an additional 150-hour specialism in either workplace safety, psycho-sociology and ergonomics or occupational hygiene. For safety consultancies to operate they too must be certified, after demonstrating the ability to undertake industry specific expertise, in each of three specialisms mentioned above.

Unfortunately, this highly bureaucratic and regulated system is in its infancy and the technical 'experts' have very little practical experience. Accordingly, in Spain and other European countries, having no track record, the 'problem' becomes one of technical over-regulation, instead of relying on the organisation to control its own risks, using standard management systems. It would appear, therefore, that although each country has developed its individual method of adopting safety and health principles, the dichotomy lies at the point of intervention, at either the workface (e.g. machine guarding, safety barriers etc.) or management (e.g. policy, evaluation and control mechanisms etc.) levels.

Either way, for any British company considering expanding or moving into the European market place, the moral of the story is that, if you are delivering a 'reasonable' level of safety now you will have nothing to worry about, as far as standards go (with the possible exception of health surveillance measures which are generally higher on the continent) but you will need to get 'competent advice' from an organisation or individual that can guide you through the necessary bureaucracy and paperwork.

Article written by:

Malcolm Tullett, BA(Hons), MIIRSM, MIFireE
Managing Director of I.R.M. (UK) Ltd.

the car in front is a

What does 'hybrid' mean?

61.4 mpg around town.*
The revolutionary petrol and electric Prius.

THE NEW TOYOTA PRIUS FROM £16,430

The Toyota Prius doesn't look like a radical departure from the norm, does it? But beneath its smooth and relatively conventional lines is one of the most revolutionary developments yet in the drive towards cleaner motoring. It's the world's first hybrid battery/petrol family car, and it's a breath of fresh air for us all.

5 YEAR/60,000 MILE WARRANTY

- Full Map Satellite Navigation†
- Driver & Passenger Airbags
- ABS with Electronic Brake Distribution
- Electric Windows
- Climate Control Air Conditioning
- Single CD Player
- Alloy Wheels

DEALER NAME
Anystreet, Anytown
Telephone: 01234 56789
www.toyota.co.uk/dealername

- **Contract Hire**
- **Leasing**
- **Motability**
- **Service**
- **Bodyshop**
- **Parts**

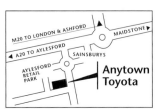

Model and specification shown Toyota Prius Hybrid £16,430 on the road. Price includes VAT, delivery charge, number plates, 12 months vehicle excise duty and £25 first registration fee. †Optional extra. *Fuel economy (93/116/EEC). Urban 61.4mpg–4.6L/100km, Extra urban 55.4mpg–5.1L/100km, combined 57.6mpg–4.9L/100km.

INTRODUCTION

We all want to see successful economies in Europe. The member states of the European Union declared at the Lisbon summit in 2000 that they wanted to see the EU become the most dynamic, competitive, sustainable knowledge-based economy in the world. These are fine words, but will it happen? This book sets out to answer that question, and to give practical advice on expanding businesses in Europe.

The first section looks at the economic prospects for high growth. In the short term, the prospects are clearly not good, but in the longer term, factors other than the business cycle will come into play. Above all, businesses need to be left free to get on with their job, without burdensome regulations. There has been progress in some countries, and in November 2001 the Mandelkern Report made a major contribution to the debate on better regulation within the EU. The Commission responded positively, but it is too early yet to say how much real change will come of this initiative.

Business could also benefit from reforms to financial markets. The Lamfalussy proposals to speed up reforms have at last gained the approval of the European Parliament (in February 2002), but again business will have to wait and see whether we will indeed see an integrated securities and risk capital market by 2003, as planned. Whether the liberalisation of energy and communications markets will be achieved quickly also hangs in the balance. Free markets are good markets, but sometimes they can be hard to achieve.

The enlargement of the EU to the East will be a major challenge. In theory, up to ten countries could join within the next three years, but the financial and institutional strains, both on the existing EU and on the new members, will be considerable.

The book then turns to three other major departures in the conduct of business: the network economy, climate change and the euro. Some technology-based businesses have gone from boom to bust, but the rate of change in the network economy is not slowing. As the large businesses with well-established brands and deep pockets get more involved, we should see a new wave of change. The regulatory environment which the EU creates will be critical to its attraction as a location for this type of business.

The EU has taken upon itself a heavy burden in meeting climate change targets. The burden will largely fall on business: business has to be ready both for new taxes and for new restrictions on its activities.

The euro has two major impacts on businesses. Firstly, there will be increased price transparency within the 12 member countries in the euro zone: charging different prices to, for example, German and Italian consumers will be difficult. Secondly, it fundamentally alters the parameters of economic management. In their day-to-day operations, businesses may not think much about monetary and fiscal policies: but they will soon notice if movements in the economic cycle become more pronounced, or different countries in which they operate react differently to external economic developments, as a consequence of the single currency.

Corporate mergers and acquisitions may have slackened off in the past year, but they have not stopped, and could well pick up. Developments in the tax and regulatory environment within the EU will influence the deals which are done. Relaxations in both German and UK law on the taxation of corporate capital gains, for example, will encourage the market. Competition law may either help or hinder progress, depending on how it develops.

The arrival of the European company will be a significant milestone. After 30 years of negotiation, a statute was agreed in 2001. It is designed to create a more efficient structure for businesses operating across the EU, which should be available from 2004.

Despite all of these potentially very significant developments, labour market rigidities remain a serious concern for businesses. If the labour market could become more de-regulated, that would be a tremendous boost for European business. But this is the biggest 'if' of all.

This book highlights recent and forthcoming changes in Europe's competitive performance and assesses the extent to which they can benefit high-growth enterprises. The IoD is grateful to all the contributors, who have given so freely of their expertise and experience.

George Cox
Director General
Institute of Directors

CIMA - The Complete Solution

Representing over 54,000 members and 73,000 students in all business sectors worldwide, CIMA (The Chartered Institute of Management Accountants) is recognised as *the* financial qualification for business.

Key to CIMA's success is ensuring that business relevance is at the heart of everything we do. Driven by research into the business trends of today and tomorrow, our syllabus is constantly revised and updated. CIMA offers, quite simply, the most practical financial training for business.

What makes CIMA unique is our focus on management. Our members are strategists providing timely and accurate financial information, and making the decisions that drive their businesses forward. They have the skills and knowledge to succeed in the global marketplace despite intense competition.

Flexibility is CIMA's strength. Our global network provides a high standard of financial training in 156 countries – and we're rapidly expanding into new territories. Wherever they train, CIMA students follow an identical syllabus, and our members have the expertise and skills needed to work effectively in any country and any business sector.

The CIMA syllabus includes business, financial and information strategy for management accounting. Starting with financial and management accountancy fundamentals, students then develop key management competencies, and complete their studies with a strategic management accounting case study.

Practical experience is viewed as essential by CIMA; that's what makes the qualification so relevant. To become a CIMA member requires three years complimentary experience in addition to successfully completing the syllabus.

Business Resources
Keeping abreast of business issues does not end at CIMA membership and CIMA recognises and supports the need for continued professional development. As part of its drive for life-long learning, CIMA provides a range of products and services available to businesses.

CIMA Publishing
Covering everything from benchmarking and financial reporting through to marketing and supply chain management, CIMA Publishing's books and CD Roms will ensure your business is kept informed of the key issues.

As a specialist provider of business information, supplying innovative business guides, research reports and study materials, CIMA Publishing can assist in the development of business libraries and resource centres.

CIMA Mastercourses
Used by over 2,000 organisations, CIMA's programme of short courses comprises more than 400 quality seminars and workshops. Topics covered include the latest advances in management accounting and corporate strategy, financial management, commercial decision making, updates on accounting techniques, IT, personal and management skills. CIMA Mastercourses are available through the scheduled open-access programme or can be tailored to your organisation's needs, and held on your company's premises. The CourseMaster corporate discount scheme offers a cost-effective way to show commitment to training; points collected can be used to claim a discount on any open-access or in-company training course.

Business Events
CIMA hosts a range of forums, seminars, conferences and debates around the world to discuss key business issues. Speakers are sourced from a wide variety of organisations and the events provide networking opportunities and assistance with career development.

Financial Management and CIMA Insider
Published 11 times a year, these professional magazines explore all the latest issues affecting accountants, financial managers and the wider business community.

Training CIMA Students
Developing a career and training go hand in hand, but time pressures can make committing to both difficult. Training Through Partnership is a scheme aimed at helping organisations support CIMA students. A team of experienced managers is available to offer assessment and advice on the development of an integrated training programme. By meeting the CIMA Training Through Partnership Quality Standards you will benefit from an established communication link to CIMA and publicity as a CIMA Quality Partner – not to mention well-trained CIMA qualified professionals.

Directory of Opportunities
Organisations with vacancies that involve joining a CIMA training scheme can advertise free in CIMA's Directory of Opportunities, a continually updated vacancy list available on the CIMA website.

Contact CIMA
For details of any of the products or services mentioned above, visit the website on **www.cimaglobal.com**, or send

Your enquiries about the qualification to
student.services@cimaglobal.com

Publishing enquiries to
publishing.sales@cimaglobal.com

Mastercourses enquiries to
mastercourses@cimaglobal.com

Financial Management and Insider enquiries to
financialmanagement@cimaglobal.com

All other enquiries to
marketing@cimaglobal.com

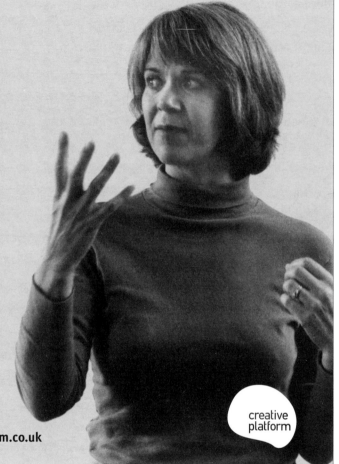

Part 1
Europe's Enterprise Model

ENTREPRENEURSHIP: DRIVING A COMPETITIVE EUROPE

An economically healthy and competitive Europe is inextricably linked to entrepreneurial health and high-growth companies. Employment boosts the economy; entrepreneurial activity boosts employment. However, Europe does not have enough entrepreneurs or high-growth companies and European legislators do little to encourage entrepreneurship. Suitable and accessible funding, taxation, burdensome social charges, incumbent bureaucracy and intolerance of failure are just some of the obstacles facing European entrepreneurs and inhibiting growth, says Nikki Walker at GrowthPlus.

In March 2000, during the European Council Summit in Lisbon, EU leaders established a new target for Europe: that the European Union should become the most competitive economy in the world. Just over a year later, European Commissioner Erkki Liikanen, responsible for Enterprise and the Information Society, remarked at the UNICE Conference for SMEs in May 2001, 'To achieve the Lisbon goal, we must use the full potential of entrepreneurship. Europe will never be really competitive as long as we are less entrepreneurial than our competitors.'

He added that it was essential not only that enterprise issues continue to remain high on the political agenda, but also that 'we pursue the necessary reforms with urgency and determination'.

Entrepreneurs leading high-growth companies and belonging to the GrowthPlus network can only agree with him. If Europe is to become the most competitive economy in the world, it needs to nurture the creation of new, innovative businesses and allow them to flourish, according to GrowthPlus president, Leendert Bikker. To help European legislators and policy-makers focus on the areas that most urgently need improving, GrowthPlus and Andersen conduct an annual benchmark analysing the tax and legal framework surrounding funding, people and the general business environment. The issues studied are those identified by high-growth entrepreneurs (members of the GrowthPlus association) as most affecting entrepreneurial activity, innovation and growth.

Funding growth

Vital to stimulating new and innovative business in Europe is access to finance. Capital of the right type and in sufficient quantity is critical if entrepreneurs are to invest in the physical, human and intellectual resources needed to exploit new opportunities. For start-ups and early stage companies, risk capital (from families, business angels and venture capitalists) is crucial while more mature fast-growth companies rely on retained earnings and, increasingly, on the stock market.

Greater entrepreneurial activity and growth could be stimulated in Europe if special tax regimes were applied to attract either private investors/business angels or venture capital funds to invest in growth companies. Similarly, tax incentives should be provided to encourage internal funding, in the form of retained earnings, or investment in research and development. It is apparent from the GrowthPlus/ Andersen benchmark 'Not Just Peanuts: Stimulating an Entrepreneur-Friendly Europe' that legislation in half of the countries analysed (Belgium, Germany, Italy, Sweden and the United States) does not provide for any tax incentives for private investors investing in growth companies (besides regular tax treatment) or for significant tax incentives for venture capital funds. Furthermore, neither a lower tax rate for retained earnings nor additional tax incentives for R&D expenses (besides full deductibility in the first year) are available in these countries. Clearly, reform of taxation with regard to external or internal funding would improve conditions for entrepreneurial growth within these countries.

Attracting the right people

In modern, knowledge-driven economies, entrepreneurs succeed because they recruit, retain and develop high-calibre people who can utilise financial, intellectual and technological resources to exploit new opportunities. In early stages of growth, when funds are limited, entrepreneurs look for innovative ways to remunerate staff, such as stock option and incentive-based schemes, but European taxation often negates the value of such programmes. In addition, entrepreneurs use employee share ownership programmes (ESOPs) as a key management tool to create an entrepreneurial spirit throughout their company.

However, only three of the countries analysed in the 'Not Just Peanuts' report (Italy, Belgium and the United Kingdom) provide a favourable regime for share and stock option plans, with a potential exemption of social security charges on the benefit that employees realise from stock options. Conversely, in Sweden the employee is heavily penalised. The profit derived by individuals on the exercise of stock options is taxed in this country at the individual's marginal tax rate (as much as 53–59 per cent).

While entrepreneurs consider stock options as a growth tool and an alternative to large salaries, many governments tax the options as income rather than capital and subject them to social security charges. Another problem is that each EU country taxes stock options in a different way, which can have a negative effect on a mobile workforce or companies wishing to expand their businesses across national borders.

Bureaucracy that facilitates entrepreneurship

More entrepreneurs willing to create new businesses and take risks are key to Europe's economy and its ability to compete globally. An overall business environment that stimulates entrepreneurship from start-up to growth (and one that tolerates failure) is therefore critical. Excessive costs and bureaucratic demands linked to setting up and running a new business, as well as high levels of tax on income and capital gains, often act as disincentives. Similarly, corporate and labour law regulations, together with social security charges, represent substantial burdens for growth businesses in many European countries.

In addition, the diversity across EU member states further complicates these issues. Corporate income tax rates range from 26 per cent in the United Kingdom to more than 40 per cent in Italy; capital gains tax from zero in Belgium to approximately 40 per cent in Sweden; social security charges (payable by the employer) differ from 4 per cent in the Netherlands to 45 per cent in France; costs for the foundation of a limited liability company range from €1.000 in the United Kingdom to €10.4000 in Italy; the time period necessary to fulfil all applicable legal requirements when registering a new company varies from one day in the United Kingdom to up to one month in Germany or Spain; wealth tax is applied in France,

Sweden, the Netherlands and Spain, but not in other countries. Successful entrepreneurs in Europe are known for their ability to expand their business beyond national frontiers. It is obvious, therefore, that harmonisation and cross-fertilisation of the legal, fiscal and social environment among EU member states would facilitate the continued development of high-growth companies and encourage more start-ups to expand across borders.

United Kingdom leading the way, Sweden lagging behind

Having analysed 19 issues that affect the ability of European entrepreneurs to grow their businesses, the 2001 edition of 'Not Just Peanuts: Stimulating an Entrepreneur-Friendly Europe' found the United Kingdom to provide conditions that most foster growth companies. The United Kingdom even out-ranked the United States. Close behind are Spain and the Netherlands, while Austria and Sweden appear to be doing the least (out of the 10 countries studied) to encourage growth companies.

If European governments were to modify existing legislation and greater harmonisation were to exist across member states, more entrepreneurial companies would start, grow and flourish. More risk takers would help secure the European Council's vision of Europe as the most competitive economy in the world.

Nikki Walker is director of communications at GrowthPlus, the pan-European association which brings together Europe's most dynamic, job-creating entrepreneurs to form a single voice for entrepreneurship in Europe. It aims to promote entrepreneurship throughout Europe and to advise policy-makers so as to improve the environment for growth companies. A full copy of the 2001 benchmark 'Not Just Peanuts: Stimulating an Entrepreneur-Friendly Europe' is available at www. notjustpeanuts.com or via www.growthplus.org.

GrowthPlus, Avenue des Gaulois, 7, B-1040 Brussels, Belgium. Telephone +32 2 743 1588.

Key findings
Overall summary   (maximum score possible = 57)

Country	Score
United Kingdom	48
United States of America	43
Spain	43
Netherlands	40
France	39
Germany	39
Belgium	38
Italy	37
Austria	36
Sweden	30

Section interim results	Austria	Belgium	France	Germany	Italy	Netherlands	Spain	Sweden	United Kingdom	United States
Funding	7	6	9	6	6	7	7	6	8	6
People	12	14	12	13	15	13	12	8	14	11
Business environment	17	18	18	20	16	20	24	16	26	26
Total	36	38	39	39	37	40	43	30	48	43

Additional findings
Funding – key findings

Topic	Austria	Belgium	France	Germany	Italy	Netherlands	Spain	Sweden	United Kingdom	United States
Tax incentives for venture individual investors	2	2	3	2	2	2	2	2	3	2
Tax incentives venture capital funds	2	2	3	2	2	3	3	2	3	2
Investment incentives	3	2	3	2	2	2	2	2	2	2
Total	7	6	9	6	6	7	7	6	8	6

People – key findings

Topic	Austria	Belgium	France	Germany	Italy	Netherlands	Spain	Sweden	United Kingdom	United States
Tax framework related to share plans	2	3	2	2	3	3	3	1	2	2
Taxation of stock options	2	3	2	1	3	3	2	1	2	2
Social security charges on stock options	2	3	3	2	3	2	2	1	3	2
Deductibility of stock option expenses	2	1	1	2	2	1	1	1	2	2
Special legal requirements related to stock options	2	2	2	3	2	2	2	2	3	1
Accessibility of foreigners to the labour market	2	2	2	3	2	2	2	2	2	2
Total	12	14	12	13	15	13	12	8	14	11

For the business environment chart, please see http://www.notjustpeanuts.com/execsum.htm

ECONOMIC FREEDOM IN EUROPE

If economic freedom is the highway to the wealth of nations, how does Europe measure up? asks Erwin Bendl of TIGRA.

How easy is it to set up a business in Europe? Which country is most attractive in terms of free trade and labour market regulation? How much of the wealth created by individuals is taken away by the taxman and spent by the government? If you are looking for answers to these and similar questions, the annual report of the 'Economic Freedom of the World' provides an excellent way to start.

Since 1996, the US economists James Gwartney and Robert Lawson have published a series of economic freedom indices, representing the state of the art in the measurement of free choice. Supported by the Fraser Institute and its World Economic Freedom Network, a group of more than 50 institutes around the world, Gwartney and Lawson have compiled convincing evidence that economic freedom is the prerequisite for growth. Their combined efforts led to 'the best way yet to define and measure economic freedom' (*The Economist*).

On average, countries with more economic freedom have a higher per capita GDP. Not only do countries with more economic freedom have a higher GDP, but they also generally grow more rapidly, says the report. The growth rate of the persistently high-rated countries are also positive, while those for the low-rated nations are low and often negative. In other words, economic freedom is the highway to the wealth of nations.

In terms of economic freedom as defined by Gwartney and Lawson, Hong Kong (number 1) has for years been the highest rated country in the world. Singapore (2), New Zealand (3), the United Kingdom (4) and the United States (5) follow closely. Oppressed countries such as Algeria (122) or Myanmar (123) have scored lowest.

In this article, a quick overview of the results for western European countries is given. Although the two researchers have published economic freedom data for 123 countries, they have also compiled a

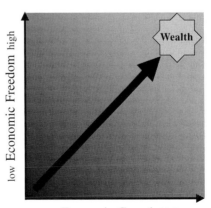

Figure 1 Highway to the wealth of nations

more detailed measurement for 58 countries. The figures presented here stem from this 'comprehensive' index.

Among the western European countries, the United Kingdom (8.0 points on a scale of 10), Ireland (7.9), and Switzerland (7.8) were ranked highest in the overall summary ranking of economic freedom. These countries provide more choice as regards economic freedom than France (6.4), Italy (6.3) and Greece (6.1), which are the lowest-ranked nations in Europe. The United States (8.2) is marginally ahead of the United Kingdom.

In general, the highest-income industrial countries of Europe score well in all major categories except two: size of government and regulation of labour market. France (3.6), Belgium, Austria, Denmark (each 4.0), Sweden, Norway, Italy (each 4.2), and Spain (4.5) are ranked in the 'bottom 20' of the size of the government area. Only the Irish Republic (7.3) and Iceland (6.3) manage to make the 'top 20'. By comparison, the United States scores 7.4. A large government usually undermines the private sector via price controls, large transfers and subsidies. In addition, a large government usually coincides with favourable rules for public enterprises and a lack of competition. Therefore, the higher a country's reliance on personal choice rather than political decision-making, the higher the scores in terms of economic freedom.

In the labour market regulation area, Germany (1.8) and France (2.2) received the lowest scores of 58 countries. Sweden (2.3), Finland (2.8), and Italy (2.9) are slightly higher ranked. Denmark (3.0), Belgium, Austria (both 3.1), Greece (3.3), and Norway (3.5) also ranked in the 'bottom 10' in the area of labour market regulation. The United Kingdom (6.1), Switzerland (6.0), Iceland (5.8), and the Irish Republic (5.2) are the only western European countries with above-median ratings in this field. From an economic freedom point of view, centralised wage-setting structures, lucrative unemployment compensation systems and overload of labour regulation in general reduce choice and are therefore unjustified. Again, the United States (6.8) outperforms Europe.

In the field of freedom to operate and compete in business – an integral component of economic freedom – northern European countries are substantially higher ranked then southern European countries. Obviously, while the government spending in northern Europe is high, its regulatory climate seems to be more open-minded toward private business and competitive markets. The set of variables used in this area are administrative conditions, time spent with government bureaucracy and irregular payments, among others. Finland (8.2 tied with the United States), Iceland and the Netherlands (both 7.9) ranked on top. Italy (5.3) seems to be the most burdensome western European country in terms operating a business – at least according to the figures.

As regards economic freedom in other important areas such as capital and financial markets, trade with foreigners and access to sound money, western Europe achieves high ratings. With the exception of Greece, the same holds true for legal structures and the security of property rights.

During the 1990s, economic freedom substantially grew in Europe. The report reveals big leaps – partly

Table 1 Access to sound money

	Rating	Ranking (western Europe only)	World ranking (58 countries)
Sweden	9.9	1	1
Belgium	9.8	2	2
Denmark	9.8	2	2
Germany	9.8	2	2
United Kingdom	9.8	2	2
Austria	9.7	6	7
France	9.7	6	7
Italy	9.7	6	7
Luxembourg	9.7	6	7
Norway	9.7	6	7
Netherlands	9.6	11	13
Spain	9.6	11	13
Finland	9.5	13	20
Irish Republic	9.5	13	20
Portugal	9.5	13	20
Switzerland	9.5	13	20
Iceland	9.3	17	29
Greece	9.1	18	31
United States	9.8	2	2

Source: Economic Freedom of the World (2001 report)

from low levels – for Greece, Portugal, Spain, the Irish Republic and Iceland. Compared to other European competitors, Germany, France and Sweden seemed to make little headway.

The current report of Gwartney and Lawson is the culmination of a process which began at the 1984 meetings of the Mont Pelerin Society in Cambridge. There, a discussion about the relationship between economic and political freedom ensued. As a result of this debate, Milton and Rose Friedman agreed to co-host a symposium to investigate these relationships. In the following years, economists around the world contributed to finding a way to measure economic freedom. Finally, in 1996, the first version of the index was published.

The rankings might best be viewed as approximations rather than precise measures. As a consequence, small differences between countries and across time periods should not be taken very seriously.

To sum up, the index developed by Gwartney and Lawson provides the most comprehensive measure of economic freedom. It should help policy-makers to better understand the relationship between the underlying factors of growth.

The tables used in this article have been slightly adopted from 'The Economic Freedom of the World' for the purpose of focusing on western European countries only. More details on the report, its concept and history can be found at http://www.freetheworld.com or http://www.fraserinstitute.ca.

Erwin Bendl (e-mail bendl@erwin.tc) is a member of the Board of Directors of TIGRA, the Think-tank for International Governance Research Austria.

FLEXIBILITY AND GROWTH

There is clearly a need for improving flexibility in Europe to enhance growth, says Professor Ray Barrell of the National Institute of Economic and Social Research.

The level and growth of output depends upon the quantity and quality of factors of production available, the efficiency with which they can be used, and the technology they can utilise. The nature of economic institutions and economic policy has a significant impact on the operation of any economy. European economies are often seen as inflexible, and one of the chancellor's five tests for EMU membership asks whether there is sufficient flexibility to deal with shocks to the Union. There is clearly need for improving flexibility in Europe in order to enhance growth. The European Commission has recognised this with its desire to transform labour markets and encourage the integration of product markets. Reforms are always needed because the nature of the economy and of the technology used also changes over time, and institutions in labour and product markets that are suitable for one era may be inappropriate for another. Greater flexibility may be needed to produce new technology-based niche products than was required to deal with traditional mass production in manufacturing.

The process of labour market reform has been under way in Europe for many years, with some successes.

In recent years, the Dutch, for example, have introduced a more flexible labour market, with some success, and unemployment there is now below 3 per cent of the workforce. Unemployment remains high in much of Europe, but it has come down from an average of around 11.5 per cent in 1994 to around 8.5 per cent currently. UK unemployment has fallen from 8.7 per cent to just over 3 per cent currently, and the country has clearly done better than its EU partners. It attempted different reform strategies in the 1980s and 1990s. The 1980s saw a wave of free market reforms that changed social institutions. In the 1990s, the strategy continued to develop and the Commission proposals effectively suggest that other EU countries should follow the United Kingdom's example. There have clearly been successes, particularly recently with the New Deal and Welfare to Work programmes, and there are lessons for other countries from the UK experience.

Comparisons are often made with the United States, where output per capita is 30 per cent higher than in the European Union or the United Kingdom, as can be seen from Table 1. US labour markets are more flexible and employees less protected; skill levels are both different and probably higher. The more flexible labour market is clearly part of the reason why Americans are better off, but they also work longer hours than their European counterparts. Those in work put in 16 per cent more hours than in Europe, and the participation rate is 12 percentage points higher than the European level. The United Kingdom is placed somewhere between the US and French and German levels of effort, but French and German output per capita and living standards are markedly higher. Clearly, there are lessons to learn from European partners also; they are more productive because they are more skilled, and increasing the skills of the workforce takes time. However, not all problems for employment and growth can be isolated in the labour market.

There are other reasons why the United States is productive and Europe is learning lessons there also. US product markets are more integrated and probably more competitive and US financial markets are significantly less segmented than in Europe. These give producers more scope for their activities and easier access to capital to finance them, and this in turn encourages enterprise and innovation. As the Single Market Programme expands and makes Europe more flexible, so the gains from specialisation and scale should be more fully reaped.

Comparisons between US (and UK) and European labour markets normally focus on greater flexibility in the United States (and the United Kingdom), with greater mobility of labour. Individuals have shorter tenure in jobs and shorter spells of unemployment in the United States (and the United Kingdom) than

in Europe. They also move longer distances when they migrate, and they are more likely to migrate between major regions than Europeans are likely to migrate between countries. The greater overall level of flexibility in the United States clearly makes it easier to match individuals to jobs, and labour is thus used more efficiently. Institutions in the two major economies differ and these may explain some of the significant differences that can be observed. The lack of employment protection and the rather limited level of social protection in the United States are clearly factors behind shorter job tenures and shorter unemployment spells. The stronger role of trade unions in the majority of European labour markets may also reduce the speed of turnover in employment and the dispersion of earnings in a number of European countries as compared to the United States. Limited social protection and a low minimum wage may also help explain the higher level of participation in the US workforce. The United Kingdom is in many ways between the European and US models, and many Europeans are slowly trying to move in that direction. More rapid movement would help them adjust to shocks to the economy and also improve their growth performance. However, removing European social institutions may increase flexibility, but it may also increase inequality, and our European partners see this as a cost to be set off against the gains.

Table 1 Output employment and hours indicators

Country	1998 Output per capita[a]	Unemployment 2001q2	1998 Employment ratio[b]	1998 Hours worked[c]
France	74	8.7	59.4	1604
Germany	77	7.8	64.4	1554
Italy	68	9.6	51.8	1648
Netherlands	73	2.0	69.4	(1365)[d]
Spain	53	13.2	51.2	1833
Sweden	69	5.0	71.5	1628
United Kingdom	70	3.2	71.2	1731
European Union	67	8.4	61.5	1671[e]
United States	100	4.5	73.8	1955

a) Real GDP per capita, USA =100, source United Nations Economic Commission for Europe *Economic Survey of Europe 2000, no. 1*

b) Person aged 15 to 64 who are in employment divided by the working age population. Source OECD *Employment Outlook June 2000*

c) Average hours actually worked per person in employment (including part time employees) Source OECD *Employment Outlook June 2000*

d) Dependent employment in 1997

e) Labour force weighted average of all members

Ray Barrell is a senior research fellow at NIESR and a visiting professor at Imperial College, London University. He leads the Institute's world economy team, who undertake a variety of academic work on growth and globalisation. His research interest have focused on European integration and the determinants of output and employment in the UK and elsewhere. The Institute is a major centre for applied economic work, with the objective of intervening in the debate over policy in a rigorous and comprehensible way.

Prof Ray Barrell NIESR, 2 Dean Trench St. Smith Square London SW1P 3HE Tel 00 44 207 654 1925 Fax 00 44 207 654 1900.

WHY BRUSSELS MATTERS TO BUSINESS

The EU is evolving into a regulator with global clout, says Elaine Cruikshanks at Hill and Knowlton, and its day-to-day role activities could affect any business that operates in Europe. So do not allow yourself to be taken by surprise.

September 11, economic downturn, redundancies, bankruptcies. . . The challenges facing business in the marketplace are multiplying daily. And under such circumstances, managers increasingly focus on the short-term operational issues far away from what might seem to be the 'ivory towers' of Brussels and Strasbourg.

But businesses ignore the European Union's institutions at their peril. The process of regulation continues daily at European level. Moreover, as the world's largest trading block, the European Union is an extremely important player in the context of multi-laterial or bilateral trade negotiations. With the arrival of the euro, the concrete manifestation of Europe as an economic power becomes evident. And, as merger cases like GE/Honeywell illustrate, the European Commission wields considerable executive powers in areas such as competition policy which can determine the very future of a business.

The European Union in context

Since its establishment, the European Union (EU) has progressively developed its influence and power on the global stage. In recent years the most striking feature has been the evolution of the European Commission, the European Union's executive body, from a technocratic to a powerful body, in particular in respect of economic regulation.

A meticulous regulator

In terms of its daily impact on business, the most high profile power of the European Union is in the field of competition policy, where the European Commission is the final arbiter on significant mergers affecting the EU. Over the past several years, it has also been the driving force in fundamentally restructuring important industry sectors by revising the competition rules under which they operate. The Commission is also currently seeking a substantially strengthened role in the pursuit of cartels and other anti-competitive activities.

M&A strategies that corporations are considering may be subject to the scrutiny of the EU competition authorities. Understanding the legal, political and communications challenges inherent in a major proceeding is essential to ensuring that regulatory hurdles can be overcome.

In addition the Commission exercises sweeping regulatory powers that touch upon every important economic sector. These powers derive from the Commission's role as the 'guardian' of the EU Treaties (for example in respect of infringements of EU law), but also through Committees set up under legislation (so called Comitology Committees) or through its role defined in secondary legislation.

These powers mean that the Commission has a day-to-day role in regulating the environment in which any business operates in Europe.

An economic powerhouse?

In terms of economic policy the 1991 Treaty of Maastricht signalled a considerable shift of power to the European Union and its institutions. The interlocking of Europe's currencies in the euro (€) at the beginning of 1999 – soon to be followed by the launch of notes and coins on 1 January 2002 – will lead the European Union to become a major economic power on the world stage. The creation of the European Central Bank with the sole responsibility for setting interest rates for a single market of over 300 million consumers will reinforce these developments.

The European Union – with the European Commission as the chief trade negotiator – has also carved out a role as a leading advocate of trade liberalisation, aggressively pursuing both a new global trade round and bilateral free trade agreements.

These trade powers, together with the EU's role in setting macro economic policy, shape the environment in which businesses operate in Europe. This will clearly impact upon investment decisions, as well as the economic environment in which corporations operate.

Europe's legislator

The European Union continues to be the pre-eminent legislator in Europe. The regulatory environment in which businesses operate across Europe invariably originates from Brussels. Through the adoption of Directives, Regulations and Recommendations, the EU lays down the framework for inter alia environmental standards, consumer protection, electronic commerce, financial services, telecommunications,

social and employment law and manufacturing standards and process. Although these rules often need to be implemented by national law, the parameters are set in Brussels. The prediction of former Commission President Jacques Delors that 90 per cent of legislation would eventually originate from Brussels is not far from the truth.

If corporations want to be aware of or influence the regulatory environment in which they operate, then a presence and an understanding of the European Union is a necessity.

The world's largest press corps

A good indicator of the EU's growing influence and importance is the fact that Brussels is now home to the largest press corps in the world. As a result, decisions taken in Brussels reverberate all over the world and in particular in financial markets. However, the presence of the media also provides opportunities to raise corporate profiles and drive the public policy agenda.

Corporations need to be in a position to communicate with the Brussels Press Corps as and when threats and opportunities arise on the public policy agenda.

Link to national government

Despite the central role of the European Commission in shaping the EU, the power of the member states remains extremely important. Not only are they key to the legislative process by virtue of their presence and votes in the Council of Ministers, but they also determine the political direction of the EU at the twice yearly European Summits. Since September 11 this has been particularly noticeable with the UK, France and Germany taking control of the political agenda.

The member states continue to influence the direction of the Commission both formally – for example through the appointments of the Commissioners themselves and informally – through the day to day negotiations between the member states and the Commission. In addition much of the legislative agenda agreed in Brussels requires detailed implementation at the level of the member states.

Corporations therefore need to be aware of the political and economic priorities of the individual member states and how they will shape the broader European agenda.

How are businesses represented in Brussels?

Brussels is now home to 10,000 public affairs professionals and has evolved along the Anglo-Saxon model first developed in Washington and London. However, a number of differences remain, largely due to the multinational nature of decision-making in Brussels.

Corporations have taken different approaches to managing EU public policy. Below we have listed the three most common approaches and where possible have given examples of corporations that have followed these models:

- **Fully staffed representative office** – this model has traditionally been favoured by corporations in highly regulated sectors, such as the telecommunications or automotive sectors, and by major multinationals. These offices can range from 5 to 20 staff with specialist expertise on key issues.
- **Brussels-based representation (1–2 executives)** – some corporations appoint a senior executive to represent them at official level with the European Union. In such cases the executive often acts as a disseminator of public policy developments and draws on the expertise of business units to help communicate the corporation's objectives. Corporations that have adopted this approach include financial services companies, airlines and media companies.
- **Non-Brussels based EU public policy executives** – a number of corporations have chosen to locate the EU public policy function outside Brussels (normally in London, Paris or Geneva) and keep close contact with either European headquarters or with specific business units.

In addition the management of the EU public policy function is often carried out in conjunction with memberships of trade associations and interest groups. However, companies have also recognised the need to safeguard their own interests and do not rely exclusively on trade associations. In addition, all major corporations have recourse to external public policy and communications advisers.

What should businesses do?

The different approaches to managing the EU public policy function reflect the differing priorities and objectives attached to EU public policy and the associated threats and opportunities that it provides to corporations. In the case of highly regulated sectors, corporations have been more or less obliged to provide resources to ensure that their interests are safeguarded. Other corporations have invested in the function as an 'insurance policy' for future major public policy initiatives that could impact their business in the knowledge that the resources invested up front will ensure that they are properly able to manage the threats and opportunities that public policy may create.

On this basis we would counsel corporations to undertake the following to assess how they should manage European Union public policy:

- Undertake an EU public policy management audit. This would include familiarisation workshops for senior executives on the European Union, its institutions, players, policies and impact on business. These workshops would be used to identify tailored objectives and requirements for managing EU public policy.
- Benchmarking with other corporations – both in the same but also other sectors. Hill and Knowlton can assist corporations by examining how other corporations are managing EU public policy and/or by facilitating dialogue with other corporate stakeholders in order to gain first hand knowledge of how other corporations have approached the challenges of EU public policy.

More than ever, having the right strategy for dealing with European Union public policy issues forms a key part of any company's corporate communications strategy to support its business objectives.

Elaine Cruikshanks is the H&K CEO and chairman for Western Continental Europe. She is also the vice chair of H&K's Public Affairs Practice Worldwide providing strategic communications advice to multinationals, trade associations and governments including lobbying, crisis and issues management and corporate communications.

H&K Brussels is a leading communications agency with some 52 international employees. It has specialists in public affairs, crisis and issues management, EU press corps media relations, corporate communications, public policy communications and marketing communications on the EU and Belgian markets. H&K Brussels is part of H&K's global, integrated network of 68 offices in 34 countries.

FINANCIAL PROSPECTS

François David, chairman and chief executive of Coface Group, assesses how European markets are likely to perform in a global context in 2002.

The September 11 terrorist attacks occurred amid intensification of the US economic slowdown. They came after a previous downward revision of forecasts in the United States and Europe and an already recession-gripped Japan. Expressions of doubt about the end of the cyclical downturn in electronics were becoming increasingly commonplace and weighing on the buoyancy of Asian economies. Uncertainty about the solvency of Argentina and Turkey and the weakness of international stock exchanges spurred strong volatility in risk premiums in financial markets.

While the September 11 events accentuated trends already underway, they did not fundamentally undermine the outlook. The main questions concern the economic downturn's amplitude and duration. Forecasts now place recovery in the 2002 first half at best.

Since September 11, the slowdown in the United States has tightened its grip (A1 watch-listed with negative implications). Household spending, particularly on property investments, which had remained firm despite the depreciation of security holdings,

the increasing number of layoffs and high level of indebtedness, is now suffering the after-effects of the attacks. Now that the remaining dynamic factor is disappearing, the economy should weaken. The downturn's amplitude and duration will depend essentially on household confidence and consumption, which should derive support from the loosening of budgetary and monetary policy. The upturn of sectors rebounding from their cyclical low points and benefiting from renewed demand (eg electronics) could ultimately offset the slowdown in sectors recently affected by the attacks (eg tourism, air transport). Company solvency should nonetheless remain shaky during coming months.

Increasing signs of a slowdown in Europe

In Europe, signs of a slowdown are increasing and it seems unlikely that the continent will avoid a new downward revision of its growth prospects. Germany (A1 watch-listed with negative implications) and Italy (A2) are facing sluggish household consumption while the world economic slowdown hampers their exports. The easing of tax policy does not appear very effective with sizeable deficits limiting the authorities' room for manoeuvre. After several years of robust growth, Portugal (A1 watch-listed with negative implications) is experiencing a sharp slowdown. In the United Kingdom (A1 watch-listed with negative

A seven-tier scale provides the basis for Coface country ratings:

A1   A steady political and economic environment enhances a generally good company payment record with very low default-probability.

A2   Although the political and economic environment or company payment record is not as good as in A1-rated countries, the default-probability remains low.

A3   Changing political or economic conditions could exacerbate a payment record that is generally lower than in A1- and A2-rated countries. Default-probability should nonetheless remain low.

A4   The political and economic environment could deteriorate and exacerbate an already mediocre payment record. Default-probability nonetheless remains acceptable.

B   A shaky political and economic environment is likely to exacerbate a generally poor payment record.

C   A very shaky political and economic environment could exacerbate a generally bad payment record.

D   A very risky economic and political environment will exacerbate a generally very bad payment record.

implications), the manufacturing sector remains handicapped by sterling's strength and a lack of competitiveness.

Spain, France and the Netherlands have sustained higher growth rates, although largely revised downward.

In these not very favourable conditions, late payments have become more frequent and recent events have sparked fears of further deterioration in coming months. All economic sectors are concerned. The recent attacks are expected to impact on tourism, air transport and housing construction, all sectors that were growing strongly until now in many countries.

In eastern Europe, difficulties persist in Poland (A4). Payment defaults by companies are commonplace.

South east Asia suffers from less buoyant sales to the United States and Japan

In Asia, Japan is already in recession and its difficulties are expected to intensify in the near term. Household demand remains sluggish and company earnings have been falling, with the scale of public debt limiting the government's room for manoeuvre. Far from completed, restructuring efforts continue in depressed economic conditions. The accelerating pace of bad debt write-offs by banks should trigger a new increase in the number of bankruptcies.

It is thus not surprising to observe the high number of company bankruptcies or scope of the corresponding liabilities particularly in the finance, construction, property, wholesale and retail trades, leisure and hotel/restaurant sectors.

Emerging countries in south east Asia are suffering from less buoyant sales to the United States and Japan and the cyclical downturn in electronics. The recession beginning to grip the United States will intensify the regional economic slowdown.

Taiwan (A1 watch-listed with negative implications) and Singapore (A2 watch-listed with negative implications), both very dependent on conditions in the United States and the electronics sector, are already in recession. Hong Kong (A1) is not far behind. Indonesia (C), the Philippines (A4) and Thailand (A3) are faced with political uncertainties which hamper efforts to implement much needed structural reforms. Conversely, China (A3), more isolated and less vulnerable to the international environment, is faring better.

Financial market instability in Latin America

In Latin America, growth is sagging due to the slowdown in industrial countries, the Argentina crisis and the increasing cost of external financing. The recent events in the United States have only intensified financial market instability and further clouded prospects for regional recovery.

Mexico (A4), particularly dependent on US growth, cannot avoid a slowdown in its export sector where

90 per cent of sales flow to the United States. The country is undergoing a sharp slowdown. With its GDP dropping for two quarters, the economy should register flat growth for 2001, coupled with reduced inflation. Looking ahead, economic activity in 2002 remains dependent on renewed growth in the United States.

Argentina (C) remains very worrying where, despite financial aid, fears of a payment default by the state persist. The country's GDP will contract again this year, its third consecutive annual contraction. The events of September 11 have only set back prospects for recovery even further with the outlook already clouded by financial market skittishness, a worrying social and political situation, and an unsustainable foreign exchange system. In that respect, the current government's expected defeat in the upcoming October elections increases the likelihood of devaluation.

The Argentina crisis also affects Brazil (B watch-listed with negative implications), where the situation is deteriorating on all fronts. Hampered by the energy crisis and the real's depreciation, growth for the year will be much weaker than forecast. Recovery in 2002 remains dependent on an upswing in the United States, resolving the Argentina problem and an easing of financing costs, all very tentative hypotheses at this present time.

Turkey should continue to enjoy the financial support of western countries

In the Middle East, company payment behaviour trends are favourable overall, bolstered directly or indirectly by the firmness of oil prices. Discounting the possibility of generalised conflict in the region, the September 11 events should not alter the existing situation. However, the Israeli-Palestinian conflict and demand slowdown in the United States for high-technology goods are spurring a sharp business downturn in Israel (downgraded to A3 in June 2001).

In Turkey (C), the recession has proven to be more severe than expected and forecasts are now betting on a 7 per cent decline in GDP. Although its external accounts have turned around, the state's financing needs remain high and, considering the banking sector's financial weakness, it can only obtain the needed capital at high cost on international markets. However, the September 11 events underscored the country's geo-strategic situation. With its special importance to western countries, Turkey should continue to enjoy their financial support.

The slowdown, which was evident in several sectors, has spread to other industries

Industry forecasts have deteriorated. Companies' margins are being squeezed. Restructuring is accelerating. Once again, bankruptcies are increasing in various countries and sectors. The slowdown, which was already evident in several sectors before 11 September, has since spread to other industries. The chronology of the slowdown does not leave much room for industries so far unaffected or those that are benefiting from the new economic and political context.

- Information technology, telecommunications, electronics, pulp, iron and steel have been affected since the second half of 2000.
- Automobile production, mechanical engineering, paper and packaging, textiles, chemicals and aeronautical transportation have been affected since the first half of 2001.
- Aeronautical transportation, tourism and duty free sales have been directly affected by the events of 11 September.
- Non-alimentary consuming and construction have been gripped by a slowdown.
- Alimentary products and distribution, pharmaceuticals and cosmetics remain firm.
- Security and defence could meet a revival of their activities.

The current conditions of world economic slowdown have prompted:

- watch-listing of Hong Kong (A1) and Mexico (4) with negative implications;
- Germany (A1), United Kingdom (A1), and Portugal (A1) to have already been negatively watch-listed in early September.

The rating of 140 countries can be checked freely at http://www.cofacerating.com.

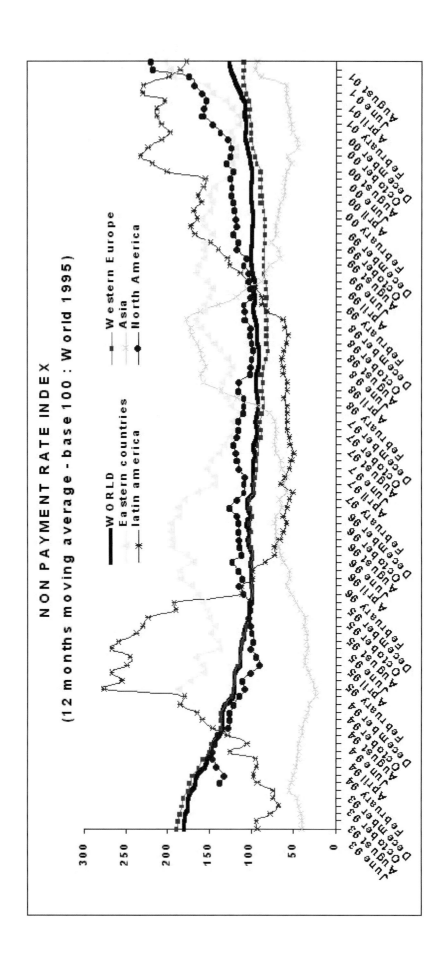

NON PAYMENT RATE INDEX

(12 months moving average - base 100 : World 1995)

WORLD
Eastern countries
latin america
Western Europe
Asia
North America

François DAVID is Chairman and Chief Executive Officer of the Coface Group.

Rated AA par Fitch, Coface Group is one of the world leaders in credit insurance, number one in insurable ratings with @rating via www.cofacerating.com, a leading provider of credit information worldwide, and manager of the French government's export guarantee programme. Listed on the Paris Bourse, the Group's shares are included in the SBF 120 and Euronext 150 stock indices.

The Coface Group's services and guarantees foster development of business-to-business commerce worldwide. It provides 78,000 customers in 99 countries with solutions drawing on the Group's expertise in domestic and international credit insurance, guaranty insurance, prospecting and credit information, receivables management and collection. Customers enjoy access to two global networks, CreditAlliance and InfoAlliance, which are based on shared risk management (Common Risk System) and an integrated product and service offer: @rating Solution.

RISKS OF EXPANSION

There are myriad risks in leaving behind a market that you know well for the risks of the unknown in continental Europe, says Pat Drinan of Royal & SunAlliance ProFin.

When any business starts to examine the maturity of its own market and decides that it is time to expand, it has to take a moment to consider the myriad risks it is thus taking in leaving behind a market that it knows well for one that is unknown. Leaving aside the obvious pure business risks of knowing your potential market, and assessing the saleability of the product, you are left with a number of 'common' risks that take on a greater significance in a foreign market.

Perhaps the first consideration is how you are actually going to move into the market. Many people are familiar with corporate structures in the United Kingdom. Whether you are a sole trader or a plc, thought will have to be given to how best to establish yourself in your target state. If it is your wish to provide services that do not require an establishment in that target state, then familiarity with the increasing regulation of distance selling and the Internet will be essential.

When considering your corporate structure, thought will have to be given to the different ways in which our continental neighbours manage their businesses.

Although as a director in the United Kingdom you have, for example, fiduciary duties to the company and certain responsibilities to the state to safeguard the interests of others, those duties may well be different in your target state. The penalties for misfeasance may be much greater and liability for different acts may be wider. Another aspect may be the manner of management: it may well be that you do not have as much flexibility in managing your business, as local legislation may require oversight by other stakeholders, such as employees, in your business.

Whatever the nature of the business, control must be maintained of the new unit. Even with modern telecommunications it can be difficult at times to keep track of what is being done and by whom. Effective reporting and control requirements will be the primary tool in ensuring control of and compliance by distant arms of the business.

Exerting effective control over foreign business units requires management to have clear procedures in place. Although UK business has experienced much in the way of corporate governance reform, business leaders will have to be aware that their existing methods of corporate governance, from the constitution of the Board through to rules on disclosure and decision-making, may be different to those in the target state. They may have to comply with potentially higher and possibly different standards in their target countries, but in all likelihood there may be a need to ensure that local standards are lifted to match the company's existing levels.

Once you have established your company, all thoughts will turn to operating it effectively. You have your new offices, either owned or leased. Companies will be used to insuring their own property (and business risks) in their home state, using brokers who are familiar with the manner in which insured values and losses are calculated under the domestic legal regime. When expanding into Europe, it is worth thinking about the different ways in which insurance in particular is treated. If your business is expanding into more than one country, a broker or company with international experience will be able to advise on the broad range of issues resulting from multinational risk. Considerations will include: the utilisation of local policies (which will help to take into account the peculiarity of local risk conditions), while still retaining a master policy for the group to cover the differences in limits or conditions between your local policies and what your business requires; the need perhaps for locally admitted security to 'front' for your preferred carrier because your trading partners demand it; and finally, if the risk is large enough, perhaps to consider setting up its own captive insurer using a tax-efficient domicile and more available reinsurance capacity.

In your new offices, your new employees are ready to work. They will be used to working under local standards and will expect you to know how to apply those standards from day one. Although there is much harmonisation across the European Union with respect to employment law, there is plenty of scope for additional requirements. Although a relatively new subject in the UK market, employment practices liability is progressively making its way on to the agenda in many boardrooms. Such exposures take on a whole new meaning where there is the possibility of a clash of cultures and inexperience with the application of local rules.

Those same employees are also going to expect their employer to take care of them in the same way an indigenous employer would. Although UK health and safety legislation draws much of its current impetus from EC law, there are going to be differences in interpretation, which cannot be avoided. Businesses will have to ensure that they comply with the

local spirit, as well as the exact interpretation of the rules. One aspect of security is more poignant following the events of September 11. While we may refuse to be cowed by such terrorist acts, business is going to have to think carefully about what it expects of its employees in times of potential danger. Many businesses in major UK cities will be familiar with the need to have contingency plans for business continuity and personnel safety. These plans cannot be left behind and companies must be ready to translate those plans to their new offices, wherever they are in the European Union.

Although EU member states have become more constricted in the exercise of state discretion where there has been harmonisation, unless legislation is directly effective (and therefore requires no further action on the member state to be implemented) there is always scope for a member state to be lax or inaccurate in its implementation of 'common' rules. While a business may be confident in its ability to provide a service or sell goods in its home state, it would be well advised to ensure that the parallel legislation permitting it to do so in the target country has been implemented in the same way, as otherwise, costly changes in strategy or challenges to government may be necessary.

On a practical note, businesses that are used to the legal theory and practice of English, Welsh, Scottish or Northern Irish courts will find that doing business in continental Europe brings with it legal practices which can be quite different to our own. It will surprise many that in the French courts for example, there is no equivalent of disclosure of documents in the course of litigation. Neither is the choice of an expert left to each party, or jointly between them, but it is in fact up to the magistrate who will also act as inquisitor, rather than take the more 'hands-off' approach of an English judge. The time that it takes to get matters resolved can vary widely from country to country, and knowing how the system works before agreeing to a jurisdiction or law for contracts is essential.

One subject that cannot be ignored in any European expansion plan is the new European single currency, the euro (€). Although continental Europe has been dealing with the euro as a scriptural currency for nearly two years, with effect from 1 January 2002 real banknotes and coins will be in circulation, and the former currencies will be phased out by the end of February at the latest. All governmental transactions will take place in euros from that date, and the physical withdrawal of legacy currencies will actively take place during the very short dual-currency periods. Anyone dealing with cash will have to ensure that they not only have sufficient stock of such notes and coins when they open for business post 1 January, but will also need to ensure that their hardware and systems can cope. There will of course be scope for fraud when any change in currency occurs. The European Union has planned an education campaign for all participating member states, which naturally has not been replicated in the United Kingdom. UK businesses will have to make a real effort to familiarise themselves with the new notes and coins if they are to avoid losses, remembering that each of the 12 member states' notes are legal tender in each other state. Spanish euros used by a German are as good for a baguette on the Champs-Elysées as for chorizo sausage purchased by a Belgian in Barcelona.

It may be trite to say that there are many good opportunities in the new markets, but while some states will offer more security than others for the new entrant, all will require the business leader to manage the risk in the context of a different, challenging and hopefully profitable environment.

Royal & SunAlliance has recently launched 'Management Assurance', a packaged product providing specialist insurance protection with bespoke cover to suit the needs of each and every business, public or private. It covers risks such as Directors' & Officers' Liability insurance, Employment Practices Liability insurance, Crime, Kidnap Ransom & Extortion, Pension Scheme Liability insurance, Professional Indemnity insurance and Libel insurance. The product includes unique value-added services designed to help insureds avoid distracting and time-consuming losses and ultimately support the insureds in managing their future with confidence.

Pat Drinan, UK areas practice leader, Royal & SunAlliance ProFin. Telephone +44 (0)20 7337 5986. http://www.profin.royalsun.com

Part 2

Markets in Change

TEN MARKETS IN WAITING

The European Bank for Reconstruction and Development (EBRD) gives its assessment of progress among the 10 candidates for EU membership in central and eastern Europe.

The objective of acceding to the European Union is a key political priority in almost all countries of central and eastern Europe. This aspiration stems from both security concerns and political and economic ambitions to join the West.

At the Luxembourg European Council in December 1997, it was decided to open accession negotiations with all 10 candidate countries from the region and to start early negotiations with five countries: the Czech Republic, Estonia, Hungary, Poland and Slovenia. Subsequently, at the Helsinki European Council in December 1999, the decision was taken to open accession negotiations with the other five candidate countries: Bulgaria, Latvia, Lithuania, Romania and the Slovak Republic.

At the June 1993 Copenhagen European Council, the EU member states agreed that certain countries in central and eastern Europe could become members of the European Union. Accession would take place as soon as each country was able to satisfy the necessary conditions. These economic and political conditions include:

- the stability of institutions guaranteeing democracy, the rule of law, human rights and respect for and protection of minorities;
- the existence of a functioning market economy as well as the capacity to cope with competitive pressure and market forces within the European Union;
- the ability to accept the obligations of membership, including adherence to the aims of political, economic and monetary union.

Membership also requires that the candidate countries incorporate EU legislation (the *acquis communautaire*) into national legislation and implement this effectively through appropriate administrative and judicial structures, and that the European Union has the ability to integrate new member states without endangering the momentum of European integration.

Accession negotiations with the EU candidate member countries are conducted individually and the pace of negotiation depends on the degree of preparation by the country and the European Union and on the complexity of the issues involved. The negotiations cover both the political and economic aspects of the Copenhagen criteria. They also focus on the incorporation of EU legislation, which is divided into 31 chapters, with each covering a certain area of the economy such as free movement of capital, labour, services and products. The actual negotiations take the form of a series of bilateral intergovernmental conferences between the EU member states and each of the candidate countries.

Responsibility for assessing the extent to which EU candidate member countries fulfil the Copenhagen criteria rests with the European Commission and these assessments are made in the context of the annual progress report prepared by the Commission. The 2001 report is due to be adopted in November. The Commission has recently provided the European Parliament with a preliminary assessment of this ongoing work. According to this assessment, all negotiating candidate countries continue to meet the political criteria, recognising that the position of Russian minorities in the Baltic region continues to improve and that the situation of orphans in Romania has started to change. However, serious issues must still be addressed. The position of the Romany people and the cultural discrimination they face also remains a difficult issue.

In terms of the economic criteria, the Commission observed that the competitive market had made its mark in all the EU candidate countries. It noted that the competitiveness in the single European market had largely been achieved since trade in goods and services between the European Union and the applicant countries had already been widely liberalised. It is also recognised that the Maastricht criteria for the euro will have to be met in full once the Copenhagen criteria for accession have been met.

Regarding the incorporation of EU legislation, negotiations have been opened for eight of the ten candidate countries of central and eastern Europe (the exceptions are Bulgaria and Romania) on all 31 chapters except for the one dealing with the budget and institutional issues. Hungary leads the way with 22 chapters provisionally closed, followed closely by Slovenia with 21 and the Czech Republic, Estonia and the Slovak Republic on 19. However, the number of chapters provisionally closed is not a complete measure of progress because it does not take account of the varying complexities and difficulties among the chapters or the progress that has been achieved in chapters that have not yet been closed. In addition, it must be recognised that many of the more controversial issues are yet to be addressed in each of the countries, such as justice and home affairs, competi-

tion, taxation, transport, budget regional policy and agriculture. A compromise was recently reached on the chapter on the free movement of people, which balances the objectives of free movement and security as far as possible.

While significant progress has been achieved in meeting the political and economic criteria for EU accession in the 10 candidate countries of central and eastern Europe, these efforts have had significant costs and strained the scarce administrative capacities of the countries. To help meet these costs and to support local administrative capacity, the European Union adopted budget provisions to make pre-accession financing available for all membership candidates in the areas of technical assistance and training (through the Phare instrument), infrastructure and environment (through the ISPA instrument) and agriculture (through the SAPARD instrument). Total potential financial support through these instruments for the period 2000–2006 is €3.1 billion. The Phare and ISPA programmes are on track, but the SAPARD programme has had to overcome substantial start-up problems.

As the candidate member countries prepare for accession with EU financial support, so the institutions of the European Union also have to be adjusted. An important step in the process was the Treaty of Nice, agreed in December 2000. The purpose of the treaty was to remove obstacles to EU enlargement and to adopt reforms that would ensure EU institutions function efficiently after its membership expands. At the same time, the EU heads of state and government approved a plan for completing the accession negotiations. However, there are doubts as to how successful the treaty has been in preparing the EU institutions for the expansion in membership. In addition, the Nice Treaty must be ratified by each member state. It failed to clear its first hurdle when the Irish Republic rejected the treaty in a referendum. It is crucial to the credibility of the accession process and to the reform momentum in the candidate countries to ensure that EU institutions are successfully adjusted.

This article is based on an extract from the Transition Report 2001, published by the EBRD in November 2001. Copies can be ordered from the EBRD's website http://www.ebrd.com.

The European Bank for Reconstruction and Development was set up in 1991 to assist the former communist countries of eastern Europe in their transition to democratic market economies. It invests with others to help meet the changing needs of 27 countries from central Europe to Central Asia.

A EUROPEAN STOCK MARKET

Assets are already being managed on a pan-European basis, says Peter Lewis at SG Securities. When will the execution and settlement of trades catch up?

The integration of European bourses has been underway for a couple of years, believes Peter Lewis, global head of programme trading at SG Securities, the French investment bank. 'The end game is to have one or two pan-European stock exchanges and one trading platform. Investment managers can then ultimately go to one place and trade Deutsche Telecom, Vodafone, Telefonica and France Telecom. Given that all these companies are in the same time zone and in the same market, there is no reason why you should not trade and settle shares seamlessly and easily across borders without hindrance.'

'How do we get away from where we are now where we have 15 national bourses, 10 trading platforms, 26 clearing and settlement houses? In the United States, there are three national exchanges, five regional exchanges and one clearing and settlement house.'

'Something is wrong somewhere,' argues Lewis, who is responsible for electronically executing orders with values amounting to hundreds of millions of euros. 'In Europe, we have too many exchanges, too many clearers and too many settlement houses. There has got to be consolidation at the front end and at the back end. We won't end up with just one stock exchange. Maybe there will be two or three, but the question is which will they be and what is the process that gets us there?'

A number of exchanges have gone a fair way down that route, believes Lewis. Following its takeover of Liffe, Euronext is now a major player pursuing a strategy of accumulating exchanges on a friendly basis. That is how the original merger between Paris, Brussels and Amsterdam was agreed. Lisbon and Helsinki are joining in the same way in 2002.

Euronext is now running a single trading platform with three segments: the blue chip market in Paris; the small caps market in Brussels; and the derivatives side in London, which moved from Amsterdam following the takeover of Liffe. 'Ultimately it is one trading platform,' says Lewis. 'You go to one exchange to trade, clear and settle stocks with no difference between any of the markets.'

Virt-x is a rival system run on a more aggressive basis. It is a merger between Tradepoint and the Swiss Exchange. Originally set up as a pan-European platform to trade securities, Tradepoint has had a number of incarnations. It could never achieve critical mass, which inspired the merger with the Swiss exchange. Swiss blue chips are now traded on Virt-x and it also lists approximately 300 stocks in six other European markets. 'It has had some success, but the issue is liquidity,' says Lewis. 'People trade where liquidity exists and it is hard to persuade them to trade anywhere else.'

The model pursued by the London Stock Exchange (LSE) has always been one of glorious isolation. 'It has never really believed in the idea of a pan-European exchange. It doesn't believe that it will work. It remembers the days of SEAQ International in the early 1990s, when you could trade more stocks through it than on the French bourse. Those days have gone, but it does believe that no one in Europe will ever be able to trade UK stocks. It does not feel threatened by the other bourses, which is a risky strategy, because if one of them does then they have a big problem.'

The LSE pursues a three-pronged strategy. It wants to be Europe's largest exchange, attracting foreign companies that want a listing in Europe; it would like to sell its trading technology to other exchanges; and it is looking to develop its capabilities in derivatives, an ambition which has been set back by its failure to conclude a deal with Liffe.

The LSE's inherent advantages are being whittled away as time goes on, believes Lewis. 'It is still significant for international listings, but Euronext now has more clout. If you are an American or Japanese company, there is no reason why you should not consider Euronext just as much as the LSE.'

The Deutsche Borse is in a similar position. It has not extended its capabilities outside Germany and thus remains a domestic exchange. 'Maybe there is an obvious deal to be done with the LSE,' comments Lewis, 'but the problem has always been the systems, where they both think that they are better than each other. They both believe that they are the dominant exchange in Europe. It will be hard to get them to give up anything for the greater good of a merger. The LSE will never achieve terms as favourable as the iX deal in 2000. The Deutsche Borse feels that it has moved ahead since then and it does not need to give itself away to the LSE. The LSE will not do a deal unless it is in control. A lot of the other exchanges are saying we do not need you.'

The pace at which exchanges consolidate is not necessarily in their control. 'The buy-side institutions are already investing on a pan-European basis. They have the models; they have the systems to manage their portfolios. Part of the drive for consolidation is to make implementation match up with how assets are managed in the first place.'

'The arrival of the euro has allowed them to transform their business. They are no longer constrained by national boundaries. They can now say that many of their assets are truly European.'

'You don't say that I have to have a certain amount of Swiss or Swedish companies. You are more likely to say that you have to be in certain sectors matched against a European benchmark. Thus, if you are a Dutch pension fund, you are not constrained to Dutch equities, but can invest in the whole Eurozone. Deregulation in the insurance and pensions fund industries in Europe is also allowing them to be more aggressive.'

Technology is making all this possible. 'Now an exchange does not need a building. It is just an electronic network. It is just a connection like a telephone exchange. You can trade anywhere you like. Once that electronic infrastructure is in place, it is easy to connect people to it. In fact, it is in your interest to do so. It brings in more participants. It drives down commissions.'

Just as exchanges are having to reinvent themselves, so are brokers, investment banks and information providers. They are all merging into one. At SG, says Lewis, 'we have to ask where we fit in as a broker and investment bank, given that the execution process is now being commoditised. People are looking for the cheapest way of executing orders and research is being devalued in that process. Institutions may want it, but they don't want to pay for it, because it affects performance overall. There is a question of whether institutions believe in the value of research that is being pumped out. At the same time, commissions are being driven down even faster. Quality of offering used to count, but now it is a matter of price and execution. In order to survive, you have to have a critical mass of at least 4 per cent–5 per cent to survive in any particular market, which allows you to use flow and liquidity to make money.'

It will be liquidity too that is likely to determine the identity of the winner in creating a European stock exchange, thinks Lewis. 'Once there is a shift in trading, it moves very quickly. It happens for one of two reasons: the incumbent makes a strategic mistake, which allows business to be stolen away, which happened with Liffe and the Bund contract; or someone comes up with a totally new way of doing things, which is much harder in the context of stock exchanges. No one can say that they have a really superior system or offering. It is likely to come down to someone giving it up and losing it.'

SG, the investment banking arm of the Société Générale Group, is present in 50 countries and employs over 12,000 people world-wide. SG offers clients a powerful combination of proven financial innovation, deep industry knowledge, and global resources. With expertise in capital markets, advisory and origination services, structured finance and commercial banking, SG builds innovative, integrated financial solutions for its corporate, institutional and public sector clients. www.sg-ib.com

Peter Lewis is global head of program trading at SG London and joined SG in September 1998 in his current role. He is responsible for all aspects of global program trading activity in seven locations around the world.

He was previously head of program trading at CS First Boston and was global head of portfolio trading & derivative sales for Robert Fleming Securities until February 1998.

He is a graduate in Maths & Chemistry from the University of Southampton.

A SINGLE FINANCIAL MARKET

The European Union's action plan to create a single financial market needs to move fast to accommodate a spectacular build-up in savings, says Graham Bishop.

The build-up of savings for European pensions in the coming years is likely to be spectacular. The problem is that European capital markets may be too small currently and squeezing a large amount of investment into a small market can create distortions – as the United Kingdom knows only too well from its experience with the minimum funding requirement (MFR). It is therefore important that the Financial Services Action Plan (FSAP) is implemented to ensure the creation of a large – and single – capital market that remains free of distortions.

The unwillingness of governments to raise taxes to finance public pension provision means the demand for pensions is likely to stimulate increased private retirement savings. The European Commission's best assessment of the total current size of pension fund assets within the Eurozone amount to just over €1 trillion, of which about half are in the Netherlands. Thus, a key question is what effect the drive to enact the Pensions Directive will have on the scale of assets. Superficially, the directive should create the circumstances where funded pension systems will develop and create, when the funds eventually reach maturity, a pool of assets that should be at least of

the same order of magnitude relative to GDP as the United Kingdom or Denmark; that would be 80 per cent of GDP – pointing to a final Eurozone total of say €5 trillion – or five times the current size.

The savings are likely to be biased towards bonds. This is not just because of recent volatility in equity markets, which has intensified since September 11. Over the past decade, long-run returns have been higher for bonds than equities. Looking at the size of EU bond markets, it is spectacularly clear that the euro has become a major currency in the international bond market. In the first half of 2001, €509 billion of bonds were issued denominated in euro, compared to €479 billion (equivalent) of international bonds in US dollars.

However, the stock of debt outstanding still reflects the historic importance of the dollar. For example, the Salomon Smith Barney Broad Investment Grade Performance Index (with a minimum size requirement of €500 million outstanding) shows the US dollar component at €6.2 trillion (equivalent) at mid-year – about twice the size of the euro component's €3.4 trillion. That calculation includes both the domestic and 'offshore' markets and is thus an 'apples and apples' comparison.

The European Central Bank (ECB) produces data on bonds eligible for 'repo money market operations' – effectively, all euro-denominated bonds. That totals

€6.8 trillion of bonds outstanding – about the same size as the US market – although the United States would also have that tail of small issues. However, the key point is that, after quite a short period of development – only 30 months – these markets are comparable.

However, global investors are likely to look first at the government bond market because these bonds have a 'benchmark' status, as the best credit in the market. Total EU-12 government bonds outstanding reached €2.5 trillion at the end of June 2001. Japan was €1.9 trillion and the United States €1.8 trillion. Thus, the US market, at the time, was actually smaller than Japan's and thus only the third largest market. As an aside, the United Kingdom's gilt market is only €0.3 trillion, and thus the euro market is seven times its size. The government component of the bond markets is broadly capped – and properly – by the Stability Pact, and any expansion must come from the non-government sectors.

The government debt managers of the Eurozone took an intellectual and emotional decision several years ago to compete head on with the US Treasury and so set about reforming the size and types of their issues. Now the debate has moved to the minutiae of clearing and settlement as the ECB resolved the payments issues by setting up the TARGET real-time gross settlement (RTGS) payment system as a preliminary part of EMU.

Despite this success, a simple comparison between the €5 trillion predicted size of pension assets and the total corporate and government bond market shows that both markets are currently too small.

Whether, or when, the EU capital markets become large enough depends on the progress made on implementing the FSAP. The FSAP is the European Commission's update of the 1992 programme for the original single market in financial services, taking into account the coming of the euro, enlargement and technological change.

The process is fraught with difficulties, as demonstrated by the current controversy over the Prospectus Directive, but it is important to get a prospectus that is capable of launching a security right the way across Europe, eventually down to individuals via the new electronic trading platforms, if the individual investor is to be able to disintermediate the savings institution.

The heads of government have repeatedly said that the FSAP must be implemented by 2005. This is a very tight deadline for legislation, even at a European level, before turning it into national law, but the history of Europe is that these deadlines are broadly met. Whether 80 per cent or 95 per cent is done, a huge difference will have been made.

Size of euro-denominated trade – driving the reserve currency function

There is no reason in principle why the Eurozone should not develop markets on the scale of the United States. The Eurozone's 300 million people constitute a more populous currency area than the United States' 270 million. Looking ahead and including all EU members and all accession candidates, the population could top 500 million. If counted as a single economy, the Eurozone would be the second largest in the world already. Even at current exchange rates, the Eurozone approaches the United States in size, with a GDP of €6.4 trillion for 2000 compared to €10.8 trillion for the United States, in the OECD's rankings. The Japanese economy is third at €3.5 trillion.

If the Eurozone does develop the markets to meet the demand, it will be no accident or chance. The FSAP demonstrates that promoting the single financial market is a matter of explicit public policy – and rightly so, the well-being of Europe's ageing population depends upon it.

Graham Bishop founded GrahamBishop.com in July 2000 to provide independent analysis on European financial affairs and continues as adviser on these topics to Schroder Salomon Smith Barney in London. His publications provide an informed commentary from the practical perspective of a market participant. Consequently, he is a member of the European Commission's Consultative Group on the Impact of the Introduction of the Euro on Capital Markets. He is also a council member of both Britain in Europe and The City in Europe. Several continuing themes have dominated his work during his near-30 year career in the City – starting with the technical nature of the financial system and building up to the political impact of modern financial markets.

He was a specialist adviser to the Treasury Committee of the House of Commons on recent EMU Enquiries; chairman, the London Investment Banking Association (LIBA) Committee on converting London's capital markets to the single currency; member of the European Commission's Strategy Group on Financial Services (1998) and Committee of Independent Experts on the preparation of the changeover to the single currency (the 'Maas' Committee 1994/5).

A NEW ELECTRICITY MARKET FOR ITALY

The EU's liberalisation of electricity markets is becoming a reality, says Alberto Pototschnig, CEO of GME, the new Italian electricity market operator.

After almost 40 years of a vertically integrated monopolistic structure, the liberalisation of the electricity industry is becoming a reality in Italy, with reform having been introduced by Legislative Decree no.79 of 16 March 1999 (the 'Bersani Decree'), implementing European Directive 96/92/EC on common rules for the internal market for electricity.

The key innovations introduced by the Bersani Decree concern:

■ the power generation business, where the objective is to promote competition between a plurality of operators;
■ the final consumers, where a growing number of customers will be able to choose the supplier, which could be different from the local distributor.

From 2003, no operator will be allowed to control, either directly or indirectly, more than 50 per cent of the electricity produced or imported in Italy. The divestment of 15 GWh of Enel's generating assets

to comply with the new market share limit, in accordance with the Bersani Decree, will favour the emergence of new producers, although the former monopolist will continue to control approximately 50 per cent of the national generating capacity.

With respect to the liberalisation of electricity demand, currently all customers consuming, either individually or as an aggregate within a consortium, not less than 20 GWh of electricity per year can qualify as 'eligible customers' and can choose their supplier. This is the second phase of the three-step demand liberalisation programme outlined by the Bersani Decree. From 1 January 2002, the eligibility threshold will be reduced to 9 GWh per year. Furthermore, from 2002, 'multi-site' customers with a total yearly consumption of at least 40 GWh may also qualify as eligible customers. The new eligibility thresholds will enable nearly 5,000 consumers (accounting for about 40 per cent of final electricity consumption) to become eligible customers.

However, even before the demand liberalisation programme defined in the Bersani Decree is completed, Law 57/2001, passed earlier this year, set the framework for a further opening up of the market. It states that within three months after the completion of the divestment of Enel's generation assets, all consumers with a yearly consumption of at least 100 MWh may qualify as eligible customers. This is a very significant development, and one that will raise the number of eligible customers to more than 150,000, representing over 60 per cent of final electricity consumption.

To facilitate electricity trading in the new liberalised environment, the Bersani Decree also provides for the establishment of an organised electricity market.

The Gestore del mercato elettrico (GME; electricity market operator) is a joint-stock company set up in June 2000 and wholly owned by GRTN, the Italian transmission system operator (TSO), which, in turn, is wholly owned by the Italian Treasury.

According to Article 5 of Legislative Decree no.79/99, GME is responsible for organising and managing the Italian electricity market in a transparent and non-discriminatory way, so as to promote competition between producers and ensure an adequate level of power reserve.

In the electricity market, the order of dispatch of electricity-generating units, as well as the selection of reserve power plants and plants providing ancillary services, will be based on the merit-order (economic) dispatch system.

In May 2001, the Electricity Market Rules developed by GME were approved by the minister of industry. According to the Rules, the electricity market will consist of:

- a Day-Ahead Market, where electricity for each hour of the following day will be sold and bought in a way that is compatible with the grid's capability of transferring power between different geographical zones of the country;
- an Adjustment Market, for modifying the commitments resulting from the Day-Ahead Market;
- a Congestion Management Market, for economically procuring resources used by the TSO to solve local grid constraints which cannot be managed by the zonal system in the Day-Ahead Market;
- a Reserve Market, for economically procuring reserve capacity to be used by the TSO for secondary and tertiary regulation;
- a Balancing Market, for economically procuring resources to be used by the TSO for real-time balancing of injection into and withdrawals from the grid.

Both the Day-Ahead Market and the Adjustment Market will define an equilibrium price for each hour, nationally or for each of the market zones into which the country is divided. This price:

- will be paid by all consumers whose demand bids are accepted (as they are characterised by a reservation price higher than the equilibrium price);
- will be paid to all producers whose supply offers are accepted (as they are characterised by a reservation price lower than the equilibrium price).

In the Congestion Management Market, the Reserve Market and the Balancing Market, each participant providing the resources for ancillary services (congestion management, regulation and balancing) will be paid the offered price (with the only exception of the price for secondary regulation reserve where a system marginal price will be paid).

The Rules define the tasks of GME in managing each of the above markets, the requirements for admission of operators to the market and the way in which settlement is carried out. The Rules also define the procedures for the trading of green certificates through the facilities provided by GME in accordance with the Decree of the Ministry of Industry of November 1999.

The way in which the Electricity Market Rules are implemented is to be defined in Instructions, which are subject to ministerial approval. On 4 October 2001, GME published a draft version of the Instructions for consultation with an interested party. On the basis of the comments received by 30 November 2001, GME will prepare a proposal of Instructions to be submitted to the minister for productive activities for his approval, having sought the regulator's opinion.

At the same time, GME is developing the information system to support trading in the electricity market. An international tender was launched in February 2001 and a contract to develop the system (hardware and software) for electricity trading will be assigned shortly. It is expected that the system will be available for testing within a few months.

The date of the actual launch of the Italian electricity market will be defined by the minister for productive activities.

Even after the electricity market is fully operational, the market will not be the only form of electricity trading. Physical bilateral contracts will still be allowed, but they will be subject to prior authorisation of the regulator.

The advent of an organised electricity market will provide eligible customers with a menu of options for procuring electricity:

- the electricity market;
- physical bilateral contracts with producers;
- contracts with wholesale customers, which may in turn buy energy through the electricity market, or from producers on the basis of physical bilateral contracts.

Captive customers will be affected as well, albeit indirectly, by the reform of the electricity sector. Acquirente Unico ('Single Buyer'), the new company that will procure electricity for the captive market, will normally make its purchases in the electricity market, in line with the relevant minister of industry's guidelines.

As the experiences of other countries have shown, there are significant advantages to procuring electricity through the market rather than through bilateral trading. First, prices in the electricity market will be set according to a simple and transparent mechanism and, at any time, they will reflect the conditions of demand and supply, ie the purchase and sale offers/bids submitted by operators. Consequently, the transactions in the electricity market will always take place under the best conditions. No customer or producer will run the risk of purchasing or selling electricity at off-market prices and this without going through a costly search for the counterpart offering the best conditions. The electricity market, like any other market, will ensure the equilibrium between demand and supply at the market price. Bringing demand and supply together, thereby minimising the cost of searching for a counterpart, is the historical role that markets play. Furthermore, the electricity market will give operators more flexibility in making their generation and consumption pledges. In the electricity market, consumers and producers

may revise their commitments to withdrawing or injecting electricity from and into the grid until the previous day, without any penalty, and until a few hours ahead of real time, in the adjustment market.

While enjoying more flexibility in making and revising their generation and consumption commitments, market participants are exposed to hour-by-hour price variability. This risk is new to the Italian electricity sector, which has emerged from 40 years of administratively set prices. Variable market prices are the norm in many other sectors, where exchange-type markets (financial markets and commodity exchanges) have a longer tradition. In these markets, financial instruments for risk management (derivatives), such as futures and options, were developed. It is worth pointing out that, in the countries where the electricity market is already in place, financial instruments for the electricity sector – and organised markets for trading them – have been developed. GME is investigating the feasibility of developing and optimising solutions of this kind for the Italian electricity sector.

Through the combination of trading in the electricity market and an appropriate positioning in the market of derivatives, eligible customers and producers will be able to replicate the economic effects of physical bilateral trading. As a matter of fact, the economic results of operating in the electricity market will be better than those associated to trading through physical bilateral contracts, as the counterparts will benefit from the competition between producers, to the advantage of the contracting producer as well.

Since September 2000, Alberto Pototschnig has been the chief executive officer of the newly-established Italian Electricity Market Operator (Gestore del Mercato Elettrico Spa), the company responsible for organising and operating the new wholesale electricity market in Italy.

He was previously director of the electricity area at the Italian Regulatory Authority for Electricity and Gas, with primary responsibility in the design of economic and technical regulation for the electricity sector.

Before joining the Regulatory Authority in April 1997, Alberto had worked for seven years for London Economics, an international economic consultancy firm, where he was a director in charge of the Industry and Finance Team.

Alberto has a first degree in Economics from Bocconi University in Milan and a Master of Science in Econometrics and Mathematical Economics from the London School of Economics, University of London.

GME – Gestore del Mercato Elettrico Spa (Italian Electricity Market Operator) is a publicly-owned joint stock company which was established in June 2000 by the Independent Transmission System Operator to develop the rules, organise and operate the electricity market in Italy. GME operates under the provisions of legislative decree no. 79 of 1999 on the liberalisation of the electricity sector.

Alberto Pototschnig Amministratore Delegato Gestore del Mercato Elettrico Spa Viale Maresciallo Pilsudski, 92 00197 Roma – Italia tel: +39 06 8012 4755 fax: +39 06 8012 4524 email: pototschnig.alberto@mercato elettrico.org

Energy for the future

Scottish and Southern Energy incorporates the supply business of Southern Electric, Scottish Hydro and SWALEC and is now the UK's third largest energy company serving about four million electricity and one million gas customers. Whatever the size of your premises or the number of your sites we can supply your energy needs now and into the future. Our prices for both gas and electricity are highly competitive with innovative contracts matched to your needs. All contracts are clearly priced so what you see is what you pay.

To provide customers with a responsive and efficient service we have created a specialist department exclusively to manage contract sales. Our team of account managers has many years of experience of commerce, industry and the public sector. They understand your varying and often unique needs as well as the choices you have to make. Every supply contact we handle is individually tailored to match your actual requirements. In this way we make sure customers never pay more than they need for electricity or gas. Our account managers examine your pattern of use then tailor a pricing schedule to match your needs.

As well as providing you with the most cost effective energy source, we can also help you implement an impressive range of technical and strategic measures to increase your competitiveness, productivity and profits. These added value resources are the result of considerable investment by Scottish and Southern Energy and they provide high standards of service for our customers in industry, commerce, government and every type of large or small organisation for whom the economies of energy usage are important.

They offer expertise in the form of consultancy, technical and strategic support to help you identify the specific opportunities that energy can bring to your business. They are backed by technology resources from Scottish and Southern Energy, its specialist divisions and strategic partners.

For customers with a group of sites seeking quotations in the competitive market it is important to have comprehensive data so you get the best offer. We are regularly discussing offers with group customers so contact us with your site information as soon as you have it ready.

If you require more information on electricity or gas contracts or our range of added value services please call our National Sales Office on

08457 210 220

Toyota Prius – *the clean machine*

Standfirst: Many words but few deeds; a popular view about environmental action which is shattered by Toyota and its hybrid car, the Prius.

Electricity as a means of transporting individuals other than milkmen was mocked long before Clive Sinclair and his C5 in the 1980s. Even when the Toyota Prius was previewed in the UK in 1999 after two successful years in Japan, eyebrows were raised.

Now that it is on our roads not only is Prius being taken very seriously by a wide range of fleet operators, it is also attracting private buyers. So what's changed over the turn of the century to give electricity this new appeal?

Firstly, Prius is not an electric car as such but a smart marriage of electricity with fossil fuel. By substituting electrical current for petrol at low speeds around town, it forces both fuel consumption and CO2 emission levels about as low as they currently go. In our current environment of sustained high fuel prices and green tax incentives, that's an attractive proposition.

Local authorities, emergency services and public utilities have so far led the way towards cleaner exhausts and more mpg, but now central government is putting its money where its mouth is.

The Department of Works and Pensions recently became the first ministry to sign up to the Motorvate initiative, under which it undertakes to reduce CO_2 emissions by 12 per cent, cost-effectively, over the next three years. Also committed to the Sustainable Development Initiative, a quarter of its car fleet must be powered by alternative fuels by next April.

The DWP, which has added five Toyota Prius cars to its fleet to scrutinise their fuel economy, durability and comfort, "is leading the way to make sure we have a greener environment," says its Minister responsible for environmental issues, Baroness Hollis.

The Government has also backed schemes such as Powershift, offering subsidies to businesses opting to use Prius, because it is not only public bodies that are intrigued by the car.

The UK arm of Sodexho, worldwide market-leader in catering and support services, is currently trying out the hybrid vehicle in close co-operation with Toyota

Fleet. If its evaluation goes to plan, Sodexho would make Prius an option for all its 1,500 company drivers and would expect significant cost-savings to result.

So what exactly is the appeal of this, the world's first mass-production hybrid vehicle? Prius combines a 1.5 litre VVT-i petrol engine with a 30kW electric motor, which kicks in automatically to drive the front wheels below 10mph.

Around town it returns on average 61.4mpg, and emits about half the CO_2 of comparable petrol-engined cars.

Prius is also the first new car to come with a standard five-year warranty and roadside assistance package, and Toyota has launched its own leasing scheme to protect against residual-value risk, undertaking to buy the vehicle back at the most favourable price.

What really surprises people is that Prius is no glorified buggy bulging with batteries but a saloon car that concedes nothing in terms of driver appeal, performance, comfort or safety.

For a while gas-powered cars were vaunted as the way ahead, but they cannot make comparable savings on fuel or emissions and they lack the number of outlets necessary to make motorists feel comfortable. Prius, which needs no such special arrangements, has the ability to disarm driver resistance to alternative fuels, Toyota believes.

"Both private and fleet drivers are under real pressure from continued high fuel prices and emissions-based road and company car tax," says Toyota Fleet's General Manager Jon Pollock. "They are increasingly ready to consider more practical alternatives. Prius is the cleanest car on the road, offers Band A VED, maximum driver tax benefits, massive fuel savings and residual value guarantees. It's an answer to the questions being asked by many motorists and by fleet operators of every type and size."

For more information, please call
Toyota Fleet on 0845 271 2712
or send an email to
info@toyotafleetbusinesscentre.co.uk

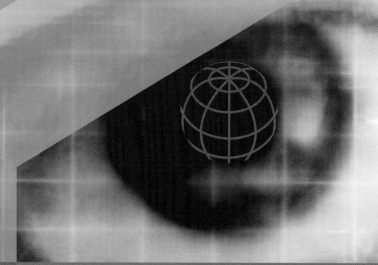

Part 3

Connected Europe

evolve~IT . . . the e in e-business applications

Evolve-IT Business Systems is focused in the development, support and promotion of a unique Business Application Development Environment, known as **evolve~IT** . . .

- Quick to market, cost effective and fully featured development solution
- Scalable for use within any size organisation, ISV or IT Consultancy
- Ease of use with Drag & Drop design features
- Data model and application neutral inbuilt features and functionality layers
- Workflow, business process automation

– **e-Server** – enables secure, real time access with a standard web browser

– **e-Manager** – an efficient & simple way for managers to have online access to your business applications

– **e-Self Service** – allows employees secure access to relevant information and data

"NO DEVELOPMENT LICENCE"

To be in e-control of YOUR e-business
Call us now on
01923 848242

or e-mail us on
info@evolve-it.com

or visit our website
www.evolve-it.com

evolve-it

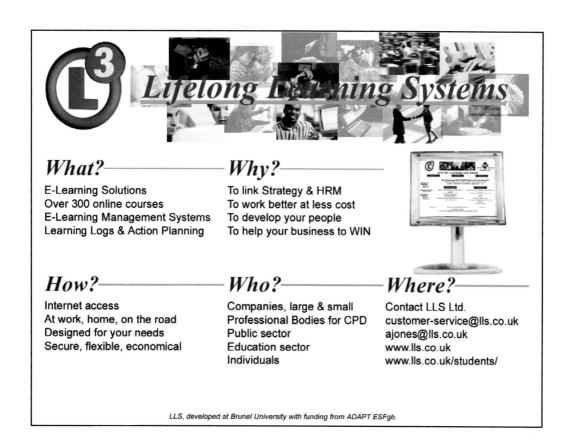

EUROPEAN BUSINESS AND THE NEW EU TELECOMS REGULATION

2002 looks set to be a vital year for determining Europe's e-future, says Andy Stern of Analytica Group, London.

The vision of an 'e-Europe' and a healthy, competitive IT sector has been stressed repeatedly by European leaders at EU summits in Lisbon, Stockholm and Gothenburg. However, with the latest report on the state of the telecoms sector showing huge barriers to free trade and new entrants making little impact on key areas of the telecoms market, 2002 looks set to be a vital year for determining Europe's e-future.

All systems go

European leaders have a stated objective to make the European Union 'the most competitive and dynamic knowledge-based economy in the world' by 2010. Establishing new regulations tailored to manage that goal has been one of the first steps undertaken by the Union.

Proposals tabled by the European Commission in Summer 2000 aimed to streamline the existing regu-

lation of Europe's communications sector. The objective of drawing up this new regulatory 'package' is also to establish a framework for the Internet-driven convergence of telecoms, technology and the media, which should be implemented by EU governments by 2002 onwards.

Devising a regulatory framework to stimulate and encourage growth in Europe's information and communications technology (ICT) sector is an increasingly complex task, given the wealth of new technologies changing the existing landscape almost by the day and the ongoing convergence between the telecoms, media and technology (TMT) sectors.

Introducing competition

At its core, the primary motivation for updating Europe's existing telecoms legislation is the belief that greater competition in access and services will result in lower prices for consumers and will fuel the growth of the information society.

Local loop unbundling (LLU) is one of the key policy mechanisms adopted by the European Commission and telecoms regulators across Europe to force competition into the local market, and with this in mind a regulation came into force across the European Union on 1 January 2001. LLU means that new entrants to the telecoms market no longer have to construct their own network to enter the local market, but can instead use the local network of incumbent operators such as BT or Deutsche Telekom. These are no longer the sole providers of data services, thus encouraging, so the theory goes, new entrants to the market.

In physical terms, the local loop consists of the last few metres of copper wire that transport voice telephony to the homes of domestic consumers. Control of these copper wires is a vitally important area for telecoms operators, as the opening of access to them coincides with the arrival of an important new technology, DSL (digital subscriber line). While high-speed data services, the key to Internet service provision, usually require fibre-optic cable, DSL offers service providers a cheaper and much easier solution for residential Internet customers.

However, LLU has so far failed to deliver the promise of competition. The process has proceeded far more slowly than planned – and very unevenly across the European Union. Foot-dragging on the part of the incumbents, as well as by some of the regulators, along with high costs and bureaucracy, have all drastically reduced the number of operators interested in providing DSL services.

The result to date has been that incumbents in most Western European countries continue to control over 95 per cent of access lines. They have also been able to steal a march on alternative carriers – many of them new entrants to the telecoms market – in the roll-out of DSL services.

Leased lines

There are other key areas which businesses feel demand more urgent action from European regulators. One crucial demand being made at present by broadband operators is that governments intervene in the market for local leased lines, the local connections that businesses require to access broadband networks and services.

For most businesses, short-distance leased lines are the only available broadband access technology and the incumbent operator is the only available provider of this key infrastructure. However, a new study issued by broadband operator Ebone showed that European businesses are curtailing their adoption of business tools such as Internet access, e-commerce, Intranets and video streaming as a direct result of the high cost of short-distance leased lines.

As with LLU, the major problem with leased lines is that despite moves by EU regulators to open the markets to competition, the incumbent operators in virtually all European countries still maintain a stranglehold on the market. Regulators, they argue, have largely neglected short-distance leased lines, preferring to focus on technologies such as DSL, which are aimed at consumers and only the smallest businesses. Redressing this balance will be one of the most crucial points for European businesses over the next 12 months.

Determining competitive forces

An important, though controversial, element of the Commission's liberalisation of the telecoms market is the competition regulation applied to liberalised segments of the market. Under normal EU competition rules, a major player in any market is perceived to be dominant when it controls over 40 per cent of that market. However, for the newly liberalised telecom markets, interim rules set the SMP threshold for telecoms at 25 per cent. Determining SMP is crucial in the telecoms market in Europe, as most regulatory obligations will only fall on operators with SMP.

The 25 per cent threshold is now set to be replaced again with the introduction of a more value-oriented assessment of SMP; draft guidelines state that operators would be regarded as having SMP if they 'persistently enjoyed a position of economic strength affording them the power to behave independently of competitors and customers', or if they had the ability to restrict access to users by other telecoms operators.

The guidelines list a number of criteria to measure market power: overall size; technological advantage; absence of countervailing buying power; product diversification; economies of scale or scope; vertical integration; highly developed distribution and sales network; and absence of potential competition. However, the guidelines have already been widely criticised by major European telecoms players for lacking coherence. This may yet convince EU decision-makers to rethink their stance, but with the new package of telecoms directives scheduled for completion before the end of 2001, the timing of interventions is critical.

Regulatory power

By issuing a set of guidelines for determining SMP in the telecoms market, the Commission has made clear that it wants national regulatory authorities (NRAs) to follow common European rules. However, the issue of Commission power over how NRAs control their own markets has proved to be one of the most divisive in drawing up the new legislation.

The Commission's initial line had been to secure for itself an ultimate veto over decisions made by national regulatory authorities. However, EU telecoms ministers voted to limit the Commission's role to merely expressing dissatisfaction with NRA rulings, rather than being able to overturn them fully.

The problem with this stance is that keeping regulatory authority at the national level retains the complexity of national frameworks and goes against the grain of a single European market for telecoms products and services. Fifteen regulators pressing fifteen individual agendas make it difficult for telecoms operators to establish pan-European efforts and bring down prices. The onus now lies firmly on EU businesses to encourage a single regulatory framework.

Conclusion

There is no doubt that moves to liberalise the telecoms sector have resulted in lower prices across all EU countries. In a recent study, the European Central Bank (ECB) found that prices had fallen most in Greece, dropping by 19.6 per cent between 1998 and 2000, with Germany showing the second largest fall of 15.9 per cent.

Table 1 Evolution of the Harmonised Index of Consumer Prices (HICP) sub-index 'Telecommunications services'[1]

Country	1996	1997	1998	1999	2000	% change between 1998 and 2000
Belgium	100.0	105.0	104.1	98.0	95.8	–7.9
Germany	100.0	96.2	94.9	84.1	79.9	–15.9
Greece	100.0	104.7	106.1	99.8	85.3	–19.6
Spain	100.0	99.7	101.6	103.7	97.9	–3.6
France	100.0	97.6	93.1	93.4	88.6	–4.9
Irish Republic	100.0	98.3	92.0	84.7	82.0	–10.9
Italy	100.0	98.8	98.8	96.8	93.5	–5.3
Luxembourg	100.0	103.2	101.6	92.7	85.6	–15.7
Netherlands	100.0	99.6	100.7	95.2	89.0	–11.6
Austria	100.0	100.3	98.8	96.6	92.0	–6.9
Portugal	100.0	102.5	99.0	95.4	90.8	–8.3
Finland	100.0	98.7	98.8	96.6	92.0	–6.9
Euroland (12 countries)	100.0	97.7	95.8	90.5	86.4	–9.9
Denmark	100.0	100.0	96.8	93.4	92.3	–4.6
Sweden	100.0	97.0	99.5	99.2	90.2	–9.3
United Kingdom	100.0	96.7	95.0	91.9	87.7	–7.7

Source: European Central Bank
[1] For Spain, Irish Republic, the Netherlands, Denmark, Sweden and the United Kingdom, the figures represent the HICP in telecoms services and equipment

The ECB's survey provided welcome news for consumers and businesses alike, with the implementation of the regulatory reforms in the telecommunications sector set to result in further decreases.

The amount of time required to reach a new overall lower level of pricing will correspond with the length of the regulatory reform process itself, the ECB says, along with a 'required adjustment period'. In real terms, this means that it could take a further 10 years before the levelling out is finished.

According to the EU commissioner for the information society, Erkki Liikanen, telecoms is now the fastest growing sector in the European Union, with growth standing at 12.6 per cent in 2000. Business needs to leverage the opportunity presented by the introduction of a new regulatory framework to determine a competitive market that provides cost-based pricing for telecoms products and services. 2002 will be crucial for the future landscape of European communications; the knowledge-based economy relies on the European Union getting this model right.

Andy Stern is managing director of Analytica Group, a business information and communications company that specialises in providing highly focused business information and communications services to companies, organisations and public sector bodies located in or with an interest in Europe.

Telephone +44 (0)20 7722 4334; e-mail andy.stern@ analytica.eu.com

TELECOMS SPEEDS UP

The future is more for less, says Eddie Murphy, senior consultant at Analysys.

Since the liberalisation of telecoms began, and the widespread use of digital technologies drove down the cost of providing telecoms, we have become used to getting more service for less money. This trend will continue into the foreseeable future, as emerging networks lead to enormous improvements in the delivery of both voice and data services. This Chapter examines a number of important areas in which developments are already underway:

- The availability of inexpensive fast access to telecoms networks.
- The increasing irrelevance of distance as a cost element in communications.
- Emerging mobile technologies.
- The convergence of networks.

Broadband access – unblocking the pipes

Probably the most significant development over the coming years will be the increased capacity, at affordable prices, in access networks. In the past, unless you were a large company and could afford to pay a large amount of money for leased lines, the copper wire between your premises and your local exchange made possible only very slow communication speeds. However, new digital subscriber line (DSL) technology allows communication at speeds of 10 to 50 times those available over an ordinary telephone line, making Internet access much faster. Other technologies, such as cable modems and fixed wireless access, can deliver similar speeds. Moreover, these technologies are all available at flat-rate prices per month. Thus, for less than £100 per month, many smaller companies will be able to communicate using fast access technologies which only large corporations can currently afford. However, larger companies will also benefit, as their employees will be able to access corporate intranets from home at speeds only previously possible from their office desks.

Although DSL and cable services are available in parts of the United Kingdom, penetration here lags behind that in other countries. For example, when looking at competing economies in the G7, the United Kingdom comes bottom of the league table for penetration of broadband access services. In Canada, the penetration of broadband access is already 10 per cent, as compared with only 1 per cent in the United Kingdom. The government is monitoring this situation carefully and is planning initiatives to improve the relative position of the United Kingdom.

Backbone network – distance becomes irrelevant

The development of optical fibre technology has allowed enormous amounts of telecoms traffic to be carried over a single fibre. In addition, other new technologies are increasing the capacity of fibre all the time. These developments are quickly eliminating distance as a cost factor in the provision of telecoms services. As more channels are squeezed into a single pipe and the cost of laying that pipe remains roughly the same, so the cost per channel is falling rapidly. In a competitive telecoms market, this decline in costs is soon passed on to the end customer. In fact, the Internet is a graphic illustration of how distance is already becoming irrelevant in communications – you can e-mail your next-door neighbour and a colleague in Australia for roughly the same price.

At the time of writing, many of the providers of telecoms backbone infrastructure are experiencing problems arising from over-capacity in backbone networks worldwide. As a consequence, a shake-out is currently underway which will see the existing infrastructure concentrated in the hands of the most efficient operators. Although the investors in many of these networks may not see any advantage, this outcome is likely to benefit customers, as operators combine innovative ideas with promotional campaigns to attract traffic on to their networks.

As competition drives prices down to reflect the costs incurred by operators, the premiums paid for long-distance and international communications will disappear. Time-of-day distinctions are also likely to become obsolete as traffic is increasingly carried over global networks.

Mobile broadband comes closer

Faster communications are also becoming possible over mobile networks. Currently, most customers have access to mobile data communications at speeds which are very slow – less than a third of the speed possible using standard telephone lines. This makes accessing e-mails a slow process and surfing the net over a mobile connection almost impossible (in addition to prohibitively expensive).

New technologies building on the existing second-generation[1] (2G) GSM standard are making faster mobile communications possible in the short term. These are often referred to as 2.5G technologies. Although, currently, these do not even offer speeds which can be achieved over a standard copper fixed line, they are expected to improve with time and handset availability.

However, until the advent of third-generation (3G) mobile services, we will not see significant improvements in the speeds at which data can be accessed while on the move. 3G will allow users to access data at speeds well in excess of those presently delivered via fixed lines, but less than those which DSL and other broadband fixed-access technologies have made possible. Indeed, the promise of 3G has been greatly exaggerated, with industry figures predicting that it will allow users to access video at speeds of 2Mbit/s. In actual fact, accessing video will be slow, expensive and a relatively rare undertaking for most users. E-mail and Internet access will be the services to benefit most from 3G, although it may lead to the appearance of new and important markets for entertainment services. In Europe alone, more than £1.5 million is currently spent each year on downloading ringtones for mobile phones, and this figure is rising – imagine what the level of spend might be on the sophisticated content that 3G will make available.

Nevertheless, there is still likely to be some dissatisfaction with the performance of 3G, as users' experience of higher-speed fixed communications links drives their expectations of 3G to unrealistic levels – and this is where 4G comes in, we might suppose.

The ability to send and receive e-mails at acceptable speeds, and access the Internet while travelling, are obvious benefits of the deployment of 2.5G and 3G technologies. In future, the combination of reasonably fast communications and innovation in handset design is likely to see a proliferation of new services aimed at businesses and consumers.

---

[1] First-generation was used for the analogue mobile phones that worked over the original Cellnet and Vodafone networks. Second-generation technology appeared in the early to mid-1990s when digital GSM mobile networks were deployed.

Voice and data networks converge

The current watchword of communications is convergence. Traditional models of communications, whereby separate networks exist for voice and data, fixed and mobile, business and entertainment, are being overthrown. Unified networks, carrying all of these types of traffic, are emerging. Cable TV networks now carry voice and Internet traffic, while telephone networks are carrying increasing quantities of data. Furthermore, what are being referred to as next-generation networks (NGNs) are starting to appear. One certainty about the definitive next-generation network solution that will be seen over the coming years is that it will be based around the IP technology on which the Internet runs today.

Converged networks will have many implications for businesses. The space in ducts will come under less pressure, fewer members of staff will be required to maintain and operate the network, the training of staff will be rationalised, services combining voice communication and databases (computer–telephony integration (CTI)) will become much easier to implement, network connection costs will fall and different terminal types will become unified into a single device. All of these developments will either decrease costs or increase the functionality of networks – or both.

The future

For the user of communications, the future is bright. Communications services that are available now are becoming cheaper. New services and working models are emerging due to the availability of fast data communications wherever people happen to find themselves. Over the next few years, users will be able to do things via communications that we could not contemplate today. The precise nature of these developments is, however, anybody's guess at the moment. Nobody would have predicted a £1.5 billion European market for downloading ringtones two years ago, but that is what has happened, even with the very limited handsets that 2G technologies offer.

Eddie Murphy is a senior consultant with Analysys Consulting and is manager of the Convergence Group at Analysys, which specialises in assessing the impact of new technologies on the convergence between the telecoms and media sectors.

Analysys delivers support and insight to the networked economy. Working with players throughout the communications and New Media value chain, it provides strategy and systems consultancy, information services and start-up support. Its services include launch phase planning and investment; corporate strategy, business planning and business optimisation assistance; economic analysis; and regulatory policy advice. Telephone +44 (0)1223 460600. Fax +44 (0)1223 460866.

e-mail eddie.murphy@analysys.com

Surrey Translation Bureau

39 West Street Farnham, GU9 7DX. Tel: 44 (0)1252 733999 Fax: 44(0)1252 733773
E-Mail: stb@surreylanguage.co.uk   Web site http://www.surreylanguage.co.uk

worden worden mots sanat palabras λέξεις worten Worter mots СЛОВА
worden Palabras 1333 CJOBA parole parole palabras mots СЛОВА
Palabras sanat Worter СЛОВА ord palabras parole mots

Lost for words?

Technically speaking....Yes!
You need a **specialist** translation service!

OUR COMMITMENT TO YOU

- Fast and accurate translations
- Competitive rates
- Professional linguists
- State-of-the-art DTP facilities
- Global network of contacts

Fax this form now to John Cooke on (0)1252 733773 or email stb@surreylanguage.co.uk and you will automatically qualify for a 10% discount.

Name: _____

Position:_____

Company Name:_____

Address:_____

_____

Postcode: _____

Tel no: _____

Fax no: _____

Please tick box below if you would like more information about our translation and related services

☐ **YES**   ☐ **NO**

EUROPE AND THE WEB

The idea of 'Internet business' has changed noticeably since 2000, says Ciaran Quinn at Virtual European Office Ltd (VEO). Business people in Europe are starting to realise that the business is not 'Internet' in and of itself, but that in reality the Internet is simply a great technology that enables companies to communicate and do business in different, additional, and more cost-effective ways.

The good old days

In March 2000, the European Internet scene was thriving. The First Tuesday networking group was turning away crowds at the doors in Paris and London, hundreds of incubators were 'helping' thousands of entrepreneurs, and pure start-ups were still getting easy money. Since then, First Tuesday has been sold twice and is but a shell of its former self, incubators have gone by the wayside and some are returning left-over capital to shareholders, and funding has dried up for so many expected entrepreneurs.

The bigger they are the harder they fall

Although the Continent was catching up with the United States, Europe never developed the same intense level of enthusiasm for 'the Internet' that was seen in the United States through early 2000 while the European Commission was launching the eEurope initiative, emphasising the promises of 'a digitally literate and entrepreneurial Europe' and 'a socially inclusive Information Society' towards European populations (citizens, homes, schools, businesses and administrations) in dire need of a persuasive motto to adopt digital technologies. The European drive started later and did not rise as high (with total e-commerce revenues reaching approximately US$87 billion in Europe and US$490 billion in the United States in 2000, according to Forrester), and therefore the rate of growth slowed, relatively speaking, less than in the United States. In fact, during the past year and a half Europe as a whole has narrowed the 'Internet gap' with the United States with respect to population on-line to less than a year and a half.

No more easy money

'Internet' initial public offerings (IPOs) are completely out of fashion and the M&A market is substantially down. At the time of writing, Credit Suisse has just announced a layoff of 2,000 investment bankers. Other investment banks are laying off staff in part because they do not see them coming back into favour quickly. Many business plans that projected wonderful yet unrealistic 'hockey stick' sales and profit growth curves simply will not receive funding. This is probably a very good thing. Businesses that were being built on the backs of venture capital money now have to try and build themselves up using revenue from (of all the wild ideas) their customers.

The decline in European investment was much less than that in the United States. The first half of 2001 saw an investment decline of 60 per cent across the United States, while the drop in France, for example, was only 15 per cent.

Cash is king again

Cash is now king once again and will stay so for the foreseeable future. Most 'pure Internet' companies that have significant cash reserves are now using them very wisely, and many are ignoring the idea of 'first mover' advantage. Instead, companies are turning their efforts towards turning a profit and not towards generating as much traffic at whatever cost possible. Business models that were built on advertising have crumbled under the twin weights of reduced general advertising spend and tremendously reduced Internet advertising spend by Internet companies themselves. Some companies are now selling what used to be available for free (eg Office.com); some are providing fee-based premium packages for additional and value-added services (eg Lycos Europe), while others are simply pulling up European stakes (eg Hoovers business information services) in order to cut costs. The subscription model is being considered and tested but has not yet found its sweet spot in the 'Internet business'. Micro-payment pay-as-you-go systems would be able to solve the general resistance to subscriptions. European mobile usage skyrocketed primarily as a result of the introduction of pay-as-you-go pricing as a complement to the basic subscription model. However, that works well in that industry because a consumer only needs one mobile phone supplier. Within the consumer Internet space, the model has to he different due to lack of ubiquity and the relatively broad range of sites that a customer may visit. There is no single solution coming to the head of the pack right now, but whatever company solves this problem will be tapping into a goldmine.

Broadband is fast, take-up is slow

Broadband is wonderful, as anyone who has experienced 24/7 rapid connections to the Internet will attest. But consumers have not taken up broadband offers nearly as quickly as expected in Europe and penetration levels remain very low. Currently, Sweden tops the chart with nearly 14 per cent, Germany and France levels are at 8 per cent and 7 per cent respectively, and the United Kingdom is only slightly above 2 per cent. This has been in part due to poor service providers. In mid-2001, BT in the United Kingdom had installed 25,000 ADSL lines but had a backlog of seven times that amount. Even though that ratio is appallingly high, the absolute number is still quite low. Until consumers have decided on 'killer' broadband services, or the initial cost difference between dial-up and broadband becomes insignificant, this penetration level will likely remain low. Music and video will be the most important such 'killer' services, but until the music and movie industries roll out decent services with attractive pricing, consumers will not take them up and the demand for home broadband will remain low. As for other promising 'in-development' technologies, such as UMTS and 3G, European operators (Orange and SFR in France; E-Plus, Mobilcom and Group 3G in Germany) are currently considering sharing their network infrastructures in order to reduce their individual costs of the rollout of their 3G mobile services.

The good news

The above paragraphs could imply that the 'Internet business' may be dead, but that is far from the truth. It is time, however, to stop talking about the 'Internet business' as if it were a stand-alone idea, and instead start talking about 'business'. The Internet is not a business unto itself, but is in fact a tool that can be used by business to better serve customers with existing and new products and services. Furthermore, the smart companies recognise that the digital revolution of the 1990s has created not just one new channel to customers but multiple channels, including digital interactive television and mobile telephones. Most European consumers had never tried any of these three channels just a handful of years ago, while today Europe has more than 20 million iTV households, more than 100 million Internet users, and more than 200 million mobile phone users. Most of Europe's

150 million households have at least one of these new channels available to them, and many have multiple channels and multiple users. These numbers will continue to increase significantly until the end of the decade when most people will have access to all three channels. In Europe, critical mass has already been reached with the Internet and mobile telephones (with penetration rates of more than 30 per cent of the population for the Internet and more than 70 per cent for mobile phones, according to IDC and Durlacher, respectively). Critical mass will be reached by iTV well before the end of this decade, as most countries have legislated an end to analogue television.

The challenge to business now is to offer excellent services to the hundreds of millions of users with these new digital channels. The explosive growth that the Internet was experiencing was given a good hard slap of reality in 2000. That slapping sound continued through 2001, but it by no means suggests that digital business is dead, but instead that it is being structured differently. It means that existing companies and entrepreneurs have been forced, thankfully, to become far better at what they do in order to attract capital and profit-generating customers. We have entered a period where it truly is survival of the fittest. Some companies will survive this period while others will thrive in it as they focus efforts not on the 'Internet business', but instead use the Internet and other digital channels to focus on their business itself.

Ciaran Quinn is a partner with VEO Limited.

Founded in 1997, VEO was initially launched to assist US Internet companies accelerate their market entry into the unfamiliar territories of Europe.

With its head office in Paris, France, and staff located across Europe, VEO now offers not only to help US companies enter Europe, but also to take European-based companies pan-European quickly. This can either be by expanding organically, or by looking for acquisition or merger opportunities.

27, rue de Solferino, 92100 Boulogne, France. Telephone +33 1 4610 9494; e-mail cquinn@veo.net; http://www.veo.net

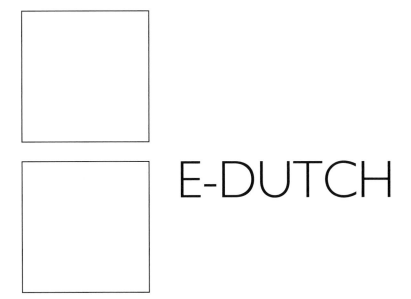

E-DUTCH

The Internet infrastructure in the Netherlands is as advanced as any in Europe, argues Mirjam Schuit.

According to a recent survey from Pricewaterhouse Coopers, Dutch dot.com companies are proving to be among the most successful in Europe. Sixty-one per cent of dot.com companies in the Netherlands will be profitable in 2001, compared to 49 per cent in France and just 24 per cent in the United Kingdom. Only Germany with 66 per cent profitability fared better in the four-nation survey.

The government supports the information and communications technology (ICT) sector in various ways. Notable is the Gigaport project, which was initiated by the government to stimulate the development of next-generation Internet. Gigaport has a speed of 10 gigabits per second, which makes it the fastest stretch of Internet in the world.

The recently updated E-commerce Action Plan contains specific policies to stimulate e-commerce. The Dutch practice of customised advanced rulings gives foreign companies the opportunity to gain insight into the tax consequences of the legal structure and type of operation being planned. Rules to determine 'permanent establishment' status are favourable for e-business operations. The Netherlands' network of tax treaties is designed to avoid double taxation.

As a result of their long tradition of transnational commerce in Europe, the Dutch are particularly adept at navigating through the complexity of a uniform global Web on the one hand, and the important differences between European countries on the other. The Internet infrastructure in the Netherlands is characterised by:

- Bandwidth availability: The Dutch communication network has the highest quality standard in Europe. The early liberalisation of the telecoms market (first on the European continent) has brought in a significant number of companies which have developed additional infrastructure, particularly fibre optics, and other high-bandwidth IP-based infrastructure. Internet service providers (ISPs) provide excellent services.
- Connectivity: The Amsterdam Internet Exchange is one of the main centres of Internet traffic in Europe. Speedy connectivity within Europe and to the United States and Asia is therefore guaranteed.
- The Gigaport project: This government initiative, undertaken together with commercial parties such as IBM, Cisco Systems, Ericsson and KPN, is one of the most advanced experimental networks for next-generation Internet development.
- Wireless e-commerce and digital TV: Mobile phone penetration and use is on a comparatively high level and provides the Netherlands with

extra growth potential in wireless communication, the next wave of Internet connectivity. The Dutch TV cable network – almost 100 per cent coverage – also provides extra e-business potential.

- Internet-ready office space: Many Dutch cities and regions have developed an attractive business environment (incubators and business parks) for start-up companies in the Internet industry. Such locations cover the needs of e-business operations: extra communication infrastructure capacity (quickly expandable), and located at public-, road- and air transport junctions. Many of these sites are linked to the so-called 'city rings' of KPN Telecom, high-quality and high-capacity double-glass fibre rings which connect important economic centres. Consequently, there is a good supply of office buildings suitable for e-businesses. The operating costs of these offices are among the lowest in Western Europe.
- Costs of telecoms and datacommunication: Telecoms in the Netherlands are privatised and subject to increasingly less regulation. Dutch national and international telecoms costs are low in comparison with surrounding European locations.

In the Netherlands, Internet access of consumers is one of the highest in Western Europe: 53 per cent of Dutch citizens are connected. Electronic banking and the use of smart cards are daily practice for the majority of the Dutch population.

Application of the Internet in business is on a higher level than many surrounding countries: around 25,000 companies in the Netherlands offer products and services through the Internet. Due to the widespread successful implementation of EDI (electronic data interchange; usually over leased lines, but now moving increasingly to the Internet), Dutch companies have already been conducting business electronically for years. Various associations and platforms have been erected. Organisations such as the Amsterdam New Media Association and Electronic Commerce Platform play an important role in setting standards and creating a stimulating meeting place.

Venture capital is growing rapidly in the Netherlands. In 1999, a growing number of Dutch Internet investors, such as Nesbic, ICOM, Gorillapark, Gilde etc, emerged. Major Dutch banks, such as ABN/AMRO and ING, established investment units for Internet-related businesses.

Mirjam Schuit is executive director of the Netherlands Foreign Investment Agency in the United Kingdom and Ireland. tel: 020 7225 1074; website: www.nfia.co.uk

E-RISKS AND EUROPE

E-commerce may be the way of the future, but do not forget risk management, says John Ryder of Royal & SunAlliance ProFin.

Over recent years, companies worldwide have invested billions of pounds in the development of e-commerce. E-enablement has been the mantra of management consultants throughout the business world. The prolonged crash in telecoms, media and Technology (TMT) stocks has certainly led to a slowdown in this process, but it would be foolish to imagine that business will ever return to the pre-Internet days. E-commerce is here to stay.

However, in the rush to e-enablement, many companies have failed to implement a risk management programme to analyse the risks associated with e-commerce and to ensure that they have adequate insurance protection in place. The purpose of this Chapter is to highlight the key risks associated with e-commerce and to consider some of the ways in which they can be mitigated.

Jurisdictional risks

One of the key drivers in the expansion of Internet use has been its multinational reach. The implication of this is that potentially its contents are subject to the laws and regulations in every country in which a site can be accessed. In a US ruling, in *Playboy v*

Playman, an Italian company was held in breach of an injunction preventing it from trading in the United States because its new website could be accessed by US consumers and orders placed for its products.

Even if the website states that a particular country's laws apply, local laws may take precedence. The European Union has plans to enable a consumer to be able to sue in his own country regardless of where the defendant is located and any agreement between the parties.

A company may mitigate the risk by targeting only specific countries – for example, where the risks and laws are considered acceptable. A company may carry out a legal analysis of each country in which it is intending to trade. A disclaimer on the website stating that the website is only intended to be used by visitors from specified countries will help reduce the likelihood of regulatory jurisdiction from other countries.

Regulatory risks

Most UK companies will be familiar with the existing regulatory regime applicable to the supply of goods and services. However, when trading over the Internet, additional regulations are increasingly being applied in the United Kingdom. For example, advertising standards apply to the content of websites, while the FSA has recently issues guidelines to the effect that it will apply its regulations to any website capable of being accessed within its jurisdiction.

An understanding of the legal and regulatory regime in the countries where a company intends to trade is essential to managing the risk of trading on the Internet.

Contractual risks

Whether trading business-to-business (B2B) or business-to-consumer (B2C), websites need the capability to create a legal relationship fairly easily. However, many sites fail to set out where 'offer' and 'acceptance' apply; through an 'invitation to treat' (ie an intention to solicit offers), a company may inadvertently form a contract. The well-publicised Argos case whereby televisions were offered for sale for a fraction of their real price is a good illustration of the potential pitfalls.

Other common failures in this area are a failure to incorporate contractual terms and/or appropriate cooling-off periods.

When developing a website capable of trading with business and consumers, it is important to understand and incorporate the appropriate contractual terms.

Content risks

The use of e-mail and websites facilitates and encourages communication with organisations and individuals worldwide. This capability, combined with the informality of e-mail, has significantly increased the risk of liability arising from the content of the website and e-mails.

There have already been a number of well-publicised defamation cases arising from use of e-mail, notably *Western Provident v Norwich Union*. Another area of increasing litigation is from the infringement of a third party's intellectual property rights. This has been for breach of copyright, in addition to trade-

mark/passing off claims, for example relating to domain names. In the United States, there have been significant patent claims arising from the infringement of patents on business processes. In order to mitigate the likelihood of such claims, companies should apply and enforce an e-mail and Internet usage policy. In addition, websites should contain disclaimers regarding their content, particularly if the website enables third parties to post information on to it.

Data risks

Data is a valuable business tool. Used effectively, it can give an organisation a real advantage over its competitors. However, it is also one of the most heavily regulated areas and easy to contravene applicable legislation particularly in the European Economic Area (EEA). In the United Kingdom, this area is regulated by the Data Protection Act 1998, under which the information commissioner has wide and strong powers.

The Act applies restrictions in relation to the notification, security and transfer of data. One particular issue for global organisations is the restriction on transferring data outside the EEA unless the state in question has adequate security measures; as yet this does not include the United States.

In order to manage the risks associated with data protection, a data protection, retention and security policy should be implemented by applicable organisations.

Infrastructure risks

The IT system supporting an organisation's business processes and website are clearly critical to an organisation's e-commerce, and failure of the part or whole could have a potentially devastating effect.

A detailed risk analysis can identify the systems risks associated with this and ensure that there are appropriate safeguards and fallback arrangements in place. These are designed to reduce the likelihood of an incident arising and to manage the incident effectively should it occur.

Conclusion

E-commerce undoubtedly brings increased risks, but many of these can be mitigated by the implementation of an appropriate risk management policy. However, there will still be risks to which an organisation is exposed, and as part of the risk management process it is important for such organisations to review such risks in relation to their existing insurance arrangements.

Most insurance policies in the market will provide a measure of cover for the type of risks described above, but organisations need to be clear where the cover ends and where their liability starts. A further complication is that there are wordings in the market which pre-date the Internet and whose language is being twisted to fit situations that were never envisaged when the policy was originally drafted. In such circumstances, it is inevitable that gaps in cover can occur.

Risk managers need to work with their brokers and insurers to ensure that their current insurance arrangements are adequate in relation to the organisation's existing and planned e-business activities.

Royal & SunAlliance has recently launched 'Management Assurance', a packaged product providing specialist insurance protection with bespoke cover to suit the needs of each and every business, public or private. It covers risks such as Directors' & Officers' Liability insurance, Employment Practices Liability insurance, Crime, Kidnap Ransom & Extortion, Pension Scheme Liability insurance, Professional Indemnity insurance and Libel insurance. The product includes unique value-added services designed to help insureds avoid distracting and time-consuming losses and ultimately support the insureds in managing their future with confidence.

John Ryder, eRisks product leader, Royal & SunAlliance ProFin. Telephone +44 (0)20 7337 5143; http://www. profin.royalsun.com

CREDIT RISKS AND THE NEW ECONOMY

With speed and efficiency come new financial risks, says Eleanor Lewis of EULER. Unknown, untested customers are ordering your goods and services over the Internet, expecting a 24/7 service. How can you keep a handle on credit decisions and payment methods?

At the beginning of 2001, the forecasts for business-to-business (B2B) e-commerce growth were fantastic. Twelve months on, the new technology bubble has been punctured and the predictions of B2B e-commerce transactions reaching levels of US$7 trillion or more within the next two years now seem optimistic. However, even though this rapid acceleration of B2B e-commerce transactions has failed to materialise, the opportunities of the new economy have not gone away. They remain to be exploited, and increasing numbers of businesses are doing just that.

One of the points about the new economy is that it is a great leveller. On-line marketplaces and exchanges bring together buyers and sellers at industry and global levels, irrespective of the size of company, offering all parties unprecedented opportunities to seek and access goods and services. They are thus causing significant change in supply chain dynamics.

All the conveniences of speed, efficiency and variety mean changing payment methods, changing customer risks and greater automation of processes such as the assessment of risk, invoicing and collection. In addition, customer expectations of delivery and service are increasing and businesses must adapt their offerings and recognise the new economy principles of speed, convenience and customisation.

Certainly, by allowing access to global markets and customers, the Internet is an empowering marketing and distribution tool. However, with this come financial risks. Gone is the knowledge of the customer, a core part of any decision to grant credit, with unknown, untested and perhaps foreign-domiciled customers accessing goods and services over the Internet. These demands, coupled with the pressures to deliver in a 24/7 environment and to meet changing customer expectations, can put great pressure on the credit manager, risk manager and sales manager within a business.

It is at this time of rising uncertainty and fundamental shifts in business practices that even greater emphasis should be placed on prudent credit management. This entails the traditional principles of assessing the customer and his creditworthiness, invoicing correctly and on time, and ensuring collection is efficient. To quote the old adage, 'A sale is not a sale until it is paid for'. Just because the delivery mechanisms and technologies that underlie the new economic models are different, this does not mean that businesses should abandon the underlying principles that prudent credit management brings – effective and efficient cash flow, targeted sales, and safe and secure business growth.

Companies should retain a traditional approach to their credit management activities. Fundamental to this is a fully-fledged credit manual. Putting together a credit manual need not be difficult: it should cover the terms and conditions of any contract and set out credit control procedures and criteria for payment. Its importance should also not be underestimated: when a (dot.com) client of EULER Trade Indemnity recently asked a bank for more funding, it discovered that it was the credit manual that the bank manager was more interested in, and not the sales plan!

There are 10 key tips on good credit management. These continue to be relevant, despite some of the substantial shifts in markets and business practices:

1. Check out prospective customers, through status agency reports, bank reports or trade references, or use a credit insurer. EULER Trade Indemnity, for example, has access to information on over 40 million companies worldwide.
2. Continue to monitor existing customers and review these at least twice a year. Most bad debts stem from longstanding customers.
3. Grade your customers by risk levels and treat their accounts accordingly.
4. Pay particular attention to those growing rapidly, and be wary of companies that have emerged from the failure of another company.
5. Before agreeing repayment plans, determine whether the customer's situation is likely to improve. Do not agree to repayment plans that would take more than six months to clear a debt.
6. Watch for sudden changes in orders – a dramatic increase could signal that other suppliers have stopped supplying.
7. Make your terms of trade clear and unambiguous. Ensure that they are agreed before despatching goods or providing services.
8. Ensure that you obtain a signed delivery note for goods supplied and always invoice on time. Failure to do so gives your customers additional credit.
9. Check the status of each account before despatching goods. Do not continue to supply if the account is overdue.
10. Give credit management a high profile in your business. Establish a credit management information system that gives an accurate, up-to-date picture of cash flow.

Whatever the forecasts of e-commerce B2B growth, one thing is certain: we are in the throws of a revolution that will change the way in which businesses and economies operate. It is simply the pace of this change that is open to debate. Evidently there will be a requirement to adapt some business practices to respond to these new market dynamics. The credit risk involved will actually be heightened because of these very dynamics: the unknown and untested qualities of the customer; the increase in the pace of change in global markets and economies; and the new-found access to markets where there is no previous experience of trading. With this in mind, the requirement for sound credit management and the use of specialist companies such as credit insurers, which have the global reach and understanding of economies, markets and companies worldwide, becomes imperative. The well-established principles outlined above have served businesses well over the years and have helped to contribute to sound business growth.

AA+ Standard & Poor's-rated EULER Trade Indemnity is the United Kingdom's leading credit insurer. It protects businesses against trade credit risk whenever and wherever it occurs.

EULER Trade Indemnity is a member of the EULER Group, the world's premier credit insurer and Europe's leading integrated factoring company (Eurofactor). In 2002 EULER will merge its operations with Hermes when the combined operations will be present in 29 countries with a 37 per cent of the world credit insurance market.

EULER Trade Indemnity plc, 1 Canada Square, London E14 5DX

Telephone +44 (0)20 7512 9333; Fax +44 (0)20 7512 9186; http://www.eulergroup.com

Need an integrated distribution service worldwide?

In an increasingly competitive business environment, ensuring consignments arrive on time and on budget is vital.

Pharos International offers a single source with the capacity to cover every aspect of mail distribution and ensure fast and accurate delivery worldwide. Our one stop service obviates the need to source different suppliers saving you a great deal of time and trouble. Another benefit is that progress can be monitored more effectively through single contact with a dedicated team assigned to your account.

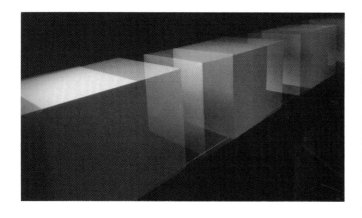

HERCULES
The strong force in international distribution

This specialist service portfolio has been extended to offer a range of UK and overseas mailing options, the latest of which is our worldwide parcel delivery service.

Tracking systems enable us to pinpoint the precise location of consignments and, in addition, monitor delivery schedules during transit.

...you need <u>our</u> stamp on your consignments.

Once we know your objectives we'll provide impartial advice on the most efficient and cost effective way to achieve them whether you require a comprehensive service or help with just one aspect of your mailing.

A fully networked IT system means we can offer a full range of electronic services including data management, analysis reporting and address enhancement.

International Mail Services
Optimum routes are chosen from a range of quality tested postal and hand delivery services

UK & International Parcel Services
See 'Hercules'

Bulk Freight
Air, Road and Sea services

Polythene Wrapping
Automated volume wrapping and addressing systems
Polythene film and polybag supply

Enveloping and Addressing
Hand & machine enclosing
Inkjet envelope addressing
Envelope supply

Computer Services
Data management
Merge/purge/deduplication
Mailsort-Presstream-Overseas Sortation
Selections
Address enhancement
Printed listings/magnetic media output
Analysis reporting
Postal address file

Laser Personalised Printing
Simplex
Duplex

Specialist Services
Pick and Pack operations
Storage

Call Simon Harris, Sales Director or Sarah Loosemore, Customer Service Manager on **01959 547900**

Fax: 01959 547901
E-mail: pharosuk@easynet.co.uk
www.pharos-international.co.uk

Pharos International Limited, 2 Churchill Court, Horton's Way, Westerham, Kent TN16 1BT.

shaping your environment

To make sure the office works for you, we mould our designs around your space, your technology and the way you work. With flexible desking, screening and storage solutions made-to-fit, we'll create a stimulating and future-proof environment to keep your business in better shape than ever.

Kinnarps

Kinnarps UK Ltd Newlands Drive, Colnbrook, Slough SL3 0DX
tel 01753 681860 **fax** 01753 683233
e-mail sales@kinnarps.co.uk **www**.kinnarps.co.uk

Part 4

Kyoto and Europe

CLIMATE CHANGE AND EUROPEAN BUSINESS

Climate change has widely been regarded as a threat to business, but Steve Sorrell and Adrian Smith of the Science & Technology Policy Research Unit of the University of Sussex argue that it can offer substantial opportunities to innovative firms.

Climate change provides society with its greatest challenge for the new century. European business has a central role to play in meeting this challenge and faces both threats and opportunities. On the one hand, business can expect increasing restrictions on fossil fuel use and carbon emissions – the cost of energy use may rise and energy efficiency will become increasingly important for competitive advantage and regulatory compliance. On the other hand, climate change will open up new business opportunities in energy-efficient technologies, renewable energy sources and carbon sequestration. New global markets in emissions trading will emerge, together with associated financial instruments for risk management. Success or failure will depend upon how innovative and adaptable European firms are prepared to be.

Kyoto Protocol

The Kyoto Protocol to the Framework Convention on Climate Change (FCCC) includes a set of commitments to cap emissions of greenhouse gases (GHGs) from 39 industrialised nations. Each national target is based on a percentage of 1990 emissions and applies to the period 2008–2012. The Protocol represents an unprecedented achievement in reconciling widely different interests within the global community. If ratified and implemented, it will form the basis for controlling climate change for the foreseeable future.

The unilateral withdrawal by the United States should not prevent the Protocol from entering into force. This requires at least 55 signatories to have ratified, and for these to represent at least 55 per cent of industrialised countries' emissions. Entry into force looks likely before the end of 2002: the European Union and accession countries are committed, Japan is happy with recent concessions, and Russia has an interest in selling emission permits. The door is open for the United States to rejoin at a later date. Many US businesses are developing voluntary initiatives on carbon abatement, in anticipation of future regulatory requirements.

The EU target is an 8 per cent cut in GHG emissions from 1990 levels. Modelling estimates suggest that reaching this target will cost €3–8 billion, or 0.06–0.15 per cent of total EU GDP. The European Commission estimates that the 'cost-effective' potential to reduce emissions is more than twice the required target, and emphasises that contributions are required from all sectors if the least-cost solution is to be achieved. The Commission has engaged with stakeholders to produce a European Climate Change Programme (ECCP) that proposes a comprehensive range of policy measures to reduce emissions. In parallel with this, member states are developing their own climate programmes, including energy taxes, voluntary and negotiated agreements, product regulations and support for renewable electricity.

Emissions trading

Central to all of these efforts is emissions trading. In an emissions trading scheme, a fixed number of emission permits are allocated to the sources responsible. Each source must ensure that its emissions are equal to or less than its permit holdings. If permits can be traded, those that face high pollution abatement costs can continue to pollute by buying additional permits, while those facing low costs can take abatement action and sell their surplus permits for a profit. In this way, each source can trade off the cost of controlling pollution with the cost of buying or selling permits. This flexibility allows each source to minimise its overall costs.

The Kyoto Protocol includes comprehensive provisions for the development of international GHG emissions trading. In addition to trading between industrialised countries, the Protocol allows credits to be generated from projects that reduce emissions in developing countries. Estimates suggest that the 'flexibility mechanisms' could reduce global compliance costs by some 50–60 per cent, with around 500 Mtonnes of carbon being traded annually. The main buyers in the carbon market are likely to be Japan, the European Union and (assuming it re-enters) the United States, while the main sellers are likely to be Russia and the Ukraine. If the United States does not re-enter, there will be a large surplus of emission permits, which will keep prices and compliance costs low.

The provisions for emissions trading in the Protocol have led both the European Commission and individual member states to develop their own trading schemes, with an EU directive planned for 2002. These schemes will involve energy suppliers and large energy users initially, but smaller firms are likely to become involved over time. Economic models suggest that a European trading scheme could achieve annual savings of €2.1 billion (24 per cent) with 42Mtonnes of carbon being traded annually.

Business opportunities and the long term

Suppliers of lower-carbon technologies will benefit once pressure to reduce carbon emissions translates into growing markets. A report for the US Department of Energy estimated a global market of US$125 billion in energy-efficient technologies and services by 2015, for the electricity sector alone. These markets will provide valuable export opportunities. New business models may also emerge, such as moving from the supply of energy commodities to the broader provision of energy services. Yet inevitably there will be losers as well as winners. Business must consider the implications of climate change now if they are to be equipped to adapt to the changes.

Kyoto and the ECCP represent only a first step towards low-carbon economies and business can expect increasing constraints on carbon emissions over the long term. There is increasing consensus within climate science on both the evidence of warming to date and the projections of global temperature rise to 2100 (1.4–5.8°C). Stabilising atmospheric CO_2 concentrations at the levels recommended by scientists would imply global emission reductions of around 70 per cent, with greater reductions in industrialised countries. Already, the United Kingdom is reviewing how a 60 per cent reduction by 2050 can be achieved.

In addition to reducing emissions, a second challenge for business is adapting to climate change. Sea levels will rise, summers could be drier, winters may become wetter, and storms and floods are likely to be more frequent and severe. This will have implications for building design, planning, seasonally-dependent business such as tourism and agriculture, insurance, transport and energy systems, and industrial supplies (eg process water). Projections of the regional consequences of climate change are imprecise and uncertain, but business cannot afford to wait for definitive answers. Business strategy and planning will have to become both low-carbon in its activities, and responsive and flexible in how it adapts to climate impacts.

Steve Sorrell and Adrian Smith are research fellows at the Science & Technology Policy Research Unit of the University of Sussex. Telephone +44 (0)1273 877067; e-mail s.r.sorrell@sussex.ac.uk; http://www.sussex.ac.uk/spru/

SUSTAINABILITY IN EUROPE

Paul Wenman, director of ERM's European corporate advisory service, discusses the levels of understanding and acceptance of sustainability across Europe, in addition to reviewing how far companies have moved towards becoming sustainable enterprises.

Sustainable development – what role for companies?

Sustainable development as a concept has been doing the rounds for more than 15 years, gradually drawing all members of society into the debate. A cascade of definitions has been called for, from the sustainable city to a sustainable lifestyle, from a sustainable national economy to a sustainable enterprise.

Meanwhile, the world continues to grow and business continues to live with the reality of its function – to understand societal needs and meet them cost-effectively through efficient use of environmental and human resources. It is in the context of this core role that we should consider the progress and contribution being made in the corporate world towards sustainability.

Rise of the business stakeholder – the agent of change

While so much debate has been focused on the sustainable development agenda, the real dynamic that has been driving corporations in Europe towards a new business model has been the rise of stakeholder influence. In the past, most corporations responded to three principal stakeholder groups: consumers, investors and government authorities. While market forces generally determined the success of consumer and investor relationships (through choice of product and the stock market), compliance with regulatory requirements was the measure of success in governmental relationships – and most environmental and social responsibility issues fell into this last bracket.

All this has been changing dramatically over the last 20 years or so, with privatisation and deregulation across the markets, freedom of information and the emergence, through better communications and educational programmes, of an environmentally informed and sensitive public. As a consequence, most companies, willingly or not, knowingly or not, have been adjusting to a new business environment – one that requires engagement with a far wider range of stakeholders across a wider profile of needs and concerns.

Corporate sustainability – external perceptions

Looking from the outside in, we can see the corporate world making commitments and taking action to adjust to the new stakeholder reality.

Commitments

Many high-profile companies, such as Unilever, BP, BT, BMW, Credit Suisse and ING, have demonstrated a willingness to adopt sustainable development principles and to make strategic commitments. These include targets to reduce CO_2 emissions, commitments towards supply chain integrity, employee rights, business ethics and investment programmes.

Recent surveys have found that many companies now accept the business link with sustainable development, even though few claim to understand it.

Surveys of FTSE-100 and FTSE-350 companies indicate that the majority of companies have put in place a basic management framework for managing and monitoring their environmental performance. The Business In the Environment annual survey of corporate environmental engagement has demonstrated a general improvement in leading UK companies across most sectors over the last four years.

There has been a significant growth in the number of 'green' or socially responsible investment funds, together with the appearance of indices such as the Dow Jones Sustainability Group Index and FTSE4 Good. This reflects a growing response from the business world towards growing stakeholder interest in the sustainable development agenda.

The concept of environmental and social reporting is also now well recognised across many European countries. Although the content and value of these reports varies considerably and a 'reader beware' caution should be attached to most, this is another measure of corporate response to the growing tide of stakeholder expectations.

However, is this all simply 'greenwash'? What is happening on the ground and is it making a difference?

Actions

Some leading companies are spreading corporate environmental and social good practice throughout their businesses and suppliers worldwide, involving adoption of better environmental technology, more advanced manufacturing techniques, higher labour standards etc in their international operations. But they are still in the minority. Surveys and direct experience suggest that action on the ground is far thinner.

Environmental initiatives are further down the road than social responsibility programmes and environmental performance is more easily quantifiable. There is therefore a better picture of progress in this area. In many ways, there has been progress in corporate environmental performance.

From cars to computers, the competitive market, coupled with regulation and taxes, has driven manufacturers to become more efficient in the use of raw materials and energy. Better product design, more innovative production and distribution systems, together with increasingly fluid and flexible supply chains (particularly now with e-business on the Internet) have opened up new opportunities for squeezing inefficiencies out of the whole value chain.

A number of companies have linked environmental performance to the overall utility of the product or service, by using integrated performance indicators eg in terms of environmental impact per kilogram of washing load or courier package delivered. These indicators are important for both driving internal decision-making and for reporting progress externally.

However, the overall trend is not one of absolute reduction in total impact on the natural environment. This reflects the fact that consumption, and therefore supply, is outstripping eco-efficiency gains and that corporate strategy remains focused on absolute growth in output as a key driver of shareholder value.

The social picture, however, is barely visible. Few companies have developed a coherent framework to evaluate their social impact, and even fewer value the business significance of social responsibility, let alone have a corporate strategy.

Corporate sustainability – the business drivers

Regardless of external perceptions, it is clear that significant changes are taking place within organisations, which relate to sustainable development. These are the result of the convergence of two stakeholder-driven trends.

Environmental management – the shift towards stakeholder engagement and corporate responsibility

Traditional environmental, health and safety programmes are broadening out to encompass a wider range of stakeholder issues under the umbrella of corporate responsibility. This is because companies have found their environmental programmes to be cost-, not value-driven – being defined on the basis of issues and driven by regulatory compliance. By relating them to stakeholder needs they can be reoriented towards value creation in the context of business strategy.

The growth in environmental reporting has reflected this. Many companies have felt the need to demonstrate good environmental performance to an increasing vocal and influential public. However, the vast majority have found these reports to be of little value in delivering assurance to key business stakeholders. Much of the reported data relates to internal operational needs or regulatory requirements and fails to connect with wider stakeholder concerns. Put simply, business has been out of touch with stakeholder concerns in these areas. Hence this one-sided communications process is now being complemented by listening.

Stakeholder engagement is driving a regrouping of issues according to the stakeholder agenda, where internal definitions as environmental, health and safety or social are irrelevant. Health and safety is more appropriately seen as an employee risk (along with diversity, career development, human rights and freedom of association etc). Social responsibility may be part of community investment and environmental issues may be grouped across governmental, community, customer, NGO and other groups.

Integrated risk management – the growing importance of non-financial measures

The core business agenda has also been responding to a shift in stakeholder expectations – particularly investors and government. Corporate risk management, once almost exclusively focused on direct financial risks, has taken a giant leap in recent years.

As analysts and investors have come to focus more on future corporate potential than past performance, they have taken a much broader view of corporate assets and other attributes for shareholder value creation when quantifying their investment ratings. Initially they focused on quality of business strategy, senior management vision and capability for strategy execution, etc. This has grown into a large set of increasingly interrelated non-financial measures. These include employee retention and recruitment, communications, reputation management and brand value protection, internal assurance and information management, supply chain integrity and flexibility, customer loyalty, business ethics, new technology investment etc.

Companies are thus redefining the concept of corporate risk management to focus not only on business continuity and financial integrity, but also on the full range of risk factors that can influence share value. This is driving a wholesale change in business culture and in the definition and expectations of corporate functions, not least corporate risk and strategy development groups. Internal audit groups have been broadening their scope, from largely financial to non-financial areas of corporate risk – increasingly including environmental and other 'stakeholder' issues. Procurement groups are reviewing supplier arrangements on the basis of total risk and integrity. Human resource groups, marketing and information management departments are all having to transform in a similar way. In the process, environmental issues and other aspects of corporate social responsibility are appearing further up the agenda across the whole spectrum of corporate functions now having to take a risk-based management approach.

This trend overlaps considerably with corporate responsibility, although few companies have yet recognised the synergies and full potential for business value creation by merging the two. Nevertheless, these two trends are laying the foundations of a cultural shift in the business world towards risk-based strategic and operational decisions which will be progressively more in tune with stakeholder concerns, more responsive to society's needs and more consistent with the concept of sustainability.

Too many companies are looking at sustainable development through the wrong lens, seeing it as an issue in its own right, somehow separate from core business strategy. Those who place stakeholders first and focus on providing value to society across all stakeholders will be the first to embrace the 'new agenda' and the first to realise the business benefits.

Paul Wenman is the director of ERM's European Corporate Advisory Service.

ERM's work in this area focuses on assisting companies to anticipate, plan for and manage the threats and opportunities arising from environmental, social and other stakeholder risks. Value is provided typically through strategic risk assessments and business planning, stakeholder reviews, business process improvement, integrated risk and assurance, public reporting and information management.

PROVIDING SERVICE
without exceptions

Millbank Environmental Limited
offers comprehensive maintenance tailored
to suit all requirements.

- Planned Preventative Maintenance (PPM)
- Predictive Maintenance
- Conditioned Based Monitoring (CBM)
- Controls
- Refrigeration
- Electrical Installation and Maintenance
- Mechanical Installation & Maintenance
- IT and Telephony

Millbank Environmental Limited is a
member of the HVCA, NICEIC and
BSRIA,ensuring our clients of a
consistently high standard of
workmanship.

Millbank Environmental Limited
Four Millbank
Westminster
London SW1P 3JA

Tel: 020 7222 8764   Fax: 020 7222 8697

www.millbank-environmental-ltd.sagenet.co.uk

info@millbank-environmental-ltd.sagenet.co.uk

THE COMPANY

Established in 1994 and operating mainly within the M25 area, Millbank Environmental Limited offers the advantage of being a privately run company with a strong commitment to customer service.

Millbank Environmental Limited is a member of both the HVAC and the NICEIC, assuring our clients of a consistently high standard of workmanship.

We specialise in mechanical and electrical installations; static/mobile site maintenance covering options from computer based Planned Preventative Maintenance (PPM) to Predictive Maintenance regimes. We utilise the latest technology in Vibration Analysis and Conditioned Based Monitoring ensuring optimum plant efficiency and cost management.

Currently over 80% of our work is from repeat customers who have used us and found us to be professional and fair, committed and honest. This is due to our entire team being passionate about providing added value and the best service possible to all our customers; their actions have a major influence on the success of the company, which in turn determines their own success.

Mobile service and routine service visits can be arranged to suit individual client and site requirements. Our 24-hour callout facility ensures that our clients can be rest assured that their premises are in good hands.

Millbank Environmental Ltd offers a range of services that cover all aspects of building maintenance and design. All our services are provided to ensure that the required level of customer services are attained and retained. MEL consider the following direction setting activities to be the essential core

constituents required to achieve a mandatory level of customer service: Strategy, Policy and Planning.

Strategy

Our strategic plan involves the development of a framework around the following sequence of events:

- Establish your requirements as our client
- As the mechanical and electrical contractor, ensure that MEL are an extension of your existing facilities team
- Set objectives and benchmarks
- Ensure the appropriate quality assurance controls are in place

- Adopt a rigid method of evaluation and measurement of our performance

Policy

At Millbank Environmental Ltd we adhere to a range of policies to ensure that on-site performance of personnel is regulated within the boundaries of our customer's constraints and wishes as well as common law.

These policies include:
- General site policies i.e. security measures and emergency procedures
- Policies to ensure consistent managerial and personnel behaviour
- Health and Safety policy
- Environmental policy

Planning

The planning of how, when and by whom each asset is to be maintained is of primary importance. The time of day, week or in some instances the month requires consideration when planning a maintenance regime.

When planning the type of maintenance regime offered by MEL various issues will be considered.

- Maintenance tasks will be co-ordinated with the assistance of your facilities management team to ensure minimum disruption
- Specific details and performance of criteria of each asset
- The performance monitoring of each operational system
- All plant environments will be developed to conform to the provisions detailed within the Health and Safety at Work Act 1974.

For more information on services provided by Millbank Environmental Limited

Telephone: 020 7222 8764 or **Fax: 020 7222 8697**
www.mel-buildingservices.co.uk

Or alternatively write to:

Mr Philip Lynn
Four Millbank
Westminster
London SW1P 3JA

ALTERNATIVE FUELS

Utopia is the first project to look at new fuels and propulsion systems on a European scale. TransportAction takes the lead in developing solutions in the UK and is participating in the Utopia project. This is its current assessment of developments in clean fuels.

The development, introduction and market take-up of new propulsion technologies, such as electric vehicles, in Europe or anywhere in the world is a continuous process. It is evident that the process is influenced by a multitude of factors and interest groups. It is also evident that the issue is generating increasing interest on a global scale among policy-makers, vehicle manufacturers and environmental interest groups.

Utopia (Urban Transports: Options for Propulsion systems and Instruments for Analysis) is the first project to aim at compiling and analysing introduction methods on a European scale. The analysis and implementation of a coherent methodology to be carried out in this project is essential to maximise output from the massive work ahead to arrest developing traffic problems.

The largest arenas for development of new fuels and propulsion systems are California, with the California Air Resources Board initiative to opt for zero-

and low-emission vehicles, and Europe, with the French cooperation between cities, governmental agencies and car manufacturers to boost electric vehicles development and get them on to the market. Several regions in Scandinavia are also advancing as proving grounds for innovative vehicle systems.

These and other contingencies have each developed distinct models to create this climate for development. Current methods employed include technology forcing, broad collaboration projects between cities, car manufacturers and energy-producing companies, international collaboration projects (eg ZEUS) and local projects to evaluate special applications.

UK participation

The Energy Saving Trust is the UK participant in the Utopia project. Its transport arm, Transport Action, promotes the use of clean fuels and the use of emissions reduction equipment by offering advice to anyone involved in the management of road vehicles (eg fleet managers, hauliers, local authorities) and also by giving financial aid in the form of grants to help them to do that via its two programmes: PowerShift and CleanUp.

The principal technologies available are liquefied petroleum gas (LPG), natural gas, electric vehicles and fuel cells, which TransportAction defines as follows.

Liquefied petroleum gas (LPG)

LPG is a very cheap fuel due to the significantly lower fuel duty imposed by the government. A litre of LPG currently costs less than half the price of petrol or diesel on the forecourt, and it allows a vehicle to travel around 80 per cent of the distance it could travel on a litre of petrol. LPG refuelling points are being introduced all over the country. There were approximately 912 in the United Kingdom as at 28 November 2001 – and the number is still increasing, with one being installed every working day.

Most types of vehicle can be built or converted to run on LPG. It is much easier and cheaper to convert a vehicle with a petrol engine than one running on diesel. LPG has proved particularly popular as a fuel for cars and vans, most of which are bi-fuel – they carry both petrol and LPG and can change from one to the other at the flick of a switch. LPG is sometimes marketed as 'Autogas'.

The typical cost of converting a passenger car or light vehicle to run on LPG is approximately £1,500 before any PowerShift grant. More vehicles with an LPG option are now available direct from the manufacturers.

LPG is mainly comprised of propane. It is a by-product of oil refining and is also associated with natural gas (methane) fields. It is often used as a bottled gas for cooking and heating where there is no natural gas pipeline nearby. LPG vehicles can be set up to run either as 'dedicated' vehicles which have LPG as their only fuel and are spark ignited (like petrol), or 'bi-fuel' (sometimes known as 'dual-fuel') vehicles – these are vehicles with petrol engines converted so that they can operate on LPG or petrol. In all cases, gas is stored on the vehicle in special fuel tanks; it is then piped to the engine and introduced into the engine intake tract, controlled by a regulator.

Natural gas

Natural gas is a very cheap fuel due to the much lower fuel duty imposed by the government. Using natural gas as a vehicle fuel can lead to significant running-cost savings. Natural gas is abundant and delivered to most parts of the United Kingdom by a sophisticated network of pipelines, thus reducing transport requirements to the point of use. To get sufficient volume of energy into a conventional-size fuel tank requires that natural gas be compressed or cooled to liquefy it. It has proved particularly popular as a fuel for trucks, buses and larger vehicles. The extra weight and cost of onboard fuel tanks makes conversion to natural gas normally more expensive than LPG for smaller vehicles. There are a limited number of public refuelling points for natural gas. Many fleets have chosen to install depot-based refuelling facilities. Refuelling options for natural gas range from cheap, slow-fill compressors which can refuel a vehicle overnight to high-tech stations which can refuel a vehicle in a similar time to petrol. Installing a larger refuelling station can be expensive, which means the economics work best when 15 or more larger vehicles are involved to spread the cost. Natural gas is currently the cheapest of all fossil-based fuels (including LPG) when fuel costs alone are considered. It costs under 6p per mile to run a smaller vehicle on natural gas (compared with 10p or more on petrol). Natural gas engines are far quieter than diesel engines, making these vehicles suitable for overnight deliveries and noise-sensitive locations.

Most types of vehicle can be built or converted to run on natural gas. It is easier and cheaper to convert a vehicle with a petrol engine than one running on diesel. The cost of building a larger vehicle to run on natural gas starts from approximately £10,000 (may be reduced by PowerShift grant). Smaller vehicles can be converted to run as bi-fuel from approximately £2,000.

What is natural gas? Natural gas is predominantly methane, mainly found in underground (or undersea) fields and often associated with oil. In the United Kingdom, it comes mainly from large fields in the North Sea and is the same fuel that is used by many people for cooking and heating in their homes.

Natural gas vehicles can be set up to run either as 'dedicated' vehicles which have natural gas as their only fuel and are spark ignited (like petrol), or as 'bi-fuel' vehicles which have two separate fuel systems and can switch between petrol and natural gas at the flick of a switch. Bi-fuel vehicles are sometimes, confusingly, described as 'dual-fuel' vehicles. However, strictly speaking, these are vehicles that run on a varying mixture of two fuels, usually diesel and natural gas. Dedicated vehicles will usually offer the best combination of emissions, performance and efficiency, though bi-fuel capability may be the most practical option where vehicles do not always return to their home depot for refuelling. A number of dedicated natural gas products are available, particularly among the heavier vehicle options. In all cases, gas is stored on the vehicle in special fuel tanks; it is then piped to the engine via special high-pressure pipes and introduced into the engine intake tract, controlled by a regulator.

Electric or hybrid vehicles

It costs as little as 1p per mile to run a car on electricity compared with around 10p on petrol. Electric cars are extremely quiet with zero tailpipe emissions. Electricity is most suited for use in city-based cars and vans with set journey patterns requiring limited range (up to 50 miles), although it has also been trialled in some urban buses. Electric vehicles can be fully recharged from any 13 amp socket in up to seven hours. Vehicles can be effectively part-charged when they are stopped for shorter breaks, which can significantly increase range. Fast-charge facilities are technically feasible but expensive. New-generation electric-petrol hybrid vehicles offer significant emissions benefits without the range disadvantage traditionally associated with electric vehicles. The latest hybrid vehicles do not require external recharging and are capable of running up to 60 miles or more on a gallon of petrol.

The extra cost of buying an electric car varies from zero to £5,000 (before any PowerShift grant). In many cases, batteries are leased rather than purchased outright at a cost of £60–£100 per month. The electric or hybrid option electric vehicles produce no tailpipe emissions. Most life cycle analyses (including electricity generation and transmission) also suggest that they contribute less in terms of carbon dioxide, the main global warming gas.

The conventional fuel system is replaced by batteries and electric motors. Vehicles may be derivatives of standard production models or purpose-built. Hybrid vehicles use a combination of a fossil fuel and electricity. The electric fuel system is used at lower speeds and for stop-start driving in urban areas. The fossil fuel is used either to drive the vehicle directly outside urban areas, or to travel at higher speeds, or to recharge the batteries. Switching fuels in this way enables the operator to reduce emissions, particularly in urban areas where most related health problems exist.

The most common battery type is still the lead-acid battery, but much research is taking place into alternative 'high-performance' batteries. Current research is focusing on batteries which are smaller and lighter and enable vehicles to achieve significantly higher range.

Fuel cells

Fuel cells are catalytic devices which convert the energy stored in a fuel directly to electrical energy. A fuel cell provides the conditions for a catalytic energy release as opposed to combustion. This occurs through the use of an electrolyte which allows the passage of ions, but acts as a barrier to the chemical reactants. Fuel cells were devised in the 19th century and were used to provide onboard electrical energy and water for the Apollo spacecraft.

Fuel cells are capable of high conversion efficiencies which compare very favourably to the thermal efficiency of petrol and diesel engines. Fuel cell vehicles are not yet commercially available but PowerShift funding may be available for innovative demonstration projects. Fuel cell vehicles have similar or improved performance as compared to a vehicle with an internal combustion engine. They are not range-limited in the way that battery electric vehicles are.

Fuel cell vehicles can be either 'pure' or 'hybrid'. The hybrid design incorporates the use of a battery for peak power loading. This also enables the vehicle to use regenerative braking, which can recover up to 20 per cent of the fuel energy utilised.

Six fuel cell buses have been operational in North America for over two years. Ballard Power Systems (Canadian market leaders) aim to commercialise fuel cell bus engines by 2002. The New Electric Car (Necar) range of vehicles has been developed by DaimlerChrysler, Ford and Ballard. This partnership aims to make fuel cell cars commercially available by 2004.

Fuel cells operate most efficiently if fuelled by pure hydrogen and oxygen. However, in practice, hydrogen can be delivered to the fuel cell using several fuel routes and air is sufficient to provide the oxygen to the cell. The method for onboard fuel storage is another system consideration. Three fuels (and storage methods) are being actively considered by most fuel cell vehicle developers. These are:

- Pure hydrogen fuel (stored onboard as a compressed or liquefied gas). The hydrogen is delivered as required to a fuel cell to provide motive power via an electric-drive train.
- Methanol fuel (stored onboard as a liquid). The hydrogen is generated from the methanol using an onboard reformer as required to provide hydrogen for a fuel cell to provide motive power via an electric drive-train.
- Petrol fuel (very low sulphur formulation; stored onboard as a liquid). The hydrogen is generated from the petrol using an onboard reformer as required to provide hydrogen for a fuel cell to provide motive power via an electric-drive train.

The pure hydrogen option operates at the highest efficiency but requires the development of a new hydrogen infrastructure. The reformer options benefit from existing fuel infrastructures, but are less efficient and more costly than the pure hydrogen option. No Proton Exchange Membrane (PEM) – the type of technology that most mass-producing manufacturers are currently developing – fuel cell vehicles are currently available. However, Ballard and partners have publicly announced bus and car engine launches for 2002 and 2004 respectively.

PowerShift

PowerShift is the part of TransportAction that aims to encourage drivers and fleet managers to switch to cleaner fuels such as LPG and natural gas and provides grants of up to 65 per cent of the conversion costs. It also contributes towards the purchase cost of new clean-fuelled and bi-fuelled vehicles such as the Toyota Prius and electric cars such as the Ford Th!nk.

There are many benefits for companies in applying for a grant. First of all, LPG is roughly half the price of regular fuels, thus giving an instant cash saving in the operational costs of running a fleet. A new LPG point is being installed at the rate of one every working day and the number of forecourts offering LPG has now reached between 900 and 1000, so company car drivers also have no problem in terms of refuelling their cars. In addition, having LPG-powered cars also offers a company an excellent environmental marketing message and demonstrates superb social, corporate responsibility.

TransportAction also recently announced plans to make it even easier to apply for financial aid to convert/purchase clean fuel cars by offering block grants, which in its simplest terms, gives a bulk of cash to convert a number of cars, rather than asking fleet managers to apply for grants on a vehicle-by-vehicle basis.

One of the only stipulations concerning the grants is that the cars a company is proposing to convert have to be listed on the PowerShift register, which can be found on the TransportAction website (http://www.transportaction.org.uk), and must be under five years old (equivalent to Euro 2 standards). The rules around the age of the car have also recently been relaxed. Until November 2001, only vehicles up to one year old and with under 25,000 miles were eligible. The announcement that funding for older cars would be made available also opened up the initiative to more private motorists as well as those running brand new fleet cars.

TransportAction has also worked hard to guarantee the quality of the conversions and this is the final rule governing the grant system. The organisation will only give money if the car is going to be converted by an approved converter. Again, a list of these can be found on the TransportAction website.

Since its inception in 1996, the PowerShift programme has funded the conversion of over 10,000 vehicles.

CleanUp

CleanUp aims to encourage drivers or operators of heavily polluting diesel vehicles such as buses, lorries, refuse trucks and blacks cabs either to convert to using clean fuels (LPG and natural gas) or to fit emission reduction technology such as oxidation catalysts and/or particulate traps. CleanUp is still a relatively young programme, having only been launched at the end of 2000, initially targeting local authority fleets such as buses and refuse trucks but expanding into the road freight market in mid-2001. The scheme has got off to a great start with many bus operators and more recently with larger fleets such as Tibbett and Brittan, Gist and Brake Brothers taking up the grants to help make their vehicles more environmentally friendly.

Again, the benefits to companies are similar to those gained through applying for a PowerShift grant, although it will also allow operators to apply for a Reduced Pollution Certificate (RPC), which means a rebate of up to £500 a year on Vehicle Excise Duty (VED). The marketing messages that companies can make use of following the fitting of a catalyst or trap are also commercially powerful.

In addition to these immediate benefits, modifications funded by either PowerShift or CleanUp may help both private motorists and transport managers get permission to drive their vehicles in low-emission zones (LEZs). These are areas which will ban the most heavily polluting vehicles from town centres and are likely to be implemented by some local authorities over the next few years.

Further info: www.est.co.uk/www.transportaction. org.uk

Part 5

The Euro Changeover

THE CHANGE TO THE EURO

Noel Hepworth, euro project director at the European Federation of Accountants, discusses the effects on British companies of the introduction of the euro and how they can be managed.

A major problem for managers of UK companies is how to make any assessment about whether the introduction of the euro within the Eurozone, but not in the United Kingdom, will have any practical effects upon them at all. Almost certainly, many companies will have opened euro bank accounts in the first flush of enthusiasm for the euro (if that is not a contradiction in terms) and then seen no activity. However, that is also true for many Eurozone companies. So far, the level of day-to-day business transactions occurring in the euro has been painfully low. A further complicating factor is that managers will be trying to make judgements about the impact that the euro might have on their company against a background of misinformation and highly prejudiced political debate. The purpose of this article is to stand away from both points and to try to make a realistic assessment of the issues that UK managers do need to consider given that the euro now exists and, most importantly, that it will be the only domestic currency available for dealing with Eurozone countries from 31 December 2001.

At the end of this year:

- The euro will be the only currency in which domestic trade transactions within Eurozone countries can be carried on. The fact that legacy currency cash will remain legal tender in some Eurozone countries until the end of February 2002 at the latest is completely irrelevant (see Table 1).

- All banking, credit and other non-cash transactions will only be carried out in euros. The only arrangements outside this would be those for the handling of legacy currency cheques and other

Table 1 Last date at which legacy currencies remain legal tender

Austria	28 February 2002
Belgium	28 February 2002
Finland	28 February 2002
France	17 February 2002
Germany	31 December 2001 – but DM still accepted until 28 February 2002
Greece	28 February 2002
Irish Republic	9 February 2002
Italy	28 February 2002
Luxembourg	28 February 2002
Netherlands	28 February 2002
Portugal	28 February 2002
Spain	28 February 2002

forms of bank transfer that started their lives before 31 December 2001.

- All contracts entered into after 31 December 2001 will also need to be drawn up in euros if the parties are to avoid the legal uncertainties that may arise from contracts drawn up in currencies that do not exist.
- In all countries of the Eurozone apart from the Irish Republic, the Netherlands and Finland, there is a specific legal requirement that internal accounting has to be in the currency of the country. From 31 December 2001 that currency will be the euro and in the other countries it will be difficult to persuade auditors and others that accounts should be compiled in a currency that no longer exists.
- All VAT payments and VAT returns relating to 2002 made by Eurozone companies will have to be made in euros.
- All payroll calculations relating to 2002 will have to be made in euros.

Do take care to understand the critical dates. The deadline date for the change to the euro is 31 December 2001. It is not 30 June 2002. That is a common misapprehension. 31 December 2001 is the date by which companies have to be ready to trade in euros. Failure to be ready means not only legal risks, but also the more serious business risk of not being able to trade at all.

There are also a number of dangers for UK companies.

There are obvious changes that British companies should make when they deal with Eurozone markets and they will leave themselves very exposed if they do not. There are also some less obvious issues that they fail to consider at their peril.

One obvious change is that the pricing of goods and services delivered in the Eurozone should be in euros where the legacy currencies were the previous pricing unit. This means changing catalogues and price lists, in addition to invoices and order forms. For some companies, a simple conversion using a fixed rate may be sufficient and particularly if that was how the conversion into the previous legacy currencies was made. However, companies do need to be aware that within the Eurozone itself, competitors may be using the change to the euro to alter their pricing structures

and therefore they may be doing rather more than a simple price conversion. Thus, an essential element to converting prices to euros is to maintain vigilance about the actions of competitors. This is particularly true where the use of attractive price points is important and where a simple conversion will result in very odd prices.

A second obvious change is that invoices should be raised in euros. Failure to do so may result in customers and clients arguing that the invoices are invalid and that payment will be delayed until a valid invoice is received.

A third obvious point is that where the two previous points apply, you should be sure that you do have the ability to not only draw up an invoice in euros but that you can also print it using the euro description, the euro symbol or the ISO code against the euro price.

Related points are whether you intend to receive payments in euros and if you are, have you opened a euro bank account? If you have previously produced different currency price lists, will one price list suffice or do you segment the Eurozone market in some way and will you want to continue doing this even though it will now be obvious what you are doing?

Another point to consider is that if you trade with several Eurozone countries and have previously maintained several foreign currency accounts, this will no longer be necessary. By amalgamating several accounts you could reduce currency costs quite substantially.

However, companies should also pay attention to a number of less obvious points:

- UK companies could be part of a supply chain beginning or ending in a Eurozone country – will the partners in that supply chain change their buying and selling habits in order to avoid currency fluctuation problems in the future? They can do this with a considerably enhanced range of new suppliers and customers from 1 January 2002.
- Your Eurozone competitors will be better placed to enter into long-run contracts without fear of currency fluctuation affecting them to your disadvantage – what will you do to counteract this competitive disadvantage?

- Up until 31 December 2001, sterling was a relatively large currency in international terms and UK importers and suppliers may have been able to insist on transactions in sterling. In relative terms, sterling will lose that status and the psychological pressure will be to switch from sterling to euros. Have you considered that possibility and how it will affect you?

- What will you do about legacy currency payment bank documents received immediately prior to 31 December 2001? You should ensure that you lodge them with the bank by no later than 31 December to avoid the risk of them being rejected with the consequent delay in payment.

- You should be concerned about the state of preparation for the euro by your suppliers and customers. Those Eurozone companies that are not prepared to operate in euros from 1 January 2002 will find themselves in considerable operational difficulty. There are plenty of them and this is one reason why there are so few trade transactions in euros. They will find it difficult to continue to supply you if you buy from them. They will find it difficult to pay you if you sell to them. Your interest is best served by finding out what the state of preparation of your key suppliers and customers actually is. If they are unprepared, you should consider the following:
  - looking for other suppliers who are prepared and who can meet your requirements;
  - altering the terms of trade with your customers to ensure that you are not disadvantaged by slowness in payment to you;
  - finding new suppliers and customers because there is a risk that your existing suppliers and customers may in the worst case go out of business if they are not ready.

- Where you have subsidiaries operating in the Eurozone, you should ensure that they too are fully prepared by 31 December 2001 for the euro. If they are not, then they too could suffer the same fate as that for suppliers and customers as described above. If you are to recover from a failure to prepare, a large amount of extra management effort will need to be put into 'fire-fighting' to restore your trading ability.

Changing to the euro is a serious business. Do not allow emotion (by which is meant political concerns) blind a manager to the consequences of a failure to be ready. That the United Kingdom does not happen to be a member of the Eurozone does not mean that UK companies can escape preparations. If they have any trading links with the Eurozone (and some may be obscure if they are part of a supply chain), they cannot.

Noel Hepworth is euro project director at the European Federation of Accountants.

e-mail noel.hepworth@ipf.co.uk http://www.euro.fee.be

NEW MONEY FOR 300 MILLION PEOPLE

Jürgen Schuhmacher, executive director of Bremer Landesbank Capital Markets, London, reflects on the early days of operating in the euro.

When the euro was introduced as a virtual currency approximately three years ago, many predicted a short life for the single European currency and a rapid implosion of this most audacious experiment in financial history. However, the Euro-Group of initially 11 countries is still bound together by the single currency and has grown to 12 with the addition of Greece in 2000.

One year before the introduction of the euro, I had a bet with an English friend, who insisted that the economic strains and political differences would be so great, that within six months of its introduction, Spain would be the first to leave the Eurozone. I won that one and with it came a magnum of champagne!

Up until now, the euro has existed only as a virtual currency in the form of central bank 'money'. From 1 January 2002, it will be introduced in the form of physical cash – coins and banknotes that people can touch, feel and, of course, spend or save. Before that happens, 14 billion banknotes and 50 billion coins will have to be distributed to 300 million people in 12 countries. While politicians and central bank officials see their 50-year-old dream of European financial integration completed, others face the logistically mammoth task of supplying the money safely to banks, shops and consumers. A bigger task still lies ahead in convincing the somewhat reluctant citizens of Europe that the newly merged money is equally good or even better than their present national currencies of marks, lira, francs, pesetas etc.

Appearance

The European Central Bank (ECB) has spent a great deal of time and effort in attempting to familiarise professionals and consumers all over the world with the design of the new notes and coins.

According to the ECB, great effort was made 'to include unique security features on the euro 1 and euro 2 coins' to make counterfeits 'extremely difficult and easy to detect'. The coins, which are bimetal (all 50 billion of them) will have 'one side common to all countries' and a reverse side that is specific to each country (this is a concept also found on the British £1 coin).

The notes come in seven denominations. When the notes were first shown to the public, the reaction was not enthusiastic, to say the least. Most people would agree that it would not be right to display national figureheads on banknotes, which were at some time in history heroes in one country but enemies in another. Thus, out went the idea of gracing notes with the portraits of 'Great Europeans' such as Napoleon, Frederick the Great and Isabella of Spain. In addition, it was decided that national monuments and victory arches would be equally insensitive reminders of past events.

Instead, the notes depict artists' designs of bridges, arches, gateways and windows, which will certainly delight architects, engineers and design students, but will not trigger the imagination of the average citizen. What does the money look like? The €5 note depicts the classical architectural period, €10 follows the Romanesque, €20 the gothic, €50 the renaissance, €100 the baroque and rococo period, while the €200 note depicts iron and glass architecture, and finally the €500 note shows contemporary 20th-century architecture.

The notes have been designed with many security features to help distinguish a genuine banknote from a fake and to make the production of counterfeits difficult. Among the security features are a 'raised' print through a special printing process. There are further watermarks, security threads and shifting images on hologram foil stripes. The iridescent stripes or colour-shifting ink on the reverse side of the notes as well as different colours and sizes should also help to identify genuine notes and prevent counterfeits.

Confusion

From 1 January 2002, citizens will carry two currencies in their purse: their national currency of drachma, schillings, escudos etc and the new euro. Supermarkets, shops and banks will have two cash registers: one to receive 'old' money and another to pay the change in euros. During the early days of the transition in 2002, it will take more time to perform even simple transactions in shops, while shopkeepers and customers have to convert prices from the old and count the change in the new currency. A recent study in the Netherlands suggests that just buying a rail ticket, for example, will take on average 30 seconds longer.

In the first couple of weeks of the changeover, there may be disorientation and confusion among the public, and longer queues at checkout counters and in banks are expected. 'Paradoxically', as *The Spectator* (6 October 2001) observed, 'the introduction of the new cash will boost the cashless economy'. Instead of waiting in long queues, customers may shop by telephone or via the Internet and use their credit cards.

Conversion

In Germany, which has a fixed exchange rate of DM1.95583 for €1, it is relatively easy to convert the currencies: simply divide the DM amount by two to arrive at the euro amount.

How about France at 6.55957? Experts say: add 50 per cent and then divide by 10. What about Holland at 2.20371? Divide by two and then deduct another 10 per cent.

In all but one country, the prices will show lower figures in euros than in their national currency – for example, the price for a bottle of claret at DM19.99 will be €10.22. What are the shops going to do? Will they reduce the price to €9.99 at a small benefit for the consumer or will they exploit the unfamiliarity with the new money to increase the price to €10.30 or more?

In the Irish Republic (exchange rate of IR£0.787564 per €1), the prices displayed in euros will be higher: a pint of Guinness costing IR£2.50 will be €3.17, indicating a higher price to an unwary drinker. Will the landlord then add a rounding difference and charge €3.20 per pint, tempting as it is?

What impact will this have on the inflation target, on monetary policy and interest and mortgage rates? If all market participants behave responsibly, the impact will be fairly small.

Many readers will remember the arrival of decimalisation of sterling in 1971. While the currency retained the same value, the pound was divided into 100 (new) pence instead of 240 (old) pence and the shilling (20 shillings to the pound) as sub-division was abolished. Old and new coins remained legal tender side by side. Despite some confusion among consumers, no lasting problems were reported. A comparison between the Imperial Pound and the single European currency may be far-fetched, as sterling still remained the national currency.

Preparation

The conversion from DM to euros does not come cheaply. How much the single currency project will cost at the end can only be roughly estimated. Who pays for the conversion? In principle, each market participant has to bear his own costs.

Costs occur from the adjustment of customer and financial accounts and electronic systems, training of staff, printing of forms and price-lists, dual pricing of goods during the transition period and much more. Many companies had already started to convert or at least prepared essential tasks during the introduction of the virtual euro three years ago. It is therefore assumed that the transition should now be fairly smooth.

Thousands of cash registers, vending machines and automated teller machines (ATMs) are just a few examples of equipment that will need to be adjusted in time for the advent of the euro. The German railway system operates 10,000 ticket machines, which have to be converted in such a way that in the first few weeks into the New Year customers may purchase their tickets in DM as well as in euros. Ticket prices will be rounded upwards or downwards to the nearest 10 cents in order to be used in machines. The railway system alone needs 350 tonnes in cash at the start, the Post Office 3,000 tonnes in coins to be distributed to its branches, which is a logistical challenge where security is of the highest priority.

The advent of the euro also makes new postage stamps necessary, which will be sold from January.

Banks hold starter kits worth €10 available from 17 December for individuals to get acquainted with the new coins and notes, while they start the general payout in euro cash from 2 January 2002. Customers have been advised early on in a high-profile advertising campaign to pay piggy bank cash and other cash reserves into their accounts to help to reduce the rush at the beginning of the year.

What about the modification to metering on petrol stations? The *Wall Street Journal* reported that in France alone there are 16,000 petrol stations with 80,000 pumps. The adjustment to metering and display systems is to be done by only 150 technicians, who are authorised by the government. They started their changeover in early 2001 to ensure a smooth transition to euros. Most customers at petrol stations that switched early did not even notice the display in euros when paying the equivalent in French francs with their credit cards.

Savings

For companies that export to or import from other euro countries, there are cost savings. There are no costs for the exchange of currencies and no hedging costs to protect against currency fluctuations. There will also be better price transparency leading to lower purchase costs and there is no currency exchange risk for capital investments in the Eurozone.

The ECB has also argued that the higher cost for the euro transition will occur only once, while the savings will be permanent.

Will the euro make a difference to the United Kingdom?

What happens to nations that are not signing up to the single currency? The United Kingdom's 'prepare and wait' policy means that the exchange of sterling from/into euros costs money while exchange risks exist. Very soon, UK sun-seekers in Spain and Greece will have their first experience of the new currency. Whether that will make any difference to the promised referendum in the United Kingdom remains to be seen.

Conclusion

For continental travellers and shoppers, the euro provides a cost-effective medium. The physical money in people's pockets may help to raise the awareness and acceptance of a hitherto unloved currency. Should they find that the new currency provides bigger advantages and conveniences than their old national currency, will they then more easily accept the change? Doomsday forecasters have prophesied that the introduction of the euro will fail. However, they also said that about Y2K and computers. As the euro is here to stay, advice to the hesitant burghers of Europe should perhaps be: 'You may not like the euro, but you will get used to it.'

Jürgen A Schuhmacher is executive director of Bremer Landesbank Capital Markets and Norddeutsche Securities Plc. Their purpose is to raise capital funds in international markets and to issue debt securities which are listed on the London and other European stock exchanges.

Bremer Landesbank, 71 Queen Victoria Street, London EC4V 4AY. Telephone +44 (0)20 7972 5450.

RETAIL AND THE EURO

The switch to the euro could be painful for UK retailers, believes Peter Williams, CEO at Selfridges.

The glitz of Selfridge's recent performance could be lost if the euro is introduced in a clumsy way. Since it was floated as an independent company in 1998, the London department store has gone a long way to winning back its reputation for glamour and contemporary design. It is now looking to repeat its Oxford Street formula in large stores in Birmingham, Leeds, Glasgow and Newcastle for the first time.

Any disruption in trading could be damaging to those plans and, as finance director for the last 10 years, Peter Williams has been responsible for eliminating any threats to the recovery in Selfridge's fortunes. The euro plainly worries him.

Williams does not express an opinion one way or the other on the principle of its introduction into the United Kingdom, nor is he overly concerned about implementing new systems and processes. Where he foresees potential trouble is in the actual changeover from sterling to euros and the effect it will have on customers at both Selfridges and other retailers. Since few people now have a face-to-face relationship with their bankers, Williams believes that retailers could well bear the brunt of helping customers get used to the new currency, which could mean lost business.

'There is a great danger that, left to their own devices, the government or others will take impractical steps which will lead to a great deal of cost and confusion. We want to avoid an implementation problem, which results in a reduction of retail sales, when people say "it is all too confusing, I'm going home". You never get those sales back.'

The costs of the changeover for the retail sector could run to as much as £2 billion, believes Williams, depending on how the euro is introduced and how prescriptive the pricing legislation is. 'It is an infrastructure change, which we are going to enable, so let's make it as painless as possible. We don't see that it is going to increase sales and it may well then decrease them.'

Williams is sufficiently worried that he now chairs the euro working group at the British Retail Consortium (BRC). Working with representatives from companies such as Arcadia, Debenhams and Sainsbury, the group concentrates on the practical implications of introducing the euro without taking any view on whether the United Kingdom should adopt it or not.

Williams does not anticipate any immediate problems at Selfridges in January 2002, when the Eurozone switches its banknotes and coins. 'As we are on Oxford Street, we already accept a number of foreign currencies at point of sale, calculating their value and giving change in sterling. Retailers in Oxford Street, as well as is ports and airports, will want to accept euro notes.'

Williams' view is that there is going to be an element of 'euro creep' in the United Kingdom. 'People who travel in Europe will find it quite useful to spend euros wherever they go. When they turn up in England, they will expect to do the same. In certain parts of the country, it will operate a little bit like a dual currency.'

Williams is far more concerned about the timing of the euro's introduction into the United Kingdom. He fears that too little time will be left to prepare. 'A few retailers may have a presence in Wave One countries. Most don't and can't be expected to persuade their Board to invest speculatively in new systems in the anticipation that it is going to happen in the United Kingdom. I won't bother putting it up to my Board. It is too vague. They would say "you have got real issues in which you should be investing".'

It is also unhelpful that there is no clear way of settling queries about how the euro might work. 'When decimalisation happened, a Board was set up 10 years in advance. It was a group that determined all the terminology, so you could go to them and say "how will this work? What will this be called?" At the moment, everyone is working in a vacuum making assumptions. It would be helpful if the government could establish a central point, so decisions could be made, saving costs further downstream.'

He is also adamant that 1 January should not be '€-day'. 'First, unlike some European countries, it is not a public holiday, but a full working day. Nor do we want to be training people in the previous three weeks, which are the busiest and most important of the year. Our view very strongly is that €-day should be somewhere in the middle of February, which is the lowest point in the retail cycle.'

'When it does happen, even with the currency in existence in other countries, there is going to be an enormous learning curve. It is not like decimalisation, where £1 equals £1 or where the old two shillings became 10 pence. £1 is going to be €1.42763. All the price points are going to be thrown out.'

'The last thing we want to do is to affect customer confidence. So we want to inform the customer as clearly as possible, both beforehand and after. There will be an element of dual pricing before, but virtually every till in the land only works in one currency and we do not want to confuse the customer over what price they are paying. Plus, it is an enormous exercise to re-ticket everything. So you will start with a pound price with a smaller euro one. As you get nearer, you will switch them.'

Williams is anxious to avoid any suspicion that the euro is being used as an opportunity for a price hike and is happy to sign up to a code of conduct that assures customers. There will still be fears, he says, simply because in people's minds £1 will suddenly be worth £1.40. 'It will be interesting to see what happens to key price levels, such as £9.95.'

One of the members on the BRC euro group, Gap, plans to convert overnight to one European price. 'They are going to have an army of people and blitz their stores and warehouses,' says Williams. 'Some of the others are introducing merchandise at funny prices now, which, when it converts, will be €9.99. For some products, it will be difficult because different prices apply in different countries.'

'The issue for Selfridges is different. We are a branded store. Everything we sell is made by somebody else. We typically sell at the manufacturer's recommended retail price. It does mean that if the United Kingdom does go in, comparisons are going to be made between Milan and London.'

'Our ideal would be to get the old currency out of the system and out of everybody's head as quickly as possible. The more it hangs around, the more confusion it will create. This is an infrastructure change. It is not a commercial benefit. We want to implement it as painlessly as possible.'

In the first days of the new currency, that could be complicated. 'The logistics should not be underestimated. The notes are not so much a problem, but the sheer weight of the coins might be. In Selfridges, the coins usually just circulate. In the first week of the euro, you will be taking sterling and giving out euro change, unless people have already been to an automated teller machine (ATM). We will then bank the sterling as there will be no further use for it. This may be only for a short period of time, provided ATMs can be converted quickly enough, but it does mean that the logistical supply and return of coin is a big deal.'

'It also assumes that the supply of notes and coins does not run out, which is a real worry in the Wave One countries. We will all get in a terrible mess if customers have euro from their ATMs and we have run out of euro change and end up having to give some in sterling. Again they might walk out of the shop.'

At Selfridges, where two-thirds of payments are in plastic, that is less of a problem than for SMEs that trade only in cash. 'A newsagent presented with a €50 note is going to need a good supply of change, otherwise he will get in a real pickle.'

'SMEs are not going to do anything on this until they have to have it,' says Williams. 'It is impossible to get them to focus on anything, unless they absolutely have to. The government says "prepare", and business says "yes, but when we know that we are going in".' It is an impasse that could cost retailers a great deal of money.

Peter Williams has been CFO of Selfridges since 1991. After qualifying as a Chartered Accountant in the London office of Arthur Andersen he has worked for Andersen Consulting, Aiwa (a division of Sony) and Freemans plc. At Selfridges he is responsible for the overall commercial and financial strategy of the business in addition to finance and information systems.

In his role at Selfridges he provided the financial justification for the significant investment in the Oxford Street store known as Masterplan, developed the multi-site strategy to open stores outside London and led the demerger team which established Selfridges as a listed plc in July 1998.

He is chairman of the British Retail Consortium's working party reviewing the practical implications of introducing the euro and has a degree in mathematics from Bristol University.

Further details of the British Retail Consortium's review of the practical implications of introducing the euro: www.brc.org.uk

CASH MANAGEMENT AND THE EURO [1]

Has the euro made the financial infrastructures of Europe the same or are they individuals acting in harmony, in the same way as tenors and altos in a choir? asks Michael Earley, global transaction services product coordinator, ABN AMRO Bank, London.

The euro has created a large market, one that challenges the United States in terms of size of GDP. As cross-border trade increases, following the increase in price transparency, so companies have to increase their efficiencies. This is not merely a cost-cutting exercise, but a change process, involving possibly a consolidation in production, a streamlining of distribution or a centralising of administration services. An alternative is to become more efficient by centralising treasury activities. Research conducted by the Bank Relationship Consultancy in conjunction with Bath University has led to estimates that 80 per cent of companies with annual sales in excess of US$500 million run local or only partially centralised cash management systems. The research also suggests that more than half of the companies will centralise their cash management.

The banks best placed to service this trend to centralisation are those that can provide a single window through which to access each of the various payment mechanisms around Europe, not only for settling invoices but also for making collections. This single window access also needs to be supported locally and provide for single pricing and single service level agreements.

Account services

The introduction of the euro has not resulted in new types of accounts, but has altered how existing accounts should be treated. What has happened though, is a move towards harmony – both in terms and conditions and in documentation. Are these euro-related or merely accelerations?

Depending upon the solution proposed by the cash management bank, accounts were offered either in-country or centralised with one office. Regardless, the result was that the client had a suite of foreign currency accounts to manage, either running overdrafts in one currency against long balances in another or swapping currencies to reverse the positions. The former meant being exposed to the banks' interest margins and the latter to the banks' foreign exchange margins. Where a series of accounts was maintained with one bank in one centre, the introduction of the

[1] This Chapter is an extract from *The Euro and the Multinational* by ABN AMRO and published by Kogan Page in 2001.

euro has brought great benefits to the corporate at the expense of the bank.

Payment methods

TARGET

In order to facilitate a single euro monetary policy across the whole of the European Union, it has been necessary to ensure that each of the national high-value payments mechanisms is capable of real-time gross settlement (RTGS), that they are linked and that they are open the same hours. With such a mechanism in place, it would be difficult to borrow euros in one country and deposit them in another to make a profit at the expense of the individual sovereign states. The next step was to bring each of the 15 local RTGS systems together through the interlinking mechanism, TARGET. This is the only decentralised RTGS system in the world operating across a range of countries.

In essence, TARGET is a highly efficient mechanism run by the European Central Bank (ECB), which interlinks all of the existing RTGS payments systems and is intended to handle high-value payments only. It is analogous to the FedWire system in the United States.

TARGET facilitates payments across Europe between 7am and 7pm (CET). Almost all EU credit institutions, and therefore their respective account holders, can be reached via TARGET, which has a directory containing some 30,000 bank identifier code (BIC) addresses.

Although originally established to facilitate monetary policy, it quickly became apparent that TARGET could be used for commercial payments. Competition commenced immediately between the primary payments systems – in particular, TARGET, European Bankers Association (EBA) and EAF2.

European Bankers Association (EBA) – Euro 1

The European Bankers Association (EBA), formerly known as the ECU Bankers Association, has approximately 100 members and 66 clearing banks, between which payments in euros can be settled with same-day value. In this respect, it very much resembles a small circle of correspondent banks. Unlike TARGET, Euro 1 has an end-of-day net settlement by the banks, with settlement being effected over TARGET. Charges for such payments are cheaper than those of TARGET due to multilateral risk sharing by members.

Under the EBA clearing's legal framework (the 'single obligation structure'), each member bank has only one payment obligation or claim on all of the other members at any given time during the day. Each member bank has both a multilateral debit and credit limit. These are binding throughout the day. At close of business, 'short' banks settle their obligation by making a TARGET payment to the ECB, as settlement service provider, and the ECB – on instructions from the EBA – transmits the requisite funds to the long banks.

Criteria for approving the application for the status of clearing bank include:

- being located in the European Union;
- having access to local national RTGS systems;
- having a short-term credit rating of at least P2 (Moody's) or AP2 (S&P).

ELS

A further alternative is ELS, originally known as EAF2, the Frankfurt-based net settlement system, which has 67 direct members, of which half are German-based. The system runs frequent batch settlements through the day, across special accounts at the Bundesbank. Banks hold an amount on their EAF accounts that serves as a limit to the excess of queued outgoing over incoming payments that can be settled in a particular batch settlement. Any payments that cannot be settled in a particular batch settlement will be held over to the next; in the meantime, a member bank may decide to transfer more liquidity across from its main Bundesbank RTGS account.

Remote access

As a result of the competition between the various clearing mechanisms, the concept of remote access to payment clearing has become widespread. Many of the larger banks have the choice of using a correspondent to act as an agent in countries on their behalf or of joining remotely. The major Swiss banks, not wanting to be isolated from Europe, joined the German ELS. A more creative membership was that of ABN AMRO Bank, New York, which joined the ELS alongside its German counterpart, ABN AMRO Bank, Frankfurt. ABN AMRO Bank, New York, is now able to sell euro clearing services to the US market, thereby ensuring local support to its clients for access to a payments scheme over 3,000 miles away.

Automated clearing houses (ACHs)

Automated clearing houses (ACHs) have developed as a means of making high-volume, low-value payments. The systems that exist in the European Union are:

- Belgium: UCV/CEC
- France: SIT
- Germany: LZB
- Republic of Ireland: EMTS
- Italy: BI-Comp
- Luxembourg: LIPS-Net
- Netherlands: Interpay
- Portugal: TEI
- Spain: CCI
- Denmark: BEC
- Sweden: BGC
- United Kingdom: BACS.

Each of the local ACH mechanisms is capable of handling euros and domestic currency. Unfortunately, no two ACHs are the same. Each has its own formats, which are not compatible with any other. The volumes transacted daily by these mechanisms are substantial when compared to the high-value mechanisms. The longer clearing cycle means that these types of payment are a fraction of the cost of their high-value cousins.

Cheques

Cheques suffer a similar problem to ACHs in that each country's cheque clearing system is unique. While it is possible to draw cheques in euros on any of the banks in the European Union, there is no linking between the different cheque clearings. The result is that any cheques sent cross-border have to be returned to the country of the bank on which they are drawn, making the transaction expensive for the beneficiary.

In order to circumvent these restrictions, a number of banks have produced their own services. Companies are now able to draw cheques on their local euro account payable in any country in Europe. When the cheque is presented, entries will be settled to a memorandum account at the local office of the bank on which the cheque was drawn. The ability to automate such a system has provided some banks with a leading-edge product. The shelf life of such a product is, however, restricted to the time until a true pan-European cheque clearing is established.

Correspondent banking

For many years, payments could only be effected where the remitting bank maintained correspondent relationships around the world. Has the euro heralded the end of correspondent banking? No longer was there a need to maintain expensive relationships around Europe because the foreign currency was suddenly the same as the domestic currency. To a certain extent this is true, but there still remains the need for domestic accounts supported locally. The role of correspondent banks is to effect introductions for corporates. It can be seen that while correspondent banking will continue, the part it now plays in the finance market has fundamentally altered. The alternative is to use a network bank where corporates make use of the spread of the branches and subsidiaries around Europe and the world.

Market solution

The Heathrow Group was established by a group of leading payment banks to agree on a solution and make recommendations to the market for which methodologies should be practised. These banks have agreed the guidelines that will be used for claims arising for payments between themselves and have agreed the compensation rate.

The wide range of settlement systems had two major consequences. First, remitters of payments – corporates – became aware of the actual charges being levied on the banks by the different systems and therefore brought pressure on the banks to reduce their charges. The second consequence was that of which method would be used for settlement. Despite agreeing standard settlement instructions (SSIs) prior to the introduction of the euro, banks could not stipulate which method of payment should be used for settlement. On the face of it, this did not seem a problem. For example, a UK bank could stipulate that it required euros to be settled direct to itself. Unfortunately, different banks interpreted this instruction differently. Some would send funds to the UK bank's account at the Bank of England via CHAPS euro, while others would arrange for book transfers with correspondents.

The euro has changed the payments world. Until 1 January 1999, currencies settled in their home country. The euro has 11 home countries and can be settled in a further four as though it were their domestic currency.

Payment and collection requirements

The introduction of the new systems for high-value payments means that improvements in speed of delivery have been readily accepted by corporate treasurers. While the early days of the euro witnessed banks not knowing where euro settlements were being made, those problems are now behind them and bank customers are beginning to see the benefits of improved service.

These methods only account for 1 per cent of all payments in Europe, however, and are typically treasury-related transactions. Almost all other corporate transactions are treated as non-urgent and the majority of them flow through domestic clearing centres. Local ACHs are processing more than 40 million transactions per day. The costs for these items is minimal when compared to the cross-border systems described earlier. It is safe to assume that the two types of system will not encroach on one another.

The multinational corporate will require access to the various systems, ideally from a 'single window'. The banking provider of that window will have to be able to access all of the payment systems, whether ACH or high-value.

Liquidity management

It is not unusual for companies in Europe to hold in excess of 1,000 bank accounts. Despite the accepted benefits of consolidating bank relationships, there often remain valid reasons for holding so many accounts. The challenge is to manage effectively balances on those accounts as one liquidity position and integrate liquidity management into funding and balance sheet management so as to maximise the returns from, or minimise the costs of, a cash position. The euro has allowed companies to net off their euro balances right across Europe. There are five main options:

- Option 1: Centralise all euro accounts at one local bank. Companies may decide to concentrate all their euro accounts with a bank in the country in which they are headquartered. While ideal from a liquidity management perspective, this structure can result in extensive cross-border cash flows for many companies. Naturally, this leads to increased costs, not only for the company involved but also for their customers. Consideration must therefore be given to the economic sense of such a structure for companies other than those with small amounts of business outside their home country.

- Option 2: Use a multi-bank solution. The strategy adopted by some of the larger multinationals in Europe is to use one local bank in each country for transactions and local cash pooling. Balances are transferred from the local accounts to a cash concentration bank through the use of a payment system which provides multi-bank access while remaining bank independent. Once concentrated, the funds are invested into the financial markets. This type of structure requires a hands-on approach from the cash manager who must be sure of receiving timely and accurate information from his bankers. Concentration of funds will also be required prior to cut-off times in order that investments may be placed. Problems often occur with varying cut-off times of different banks for different currencies. An alternative would be to pre-advise receipt of funds to the bank.

- Option 3: Use a European network bank for all cross-border transactions. In this case, the European network bank will be used for all cross-border transactions. Such a bank is therefore required to have both a presence and a local clearing capability in every Eurozone country. All cross-border cash flows will be routed through non-resident accounts held with the network bank. The local nature of these payments and collections will provide the benefit of reduced transaction costs. By the end of the day, the network bank sweeps surplus euros from non-resident accounts into a central zero balancing account from where the company can invest or fund all of its liquidity in the money market to achieve the optimum result. Any local account shortages will be covered by a sweep from the central account. Such a cash management arrangement is very efficient because it makes transfers electronically, guaranteeing a zero balance on the local accounts maintained with the network bank and therefore optimising balances.

- Option 4: Use a European network bank for all transactions. This arrangement is similar to Option 3 with the exception that the network bank also handles domestic payments and receipts. The principal benefit is that the subsidiaries work with one uniform system for transaction initiation and reporting, thus obtaining the benefits of greater buying power.

- Option 5: Use a European network bank for shared service centres. In this arrangement, the client will have centralised much of the administration, and payments are initiated by a shared service centre (SSC) rather than by local subsidiaries. Typically, the SSC would want to submit a single, comprehensive payment file to the network bank, which would execute all payments locally and provide the centre with comprehensive reports containing all required transaction details.

Reference rates

The single currency did not bring a single benchmark from which to base interest rates. The challenge for banks has been to use interest rates, which are reference rates, which their clients understand. Benchmark rates are available from several sources within the European Monetary Union (EMU) as well as from the United Kingdom, an EU member.

On the lending side of the market, EURIBOR came head to head with Euro LIBOR. The difference between the two is marginal in real terms as well as in the method of their calculation. The reason for the similarity was arguably less due to the choice for customers and more due to the effort to become the pre-eminent financial position in Europe if not the world.

EURIBOR has replaced the national IBOR reference rates for EMU currencies. It is based on a panel of 57 banks, including at least one from each EMU member state. It is the rate at which euro inter-bank short-term deposit rate are being offered within the Eurozone by one prime bank to another. The calculation discards the top and bottom 15 per cent and averages the remainder of the rates. It is fixed daily at 11am (CET) on all TARGET days for value the second TARGET day after fixing. The fixing periods are one week, one month up to 12 months. Euro LIBOR is very similar, with the main difference being that it uses rates from the 16 most active banks in the London market.

On the other side of the market appeared EURONIA and EONIA (Euro Overnight Index Average). The panel of clearing banks is the same as that of Euro LIBOR and EURIBOR. The rate computed is the weighted average of all overnight unsecured lending transactions in the inter-bank market. Rates are published daily by the FBE at approximately 6.30pm (CET).

The widely used repo rate, similar to that formerly used by the Bundesbank, was replaced by refi and is published by the ECB. This rate is more static than the market rates above and is more a matter of government policy-driven than market-driven.

As bankers and their customers become more familiar with these various benchmarks, so they become more widespread in their use. Many bank proposals to MNC clients now quote margins around EONIA for pan-European deals. The acceptance by the banks allows customers to compare on a like-for-like basis. The volatile nature of current account balances means that margins will continue to be relatively wide. For less sophisticated clients, banks will apply their own benchmark, selling it as a 'cash management rate'. This is merely a marketing exercise and provides the bankers with the ability to increase the margin, albeit less evident to their customers.

The future for euro cash management

The future of cash management will bring further demands for increased efficiencies within corporate treasuries. For day-to-day transactions, the banks are in a position to handle these, whether by formally outsourcing accounts receivable and payable, by receiving single files of payments, or by allowing the banks to conduct automated pooling structures.

Extension of EMU members will bring even more efficiencies for the treasurer. Sterling's inevitable membership and the possible inclusion of Switzerland will further reduce the number of currencies traded globally. One area of significant new potential requirement for cash management solutions concerns the major states of the former Eastern bloc: Poland, Hungary and the Czech Republic. Each of the major banks has made significant investment in these countries, with the expectation of an explosion of inward corporate investment and the possibility of EMU membership. Payment mechanisms will have to be as efficient as those that exist in EMU – RTGS will be a necessity.

The high-value clearing mechanisms are unlikely to be able to encroach on the traffic that currently passes through the ACHs. It is essential that a single clearing be established whether as a competitor to the local ACHs or through some type of interlinking. In the short term, the banks will look to take a single payment file from their corporate clients, but within the files there have to be country-specific formats. This is highly inefficient and expensive and has a limited lifespan.

While the volume of cheques is reducing, the rate at which it reduces is not great. Banks are faced with a dilemma. Should a pan-European cheque clearing be introduced whereby euro cheques may be sent cross-border and cleared in the receiving country without extra costs? If this is achieved, there will be little encouragement to reduce the volume of cheques written – Europe will start to see clever arrangements for cheque writing as seen in the United States.

Consolidation of bank accounts is expected. This will favour the large network banks. However, banks will still advise companies that make substantial cross-border payments to maintain accounts in the local countries. It should not be long before these network banks offer to receive and make payments locally to memorandum accounts with end of day settlement being made to a single euro account. The company will benefit in holding only one account and being able to effect cross-border payments as if they were in-country payments, while their buyers would also be able to settle locally.

Thus, is cross-currency pooling the Holy Grail? With the expected reduction in the number of currencies leaving US dollars, Japanese yen and euros as the major trading currencies, banks may find the task of providing some kind of interest offset for cross currencies easier to manage. Corporate treasurers will not be interested unless the banks are able to conduct the notional foreign exchange at market rates.

THE EURO AND THE SUPPLY CHAIN

The changeover to the euro in early 2002 is having a major impact on the structure of businesses and the competitive environment, not only upon those organisations based within the Eurozone, but also those outside it, such as the United Kingdom, says Carolyn Munton of the Chartered Institute of Purchasing and Supply (CIPS).

The changeover to the euro in some countries within the European Union has added another dimension to the development and management of supply chains. Although the United Kingdom is one of the few members of the European Union not to have introduced the euro, those individuals with responsibility for purchasing and supply management in UK businesses must have at least a general awareness of the issues involved, and particularly so if their organisations are included within supply chains across other EU countries.

The effects of the euro will vary according to the nature of the business, and in some sectors according to geographical location. The following advice is currently being provided by the Chartered Institute of Purchasing and Supply (CIPS) within its document 'EMU Practical Guidelines':

- A reduced supplier base may bring about a need for re-sourcing – this needs to be addressed as a priority.

- Existing contracts may need to be reviewed to take account of any such changes in the supply situation; however, the introduction of trading in euros is not sufficient cause for terminating contracts early.
- Supply chain managers should be aware of i) economic consequences to the United Kingdom and ii) the measures taken by the government to protect the UK position – in particular there is a need to monitor changes in the sterling/euro exchange rate.
- Buyers may need to adjust their procurement strategy to take into account the euro issues. The reduced emphasis on price will lead to greater interest in other criteria such as quality, which will be beneficial to the buyer.
- Price transparency will lead to stronger competition, which is good news for buyers who will be able to take advantage of suppliers' slimmer margins.

The aim of a single currency shared across many countries is to sharpen competition across Europe through lower transaction costs, the removal of exchange rate fluctuations and price transparency.

- The use of a single currency removes the requirement to change currencies when dealing in cross-border transactions. This in turn should mean the removal of a major element of transaction cost, theoretically making it cheaper to trade across borders.

- The use of a single currency removes the uncertainty of exchange rate fluctuations. The practice of 'hedging' or otherwise protecting against the risk of fluctuating exchange rates has previously been a cost incurred by companies. Long-term exchange rate fluctuations have also impacted upon business investment decisions. The single currency will facilitate better decisions that meet the needs of the business rather than minimising the currency risk.
- Greater transparency of prices should result in a higher degree of harmonisation between prices as buyers source products from the cheapest sources. However, there are many local factors that will ensure that for many goods a single European price remains for the foreseeable future an aspiration rather than a reality.

Although the above objectives for a single currency are laudable, there are many practical issues which companies must address, or at least must be thinking about, as a result of the changeover to the euro, whether the United Kingdom signs up to it or not. The following lists some of those issues to which attention should be turned (these issues are explored in full in the CIPS publication 'How to handle economic and monetary union' (Sam Tulip), which is available through the CIPS Bookshop, £10.95).

Customer-centred issues

- Can you handle the remaining exchange rate risks?
- Will you need to set standard prices for your products across the Eurozone?
- What relationship will you establish between your euro prices and sterling (or other currencies, eg dollar) prices?
- Will you need to establish new price points in euros?
- Have you taken into account the effects of the euro on your Eurozone distributors, agents and wholesalers?
- Does the Eurozone affect the choice of marketing and distribution channels?
- When will you start to reflect these decisions on product labelling, marketing, advertising and point of sale information?
- Does the larger and more integrated market offered by the euro have implications for product design (including packaging design and pack size)?

- Do you have the necessary production, distribution and support capacity to serve an expanded market?
- Are developments in the European marketplace likely to affect your UK customers' requirements?

Supplier-related issues

- Will your Eurozone or other suppliers insist on being paid in euros?
- Will your UK or non-Eurozone suppliers accept payment in euros?
- Who is handling any resulting exchange risk?
- Will increased price transparency, reduced exchange risk and lower transaction costs suggest a re-sourcing strategy?

Organisational issues

- Can your accountancy, financial and other systems handle the euro and its relationship with other currencies (not just sterling)? What base currency is your organisation going to use?
- Can you print and transmit documents using the euro symbol (€)?
- Are your arrangements for handling cash adequate?
- To what extent is it necessary to convert historical data into euros?
- What financial dealings will be based in euros?
- Are your banking arrangements appropriate?

The changeover to euros in early 2002 will have a major impact on the structure of businesses and the competitive environment, not only upon those organisations based within the Eurozone but also those outside it, such as the United Kingdom.

It goes without saying that all organisations with trading links with a Eurozone country will be affected. However, so will those, to a greater or lesser extent, whose immediate interests are confined to the United Kingdom but which are nonetheless exposed to the euro through its effects on competition or its interaction with some other part of a supply chain in which they operate.

Although there are a number of immediate operational and practical tasks that firms must carry out (as outlined above under 'Organisational issues'), it would be a mistake to see the euro issue solely in terms of compliant IT and accounting systems. Of far more strategic importance to the business is the consideration of the likely impact of the euro on your own supply chain activity, recognising that it presents both opportunities and threats.

Carolyn Munton is director of Marketing and Communications for The Chartered Institute of Purchasing and Supply (CIPS). CIPS is an international organisation, based in the UK, serving the purchasing and supply profession. With 30,000 members wordwide, CIPS is dedicated to promoting best practice and provides a programme of continuous improvement in professional standards, raising awareness of the contribution purchasing and supply makes to corporate, national and international prosperity.

The Chartered Institute of Purchasing and Supply, Easton House, Easton on the Hill, Stamford PE9 3NZ. Telephone +44 (0)1780 756777; Fax +44 (0)1780 751610; e-mail info@cips.org; http://www.cips.org

CIPS Bookshop. Telephone +44 (0)1780 761468; http://www.bookshop.cips.org

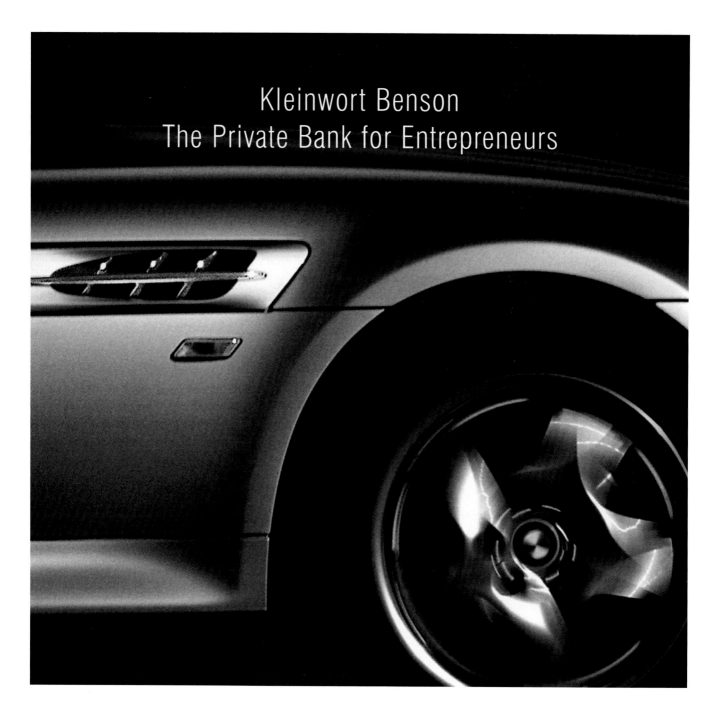

Kleinwort Benson
PRIVATE BANK

Kleinwort Benson Private Bank provides an exclusive environment for successful people in business. We offer a complete personal asset management service to owners of private businesses and access to the Entrepreneurs Club. The Entrepreneurs Club was launched in November 2000 with membership being limited to successful entrepreneurs and those seeking to reinvest in private businesses. At regular monthly events members can network and interact with like minded people and access introductions to development capital and professional services.

For more information about the Entrepreneurs Club and our services please contact Derek Wright or Tanya Jack on 020 7475 5100 or visit our website www.kbpb.co.uk.

A Member of
Dresdner Private Banking

Dubai · Frankfurt · Geneva · Grand Cayman · Guernsey · Hamburg · Hong Kong · Jersey · London · Lugano · Luxembourg · Miami · Montevideo · New York · Panama · Singapore · Zurich

Kleinwort Benson Private Bank
The Private Bank for Entrepreneurs

Kleinwort Benson Private Bank delivers a complete range of personal financial services to UK and international private clients. From our origins of advising clients emerging from the Industrial Revolution to advising entrepreneurs from today's technology led revolution, the commitment to finding bespoke solutions to meet each clients needs has remained constant throughout.

The Entrepreneurs Club

As part of our ongoing commitment to entrepreneurs in the UK, we have created the Entrepreneurs Club that provides an exclusive environment for successful people in business. The club was launched in London in November 2000 with membership being limited to aspirational entrepreneurs, and those seeking to reinvest in private businesses. At regular monthly events members can network and interact with like-minded people and access introductions to development capital and professional services. The Club will expand into Birmingham in March 2002 and then Manchester, Leeds and Scotland, so that entrepreneurs throughout the UK are never far away from an exclusive networking environment.

The Club operates in a virtuous circle of entrepreneurship. We have members as owners of emerging businesses, those who own a later stage acquisitive business, and those with a business approaching an exit by trade sale or market listing. We then help those who have exited become serial entrepreneurs as investors who wish to find a new emerging opportunity.

Members of the Club can also access Kleinwort Benson Private Banks sophisticated network of venture capital companies, corporate finance advisers, other professionals and non-executive director forums to assist in the growth of their businesses.

How we help growing businesses

We help businesses in a number of ways. Owners of new emerging businesses often require advice and a voice of experience from non-executive directors just as much as they require financial advice.

For acquisitive companies seeking to expand market share in the UK and Europe we can introduce you to specialist business advisers and individuals who have the required experience of building European businesses We can also offer private equity and mezzanine finance from vetted third party providers or our own private equity funds. A number of companies may require private investors, rather than the involvement of a venture capital company, thereby achieving added experience as well as finance. Though a network of pedigree 'business angel clubs' we can effect appropriate introductions.

For companies seeking an exit via a trade sale or market quotation we know the best advisers and those who provide entry on to the OFEX and AIM markets. Through our sister company, Dresdner Kleinwort Wasserstein entry to the official lists of worldwide bourses can be explored. After the deal is done you may wish to retire or continue in business to become a serial entrepreneur. The Entrepreneurs Club is there for you to find a new opportunity and perpetuate the virtuous entrepreneurial circle.

How we can help you personally as a director or owner manager?

We have a commodity you do not often possess – time. Time to review your personal financial affairs whilst you concentrate on building a successful business. The issues we can review and provide solutions include:

- Effective and efficient remuneration to reward and motivate key employees.
- Consequential loss cover via key person insurance, including advice on cross option agreements to acquire shares and keep control.
- Personal pensions, maximising contributions and planning into retirement.
- Keeping control but planning the succession via family trusts and discretionary wills.
- Mitigating tax on exit to protect the wealth your hard work has built.

What does Kleinwort Benson offer?

Kleinwort Benson Private Bank provides access to all forms of asset management with a proven performance track record and the ability to innovate new strategies in response to change.

In addition to our investment management services into worldwide stock and bond markets that start for funds from £100,000, we offer innovative approaches to the management of a variety of asset classes. These classes include cash, options, single stock risk management techniques, real estate and private equity, including tax efficient investment of VCTs and E.I.S arrangements. In regard to financial advisory services we have independent experts to advise you on personal pensions, trusts and tax planning. In regard to personal banking we offer deposits from £100,000, and loans against marketable assets from a similar amount.

Delivery of these services continues to be via a personal relationship from a client manager who takes time to understand your financial circumstances and aspirations. The right service is then delivered at the right time and in the right way.

The Private Bank is part of the Dresdner Bank Group and therefore can provide access to European private banking skills through specialists based in Frankfurt, Geneva, Guernsey, Jersey, Milan, Paris and Zurich.

Points of Contact

For further information on the Entrepreneurs Club visit the dedicated web site at www.the-entrepreneurs-club.com or telephone the Club director, Derek Wright on 00 44(0)207 475 5476.

For information on any Kleinwort Benson Private Bank's services please contact the business development team:
In London 00 44 (0)207 475 5100
In Birmingham 00 44 (0)121 632 5306

Or write to us at:
Kleinwort Benson Private Bank
10 Fenchurch Street
London EC3M 3LB

Part 6

Selling in Europe

MANAGING RISKS IN EUROPEAN ALLIANCES

Strategic alliances can be more effective than acquisitions as a way of expanding rapidly in Europe, say Arun Singh and Alan Shaw of KLegal, London.

The recession of the 1990s forced numerous companies throughout Europe to consider a wider range of strategic options to enable them to compete more effectively. Strategic alliances can offer an effective way to expand more rapidly, thus improving competitiveness.

Cross-border acquisitions often fail when moving into new or related businesses. Cross-border alliances are frequently preferred and are a lower risk alternative to an acquisition under these circumstances. Various studies have shown that alliances are more likely to succeed where there is little overlap between the participants. If the parties operate in the same geographical or business area, an acquisition stands a greater chance of success.

Reasons for expansion

The market-related reasons for expansion are:

■ Economies of scale: geographic expansion and economies of scale are the two most frequently cited reasons for building larger businesses.

■ Shortening product life cycles: strategic alliances can lead to the sharing of research and development, distribution and manufacturing costs, while enabling the businesses to respond quickly to changing market dynamics and government pricing and regulatory pressures.

■ High prices: the popularity of strategic alliances can result from high prices required to consummate acquisitions and financial constraints placed on many acquirers from aggressive borrowing to finance previous acquisitions.

The commercial rationale for European alliances is:

■ Financial constraints: an alliance that is floated or an alliance which combines the subsidiary of one partner with a publicly traded equity can create an independent affiliation with access to public sources of capital.

■ Initial step to buying or selling a business: studies have shown that approximately three-quarters of cross-border joint ventures result in an acquisition by one of the partners to the alliance (as opposed to a flotation, the sale to a third party or dissolution).

■ Access to new or developing technology: many companies lack the resources to develop alone the required technical sophistication. In addition, one partner can benefit from existing technological advances made by another partner.

- Access to new markets or distribution channels.
- Production efficiencies (eg sharing production and technology development costs).
- Spreading commercial risks: the costs and risks of development can be shared, while the respective partners' areas of expertise can be exploited.
- Managerial access: a parent may place a subsidiary in a joint venture if it is felt that it could benefit from the stronger management talents of its partners.

Structuring European alliances

Operational alliance

Operational alliances occur where one party provides a service or product to another. They are usually evidenced by some form of contractual agreement. Examples of such agreements include:

- Distribution/marketing agreements whereby one partner might develop and produce products and rely on the domestic partner for marketing, distribution and service. The advantages here are:

   i)   Local knowledge leads to quicker response to market needs and greater flexibility to match local circumstances and solutions.
   ii)   Reduced need for producers to manage end customers directly.
   iii) Ready presence in the market.

   The difficulties are:

   i)   Isolation from market – loss of control and customer ownership.
   ii)   Reduced capability to service special needs.
   iii) Problems of dealing with possible poor feedback from the market.

- Technology agreements whereby one party could make its technology and/or know-how available through a licence to another party, which produces and markets the product in its marketplace. The advantages here are:

   i)   Cheaper and faster market entry.
   ii)   Easier product adaptation to local needs.
   iii) Production costs are lower and can be adapted to local market prices, which leads to better margins.
   iv)   Reduced costs of exporting, particularly for low-tech and bulky products.

The difficulties are:

   i)   No control over volume or market coverage or costs.
   ii)   Minimum control over quality.
   iii) Important to ensure that the technology or know-how is protected.

- Franchise agreements whereby one party provides a concept and/or format and others bring capital with local market expertise. The franchise is licensed to use a logo, trademark or brand name and a proven business format in return for royalties and an initial fee for the know-how. The advantages here are:

   i)   Quality control.
   ii)   Diffusion of the brand.
   iii) Continuing income.
   iv)   Many outlets but a low investment.

The difficulties are:

   i)   A proven business format is needed before franchising.
   ii)   The business must be transferable and replicable.
   iii) There must be tight management and control of quality, ensuring standard levels across all units.
   iv)   Royalties are often substantially under-reported.

Manufacturer commitment to research and development is vital.

Parties can also form alliances through manufacturing agreements where one or more of the parties might provide a manufacturing service to the other in a particular market where that party cannot justify the cost of establishing its own capacity.

Equity joint venture

Alternatively, the parties may decide to establish an equity joint venture whereby partners set up a new legal entity and contribute assets, liabilities and services to it for the development of common objectives. Here, there is a sharing of financial commitment, risks and resources, together with a more competitive way of entering into unknown territory. However, there may be a loss of control, which would be highlighted if the minority interest partner has the upper hand due to market proximity. In addition, lengthy decision-making would take up management time and effort. Studies indicate that joint ventures with an even ownership split are nearly twice as likely to succeed as those with uneven ownership structures.

Selection of foreign partner

When selecting a foreign partner, it is necessary to verify the following:

- financial position and creditworthiness;
- connections;
- quality of facilities;
- people and skills;
- management style;
- credibility and image.

In order to verify these matters, professional help in the relevant country should be sought from:

- lawyers;
- country experts – consultants;
- local Chambers of Commerce;
- commercial sections of embassies;
- existing customer references;
- accountants/auditors;
- financial institutions;
- other government organisations.

Purpose of the European alliance

Various issues should be considered in setting up the European alliance, including:

- Commercial rationale: Concorde was developed as a compromise between the French plans for a medium-haul jet and British plans for a very long-distance airliner carrying fewer passengers. Its range barely allows it to cross the Atlantic without refuelling, thus preventing it from flying distances where supersonic speed would be a real advantage. In addition, the 100-seat capacity makes it uneconomical.
- Location and structure including any tax and organisational constraints on the partners.
- Financial returns and objectives including dividends, future funding and return of capital.
- Assets contributed including intangibles such as management skills and technology.

- Control: voting control need not always mirror the partners' share of the joint venture equity. Where management is shared, one partner might hold a disproportionate share of the joint venture equity and have rights to early dividends until the imbalance in value contributed to the joint ventures is corrected.
- Appointment of the managing director and chairman: they tend to determine the culture and character of the joint venture and the degree of autonomy eventually granted to the partnership by the shareholders.
- Further appointments: a partner bringing in research and development might have the authority to appoint subsequent research and development directors.
- Funding: there should be continuing financial commitment. However, consider how the lender will be taxed. Will any interest be tax deductible?
- No conflicts with other businesses of either partner.
- Mutual trust and respect: one way in which to avoid mistrust arising is to create a permanent executive committee to which each partner delegates one or two representatives.
- If the joint venture will be borrowing money, what security will be given?
- Will the third party lenders want guarantees from the parties?
- Do the parties envisage taking out know-how, income, capital growth etc?
- Can the parties to the venture use the joint venture's losses (if any) to set against their own profits for tax purposes?

Governance and interference from shareholders

To what extent do shareholders need to participate in day-to-day management? The overriding purpose should be to encourage independence of the alliance while maintaining an acceptable level of control at the parent level and minimising bureaucracy between the alliance and its owners. This is often achieved by requiring explicit approval of the partners for certain major matters while leaving management responsibility to the joint venture board. Such major matters might include, for example, an increase in equity capital or return of capital, a change in debt levels, dissolving the partnership, or mergers and acquisitions.

Competition

Competition laws will often apply to commercial arrangements, and will do so in different ways depending on the nature of the arrangement, the markets involved and the economic power of the parties, their competitors and others concerned (eg suppliers/purchasers/consumers). For example, certain types of joint ventures may be treated as mergers or acquisitions and be subject to mandatory pre-notification under the EC Merger Regulation if the parties' turnover meets the relevant jurisdictional thresholds. Others might be subject to mandatory (eg Germany) or voluntary (eg the United Kingdom) national merger control. Still others will be treated under different rules and procedures, but notification to the European Commission in Brussels and possibly to other national competition authorities for individual clearance may well be advisable.

At the other end of the spectrum will be cooperation arrangements which have no or only minor economic effects and which are treated as falling outside EC and/or national rules which prohibit anti-competitive agreements unless they are notified and cleared. In between there is a wide range of possibilities in relation to which EC and/or national competition laws may well apply and in relation to which individual notification/clearance may be advisable, or it may be possible to take advantage of block exemptions or EC guidance (eg block exemption for vertical agreements, guidelines on agreements of minor importance and on horizontal agreements).

Key issues therefore include:

■ Must my agreement be notified, and under which rules and to which authorities?
■ Should my agreement be notified, and to whom?
■ What are the procedural (eg timing of clearance) and substantive (ie is clearance, with or without conditions, likely?) competition law issues?
■ What risks do I run, in terms of significant fines (up to 10 per cent of worldwide turnover under the EC Rules), contractual unenforceability and the risk of being sued for an injunction/damages, if I fail to notify?
■ In negotiations can I resist certain provisions on the grounds that they are anti-competitive?
■ Is my, and/or my proposed 'partner's' market power such that I or we have market dominance

(roughly 40 per cent plus market share) and that the arrangement might be seen as an abuse of that dominance?

Intellectual property

It is important to differentiate between jointly developed technology and technology introduced to the joint venture by one or other of the partners. Jointly developed technology can be licensed to the parents or third parties from the joint venture for use outside the scope of the alliance. Technology introduced by the partners can be assigned to the partnership or licensed from the relevant parent.

Intellectual property (IP) rights (patents, trademarks, copyright etc) tend to be territorially limited rights so that a company which only operates in one country needs only to be concerned with IP rights effective in that one country. A trap that many companies fall into when expanding internationally is to pay too little attention to the fact that by expanding into a new market they are creating an entirely new set of competitors, with IP rights of their own. Questions for a business to answer will thus include:

■ Will my products avoid patent infringement in the new market?
■ Am I free to use my brand in the new market?
■ Is the brand commercially and culturally appropriate for use in the new market?
■ Am I protected against competitors in the new market with IP rights of my own?
■ Will I be liable for a tax charge by moving IP (assets) out of my home country?

Valuing contributions

Depending on the nature and location of the joint venture, and particular accounting and tax practices, the value of assets contributed can vary considerably. Partially allocated assets (eg a shared production facility) or services to be provided to the joint venture, add to the complexity of the valuations.

The value of qualitative items such as management or brand names or the value of cash now versus some form of royalty stream over time needs to be ascertained. In addition, how is existing technology, IP, or for example, an exclusive distribution agreement in a particular agreement to be valued?

Revenues of the businesses being contributed should be considered. How much of the growth in revenue is pricing led and how much is volume driven?

Do the companies have sustainable earnings momentum? Has the companies' performance improved significantly?

Have both companies maintained an appropriate capital expenditure programme? Is the level of working capital sufficient to service customers?

There should also be a review of intangibles. Is one party contributing a plant that has potential environmental liabilities? Are there employee liabilities such as unusual benefits or non-funded pensions? Are there likely to be significant future tax liabilities?

It is important to assess whether there are likely to be economies of scale and whether it is likely that distribution or development costs will be reduced.

Settling disputes and termination

The average lifespan of a strategic alliance is less than five years. Half of alliances with shared management disappear or are reorganised within five years.

Over two-thirds of alliances are estimated to have some form of operational difficulty during their first two years, usually as a result of some commercial misunderstanding. Therefore, in the operating agreement, provision should be made for a mechanism for settling disputes to avoid deadlock. In addition, there should be restrictions on the sale of equity in the joint venture company, as well as provisions detailing which partner has rights to particular assets and liabilities if the joint venture is dissolved (eg rights to technology and customer lists).

Key success factors

- Strong commercial logic for all parties.
- Clearly defined and achievable set of objectives.
- Similar financial expectations and timing to achieve these objectives.
- Partners will each provide complementary skills, products, technologies, geographic spread of activities, distribution capability and so forth.
- Venture should be allowed to evolve. Legal documentation should allow for changes in the market but provide protection if things go wrong.
- No conflicts with other businesses of either partner.
- Cooperation and commitment. Training such as team building, employee exchange programmes, motivation – encourage innovation and growth potential.
- Management should have a degree of independence but also a recognition that parent companies may provide guidance on key strategies especially early in its life.
- Communication link from the alliance to the parent companies to maximise the benefit of the venture to each partner.
- Continuing financial commitment, not just at the inception.

Strategic alliances can provide an effective way for European businesses to expand. However, it is essential that prior to entering into any agreement the parties decide on the most appropriate structure to enable them to fulfil the maximum potential of any alliance.

Arun Singh OBE is partner and head of commercial law at KLegal, London, the international law firm associated with KPMG. He advises companies from a range of sectors on their international operations including acquisitions and various forms of collaborations.

Alan Shaw is a solicitor in the corporate and commercial department of KLegal, London. E-mail alan.shaw@ kpmg.co.uk

PERFECTING EUROPEAN DISTRIBUTION

P&M has taken five years to find the right European distribution strategy.

P&M's lead product is the Blopen, a felt tip pen for children, which doubles up as an airbrush when you blow through it. When Douglas Eaton took over as managing director in 1996, the company had a turnover of £1.7 million and sales in 55 different countries. Its export strategy, he admits, was largely a matter of vanity.

'We would deal with anyone who was enthusiastic. All they had to say was, "We love your products, we will sell them". We did not run any in-depth checks on whether they were the right people.'

Eaton made the decision to concentrate on fewer markets, putting more energy and effort into each one. His aim in Europe was to work with exclusive distributors in Scandinavia, Benelux, Germany and France, lifting sales in each of these markets to the same level as in the United Kingdom. It has taken him five years to get this strategy right.

The first market in which the Blopen took off was Scandinavia. 'Our distributors got behind it and turned it into a fad, promoting it through videos in stores. Sales were great for 18 months but then tailed off dramatically.'

It is a familiar tale in the toy business. When a craze takes off, orders are spectacular until the bubble bursts. 'It is great for the moment you have it,' says Eaton, 'but we want to avoid the volatility of those highs and lows. If a video promotion only lasts for a months in a store, then kids are going to be disappointed when they come back for refills. We want them to buy into the brand.'

'The idea is to work incredibly closely with the retailer,' he says. 'It may not sound much to increase our pegs at Woolworths from two to five, but across 850 stores that is a lot of business.'

When Eaton went to look for a distributor in France, he wanted to find a partner that knew the retailers and shared P&M's approach. 'We had learned from our experience in Scandinavia. We did not want it to become a fad. It was imperative to gain a permanent presence in the stores.'

Such insistence has paid off. In 2000, P&M's sales in France grew by 38 per cent and they are now at the same level as the United Kingdom. By adopting this strategy in other markets, Eaton hopes to establish P&M under its Colour Workshop brand as the number two in creative colouring in each market behind Crayola of the United States.

'We are not just talking about playing at the fringes. We are on the pitch to play the game. We are going to be picking off new countries, applying what we have done in France and emulating that. How we do it exactly depends on each market.'

Eaton structures deals to allow his distributors a margin to invest in promotion over and above the usual costs of sales, marketing and inventory. 'When we find the right distributor, we spend a great deal of time working with them on marketing plans and advertising strategy. We regard them as partners – and that is not simply lip service. We deliberately do not have an export *sales* director – instead, we have an export *development* director.'

'We know that initial enthusiasm and excitement are not enough. We take the trouble to understand where our distributors are coming from. We insist on sitting down and discussing business plans. We also know that we have to stay in regular contact. However good the level of orders appears, there may be an underlying problem.'

'To retain business, we know that we have to keep the product fresh. You soon learn that space on the shelf in any retailer is fixed. There is always a competitor after your slot. Our aim is to replace 20 per cent of our range each year, ensuring that we cover all the key price ranges – £2, £5, £10, £15 – while offering really good value for money. We have the advantage, of course, that kids are kids the world over.'

Parents are a different matter however. 'The degree of involvement differs from country to country, although research clearly shows that they are concerned about the amount of time spent in front of PCs and Playstations. We benefit from the idea that creative activities are good for a child's development.'

There are also marked differences between retailers. France tends to be an early adopter of new ideas, while the United Kingdom and Germany are more cautious. One trend on which Eaton will be keeping a close eye in 2002 is the centralisation of European purchasing. Staples already has a single purchasing office in Brussels and Carrefour is moving in that direction.

What of the Scandinavian market? P&M has stuck with its original distributors and is working with them to change the style of their business. 'They were dubious at first about how we allocated space in stores. They told us, "You can't sell the product, the market is dead". They then started to see that our approach of working closely with retailers might actually be a way to achieve a larger share of the market in the long term.'

Presenting the retailers with 'planograms' as to how the product range could look on the store's shelf was a key factor in selling the way forward, to both the distributor and ultimately the retailers.

Although P&M's strategy in Europe is paying off, its performance in the United States is even more impressive. Three years ago, Eaton was seeking a distributor to buy into P&M's vision. He could not find one. Instead, P&M opted to do it itself, recruiting its own US team. The results have been spectacular. Sales in the United States are currently £20 million per year, which represents 80 per cent of P&M's total revenue. 'You must always be alive to finding the most effective and efficient way to market,' concludes Eaton.

Douglas Eaton was MD of P & M Products between 1996 and 2001, launching the Colour Workshop brand, winning the Queens Award for Enterprise, and achieving 70 per cent annual compound growth. His background includes senior international marketing and general management roles with Unilever, Reed International and Barratt Developments, as well as a number of SME's. He is now running his own development company and is seeking a few 'interesting' non-executive directorships!

FRANCHISING: BREAKING INTO EUROPEAN MARKETS

Franchising should be a natural way of expanding across Europe, say Professor John Stanworth and David Purdy of Westminster Business School, so what is holding it back?

However, whilst those promoting franchising generally tend to hold a bullish view for its future prospects, early forecasts of expansion into Europe do not appear to have materialised in full.

European markets

For UK franchisors having already established a network in the home market, the next step in developing the system might be to look to neighbouring markets. And given that the concept of franchising is well-established in many of the European Union member states (**Figure 1**), then an expansion into Europe could represent a natural progression.

Past expectations

In 1991, a trade association survey of franchisors reported that 15 per cent of British franchises were already operating in Europe and that, by 1996, the total would rise to 54 per cent (NatWest/British Franchise Association *Franchise Survey*). At the time, it was reported that there were 379 franchisors active in the UK. Thus, it was predicted that British franchising stood on the verge of an era of substantial export growth.

	Franchise Systems	Franchisees	Combined Outlet Sales T/O	
France	571	31,781	£21.3 bn	34.2 bn Euro
Germany	810	39,500	£14.2 bn	22.9 bn Euro
Italy	562	31,439	£7.8 bn	12.6 bn Euro
UK	665	35,600	£9.3 bn	15.0 bn Euro

U.S. & Foreign Commercial Service; NatWest/BFA, 2001

Figure I Franchising in the larger European economies (2000)

Similar forecasts were predicted for a number of subsequent years, and by 1998, for example, it was reported that 22 per cent of franchisors were currently active in Europe and a further 26 per cent were planning to be so by the year 2002.

But in 1997 the *European Franchise Survey*, (European Franchise Federation), succeeded in identifying only 31 'Out-Bound UK Originated Franchise Systems' operating in Europe and, of these, 17 had not in actual fact expanded beyond the UK and Eire. Whilst there are some inconsistencies between the surveys to consider – the 1991 data for franchises operating in Europe may well have included US firms operating both in the UK *and* mainland Europe – the push into Europe over the past decade appears to have encountered some critical obstacles.

Barriers

If we initially look more widely – that is, Europe and beyond – the top five barriers to the growth in franchised units outside the UK have recently been cited as being:

- Language barrier (24 per cent)
- Legislation in some countries (19 per cent)
- Lack of suitable franchisees (14 per cent)
- Cultural barriers/business culture (9 per cent)
- Lack of finance (6 per cent)

The data was derived from a poll of franchisors operating abroad or planning to operate abroad (NatWest/BFA *Franchise Survey*, 2001).

EU research

Just prior to the launch of the European single currency in 1999, the University of Westminster and the Royal Bank of Scotland conducted a survey of franchisors to help identify some of the key issues regarding expansion into Europe (*Franchising: Breaking into EU Markets*). The population of UK originated franchisors was estimated to be in the region of 450 systems at the time.

Development phase

A breakdown of the franchisor respondents revealed that 59 per cent had no current plans for expansion into the European Union (EU) countries, but the remainder were separated into two key groups:

- EU 'Activists' (14 per cent) – already active in the EU (beyond UK & Eire)
- EU 'Aspirants' (27 per cent) – planning to be active in the EU within 3 years (beyond UK & Eire)

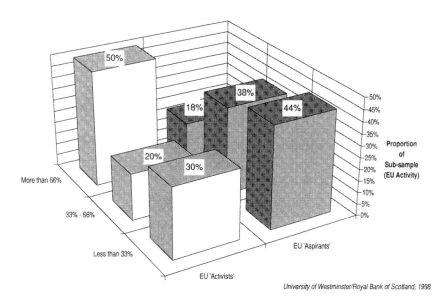

University of Westminster/Royal Bank of Scotland, 1998

Figure 2 Completeness of existing UK networks

Most importantly, the 'Activists' have prior experience in the field, offering a useful benchmark for those without such experience.

Figure 2 shows the level to which the key groups considered their UK networks to be complete. The differences are quite marked, with 50 per cent of the firms already in the EU considering that their systems were more than 66 per cent complete, compared with only 18 per cent of the aspiring firms.

Perceptions of 'completeness' varied depending on the nature of the franchise in question. On occasions, systems with 200+ outlets saw their systems as less than 33 per cent complete whilst, by way of contrast, systems with only a handful of UK outlets sometimes considered their systems as being more then 66 per cent complete.

Figure 3 illustrates the number of UK franchisees for each of the key groups of franchisors. Interestingly, there were a number of systems active in the EU that had no franchised outlets in the UK.

Nearly half (46 per cent) of the aspiring systems appeared within the 21–50 franchisees size group. Perhaps unsurprisingly, 40 per cent of the systems already active in the EU had more than 50 franchisees.

Previous research indicates that, for many franchise systems, financial break-even occurs within the 21–50 outlets range. A substantially larger proportion of EU 'Activists' than 'Aspirants' had passed that stage.

Estimated costs

New business ventures seldom turn out to be less costly than planned and frequently run over-budget. Figure 4 shows stark differences in the costs claimed by those already active in the EU and those expected by those aspiring to EU entry. For instance, 34 per cent of aspirants felt that they could stage EU entry for less than £10,000 compared to only 11 per cent of franchisors already active in the EU.

At the other end of the scale, only 17 per cent of aspirants were calculating to spend in excess of £50,000. This compared with a figure of 44 per cent for those already in the EU. Overall, 48 per cent of aspirants were anticipating spending £20,000 or less, compared with only 22 per cent of franchisors already in the EU.

Entry of partnership method

The research explored the use of three different methods – master franchising, direct franchising and joint ventures (Figure 5) – and the following descriptions for each have been taken directly from a US International Trade Commission report, *Industry & Trade Summary: Franchising* (1995).

■ Master franchising

Master franchise agreements involve the granting of a licence to an individual or firm established in the

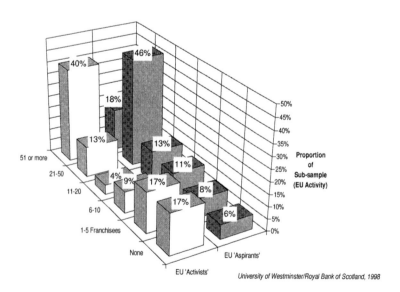

University of Westminster/Royal Bank of Scotland, 1998

Figure 3 Number of UK franchisees

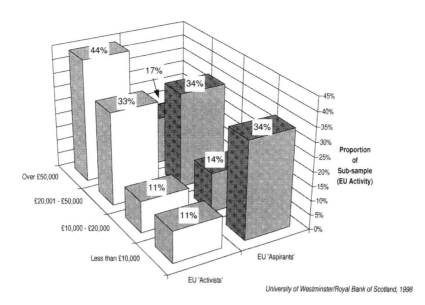

Figure 4 Actual/anticipated cost of EU expansion

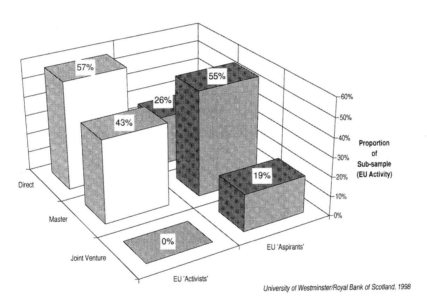

Figure 5 Partnership method used/anticipated for EU expansion

foreign country to operate or sub-franchise all franchises in a given region.

The primary benefit of such agreements is that they require less direct involvement by the franchisor. Consequently, master franchise agreements are considered to be particularly appropriate if the franchisor does not have sufficient management and financial resources to franchise directly, if the geographic distance is great, or if cultural differences are severe. Master franchising is the most common form of franchising selected by US franchisors because it offers a smaller commitment of financial and human resources than other options, shifts most financial risk to the master franchisee, and capitalises on the local knowledge of the master franchisee.

Another powerful enticement is that master franchising may offer a large payment in advance. Many franchisors find it difficult to turn away from a large sum of money, even if they are unprepared to enter the foreign market.

But master franchising also entails some ***disadvantages***, which include potential loss of control over the system and trademarks, problems enforcing franchisors' rights, and risk in choosing the right master franchisor. Franchising representatives report that selecting the right master franchisor is the most important factor in determining the success of a master franchise agreement.

■ Direct franchising

With direct franchising, the franchisor sells franchises for individual establishments directly from the home country to the foreign country without establishing any kind of a regional headquarters.

Direct franchising is effective for situations where the scope of the foreign franchise effort is small or where conditions are such that the foreign franchise system can be managed from the home country. Generally this form is selected if the foreign country is geographically close and if the respective cultures and legal systems are similar.

Direct franchising is particularly popular for franchisors operating between the United States and Canada and between Australia and New Zealand. The advantages of direct franchising include easier compliance with local regulations, greater profitability, improved control over the actions of franchisees, and lower costs than establishing a commercial presence.

Disadvantages include difficulties encountered selling establishments across a large distance, providing promised services to franchisees, obtaining financing and leases, and settling disputes.

■ Joint venture

A joint venture involves establishing a commercial presence in a foreign country in partnership with a local organisation.

The main benefit of a joint venture arrangement is that risk is shared between the partners. Another advantage is that often all of the capital is committed by the foreign partner, while the franchisor only provides the know-how.

One classic ***disadvantage*** to joint ventures is weakness in decision-making caused by the sharing of management responsibilities. Other disadvantages include the weakness of the franchisor's position because of cultural and geographic distance, problems repatriating profits, and difficulties selecting an appropriate partner.

Figure 5 indicates that there were distinct differences between the chosen entry routes.

For instance, over half (57 per cent) of those already in the EU had staged a direct entry. This compared with only 26 per cent of aspirants who preferred this route. None of those actually in Europe had used a 'Joint Venture' strategy of entry, compared with 19 per cent of aspirants who said they would. Three-quarters of aspirants intended to involve other parties (particularly Master Franchisees) compared to only 43 per cent of those already in the EU.

The findings here probably go some way towards explaining why, over the years, relatively large numbers of EU-export 'Aspirants' have not resulted in more 'Activists'. Most of the former are inclined towards the perception that any future EU expansion would take the form of some kind of collaborative exercise involving another major party.

Target countries

Figure 6 shows that, amongst UK franchisors aspiring to trade in the EU, Germany and France were the most popular. However, amongst systems already in the EU, Ireland's popularity declined quite markedly.

Language skills

Figure 7 shows systems already trading in the EU as having greater language competence in each of five different language categories – French, German, Italian, Spanish plus any other European language but English.

This research did not explore the route by which those active in the EU had gained their language competence. For instance, it may have been that existing staff already had this competence. Alternatively, they might have acquired it by means of receiving professional language instruction. Finally, they

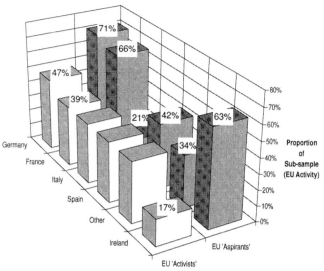

80%
70%
60%
50% Proportion
40% of
30% Sub-sample
20% (EU Activity)
10%
0%

71%
66%
47%
39%
21% 42% 63%
34%
17%

Germany
France
Italy
Spain
Other
Ireland

EU 'Aspirants'
EU 'Activists'

University of Westminster/Royal Bank of Scotland, 1998

Figure 6 New/early target countries

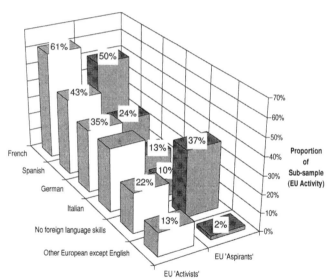

70%
60%
50%
40% Proportion
30% of
20% Sub-sample
10% (EU Activity)
0%

61%
50%
43%
35% 24%
13% 37%
22% 10%
13% 2%

French
Spanish
German
Italian
No foreign language skills
Other European except English

EU 'Aspirants'
EU 'Activists'

University of Westminster/Royal Bank of Scotland, 1998

Figure 7 Languages spoken adequately by staff

may have purchased this competence by buying-in staff specially with language skills.

Conclusion

Franchising is neither cheap nor easy and the support of professional and competent advice is considered a 'must'. But with the coming of the Internet, it is now possible to explore background issues rather more easily than before. The accompanying sources are therefore suggested as a possible short-cut to potentially beneficial insights into franchise system development. They are not intended to be exhaustive, but exploration of these should lead to other sources offering further useful information.

Further information

The following websites offer online free-of-charge information about franchising:

- **Trade Partners UK**
  http://www.tradepartners.gov.uk/
  'Trade Partners UK works alongside Invest UK within British Trade International whose role is to foster business competitiveness by helping UK firms secure overseas sales and investments . . .'
  The site has a search facility (in the process of being updated), so that visitors can look for specific items. It has information about many markets throughout the world, but in some areas, more current and detailed information can be found elsewhere, eg Strategis, below.

- **Strategis (Canada)**
  http://strategis.ic.gc.ca
  This is an example of the freely- available market information accessible via the Internet, compiled by authoritative sources, that English-speaking businesses based elsewhere might find of benefit, too. 'Strategis is produced by Industry Canada a department of the Federal government . . . The department's mission is to work with Canadians to build a growing competitive, knowledge-based economy. Industry Canada hopes to improve conditions for investment, enhance Canada's innovation performance, help make Canada the most connected nation in the world, increase Canada's share of global trade, and build a fair, efficient and competitive marketplace.'

  Example: A search for 'franchising and Spain' produced a total of 65 documents, structured under various main headings. And one of these – *Spain: Long Term Prospects* (a Country Commercial Guide) – offered an overview and sets of data for as recent as 1998.

- **British Franchise Association**
  http://www.british-franchise.org/
  The British Franchise Association (BFA) is a trade association and 'a non-profit making body responsible for developing and promoting fair and ethical franchising through its member franchisor companies.' The BFA publishes an annual survey of franchising in the UK.

- **International Franchise Research Centre (IFRC)**
  http://www.wmin.ac.uk/~purdyd
  This is based at the University of Westminster, and as well as offering access to a number of investigations into franchising, the site has links to other sources of information, such as franchise associations, magazine publishers and other academic web sites.

References

European Franchise Federation *European Franchise Survey* (1997) *European Franchise Survey Supplement* (1998)

Faria, R. M. (2001) *The French Franchise Market*, U.S. & Foreign Commercial Service &U.S. Department Of State

Gattinoni, P. (2001) *Franchising* (Italy) U.S. & Foreign Commercial Service &U.S. Department Of State

NatWest/BFA (2001) *Franchise Survey 2000*

Stirland, J., Stanworth, J., Purdy, D. & Brodie, S. (1998) *Franchising: Breaking Into European Union Markets*, University of Westminster/Royal Bank Of Scotland

U.S. International Trade Commission (1995) *Industry & Trade Summary: Franchising*

Winkler-Helmdach, D. (2001) *Franchising* (Germany) U.S. & Foreign Commercial Service & U.S. Department Of State IoD Europe Franchising 2001.pub 1-Nov-2001

PUBLIC PROCUREMENT AND THE SINGLE EUROPEAN MARKET

Europe's public sector is a huge market spending £630 billion each year, but can smaller companies realistically expect to gain access? asks Tim Williams, managing director of Tenders Direct.

Purchasing by public sector organisations represents a huge market worth £630 billion across Europe as a whole and £170 billion in the United Kingdom alone. Recognising the power of this market as a force for change, the European Community has repeatedly affirmed, most publicly at the recent Lisbon summit, that the liberalisation of public procurement is a key tool in the establishment of the single European market. Yet, less than 15 per cent of public sector purchasing in the United Kingdom is sourced through widely publicised calls for tender. This pattern is repeated across Europe, with France publishing only 19 per cent and Germany a paltry 8 per cent. This lack of access to the market is detrimental to European companies of all sizes, but is particularly disadvantageous to SMEs which lack alternative resources to identify these opportunities.

Cross-border purchasing is also lagging behind expectations. For example, the Commission has estimated that in 1998 Germany covered only 5 per cent of its public procurement needs with direct imports from other EU states and indirect supplies, such as those from subsidiaries in Germany of companies based elsewhere in the European Union. In general, the smaller European states bought more from their neighbours, reflecting their more open economies. Ireland's public authorities were the most receptive, meeting 32 per cent of their needs with direct and indirect imports from other EU members. This pattern has obvious implications for exporters trying to gain access to overseas markets.

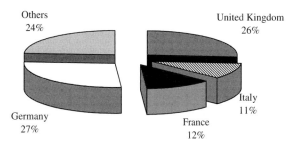

Figure I Share of public procurement expenditure in Europe

Given the importance of procurement policy to the Community, why is it that compliance with the directives is so low? Publicly, the Commission's view is that the complexity of the existing directives means that contracting authorities do not understand the obligations placed upon them. A new legislative package to address this issue has been proposed by the Commission and is currently working its way through the European Parliament and Council of Ministers. Although the Lisbon summit called for these measures to be in place by the middle of 2002, it is unlikely that they will be enacted before the end of 2003. While this initiative is to be welcomed, the degree of simplification that has been introduced is unlikely to have any significant effect on the level of compliance.

The one measure that seems to be holding back the development of an open and transparent market is the lack of an effective monitoring system, combined with an informal arbitration scheme and effective penalties for organisations that continue to ignore their obligations. In this respect, the new legislative package is distinctly lacking, as it simply carries forward exactly the same requirements as the existing legislation, which require the member states to provide statistical reports to the European Commission. These reports should include the number and value of contracts classified by product type, service classification or works classification. In principle, this should provide an effective mechanism for monitoring the level of compliance; however, in practice they suffer a number of fatal drawbacks, as follows:

■ The Commission does not know how many entities carry out procurement activities that are covered by the directives, let alone the identity of these entities. Without this fundamental information they cannot check that they have even received the correct number of reports. The Commission estimates that there are between 200,000 and 400,000 entities governed by the directives, yet less than 19,000 have ever published a tender notice in the *Official Journal.*

■ The data in the statistical reports that are provided is frequently incomplete and inaccurate, but the Commission does not have the authority to audit the contracting authority to verify the report.

■ The Commission does not currently provide sufficient resources to analyse the statistical reports – in fact, only one member of staff is assigned to review these reports.

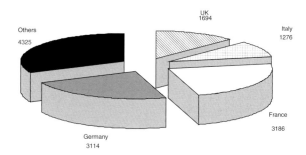

Figure 3 Number of organisations publishing tenders

The cumulative effect of these failures is that a huge amount of management time and expense is expended in generating and collating these reports, but once they have been combined at a European or even national level they are almost completely worthless.

The directives are intended to be self-policing in that an aggrieved supplier can take action in the civil courts to have the tender process set aside or obtain damages. However, the reality is that in all but the most flagrant breaches no action is taken. The most common reasons for this are:

■ It is extremely difficult for an external party to obtain sufficient information to determine whether an infringement has occurred.

■ Suppliers are frequently ignorant of the contracting authority's obligations or the arbitration and legal remedies available to them.

■ Many suppliers are reluctant to take legal action against a potential customer because they fear being blacklisted.

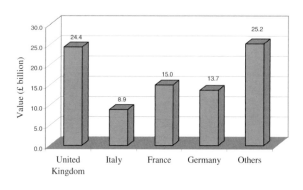

Figure 2 Value of tenders published

- Uncertainty of a successful outcome versus the high cost and protracted timescale of legal action is a major deterrent. Just to initiate a court action in the United Kingdom requires an investment of approximately £50,000 and is unlikely to cost less than £500,000 if pursued to its conclusion.

Many smaller companies are unable to participate in this market because the financial thresholds in the directives (ie a minimum of £94,000) put the contracts out of their reach. This lack of access for SMEs is aggravated by the rapidly growing trend for purchasing to be carried out by large consortia that aggregate the requirements of a number of awarding authorities into a single large contract. Only the very largest national or multinational companies have the capacity to be able to service such contracts.

In the United Kingdom, the Office of Government Commerce (OGC) under the leadership of Peter Gershon is a strong advocate of such centralised buying. Indeed, it forms an essential part of their business plan for 2001–2002. For example, the OGC has recently established a new G-Cat information technology contract, which has a predicted spend of up to £1.5 billion over three years, which is clearly beyond the reach of any but the very largest companies.

In conclusion, while the often-stated aims of the European Community and our national leaders are very worthwhile (ie value for money, a competitive business environment and equal access for small and medium-sized companies), the reality is rather different. We are faced with a distinct lack of openness and transparency, the development of cross-border trading is at a standstill and the already difficult access for SMEs to these opportunities is becoming increasingly as smaller contracts are aggregated into larger consortium agreements. However, to end on a more optimistic note, despite the problems there are nevertheless huge opportunities for companies of all sizes in the European public procurement market, and even the 15 per cent publicised in the United Kingdom is worth a staggering £25 billion per year.

Tim Williams is managing director of Tenders Direct.

Telephone +44 (0)1224 636999. Fax +44 (0)1224 636997; E-mail tim@tendersdirect.co.uk. http://www. tendersdirect.co.uk

CHANGE AND THE GERMAN CONSUMER

The more the German consumer market changes, the more it stays the same, says Eric Lynn of LCT Consultants.

In reading the German press during the last few years, one could get the impression that a revolution is underway in German consumer behaviour: changes in retailing laws, old standards being dumped, e-commerce etc. It must be agreed though that revolutions are relative. Considering that we are now experiencing the effects of changes to laws and practices with 40-plus years of substance behind them, the changes are revolutionary for Germany – and this is the key. The question remains, however, as to how much German consumer behaviour is really changing.

Significant changes

Since the 1950s, consumer behaviour in the German retail market has been greatly influenced by a series of (for the Anglo-Saxon mindset) restrictive laws on the one hand and the values underlying society activities on the other. The laws have partially changed, conditions are changing, but the values remain.

Significant changes include:

■ For many years, consumers and large retail chains campaigned for changes in the *Ladenschlussgesetz* (law on shop closing hours), which, after being introduced in 1953, restricted shop opening to 6pm on weekdays and occasional long Saturdays on which shops were permitted to remain open beyond 2pm Since the mid-1990s, shops are permitted to remain open until 8pm during the week and 4pm on Saturdays, giving consumers greater flexibility.

■ German advertising law is based on the principles of fairness towards competitors and not being misleading towards consumers. Until 1998, comparative advertising was forbidden. A court ruling of that year now permits it, providing it is not misleading.

■ In July 2001, the *Rabattgesetz* (law on price discounts) was abolished. This law dated from the 1920s and legally limited reductions on posted prices to 3 per cent.

■ The advent of e-commerce in the late 1990s.

■ The significant increase in wealth (to a large extent inherited, but also partly earned) among the younger generation.

Effects of these changes

■ While the change in the shop opening hours law undoubtedly gives consumers more flexibility in deciding when to shop and arguably more time to actually shop, it is not clear whether this has had a real effect on total consumer spending.

City centre shops generally remain open until 8pm. The majority of small retail outlets not located in city centres, however, still close at 6pm during the week and around lunchtime on Saturdays; local customers stick to their traditional hours and therefore the shop owners gain no benefit from remaining open. Old customs die hard: established is established.

- Factually-based comparative advertising of the type claiming that 'Our widgets contain seven key features while the competitors' all contain only three or four' is now permitted, but emotional appeals claiming 'Our widgets are the best on the market' are still forbidden, having been ruled as misleading by courts. Again, there is little conclusive evidence as to whether retailers and manufacturers using such advertising have gained any competitive advantage. An additional factor restricting retailers is the concept of 'unfair competition'. A well-known recent court ruling forced Land's End, a clothing mail-order company to withdraw its lifelong guarantee on product quality. The concept of equal opportunity within the community is that competition needs to be orderly.

- The new law on price reductions enables stores to compete on price more aggressively than in the past. It also permits consumers to bargain. Initial, albeit very general, questioning of the public during the first few days of the new law seemed to suggest that most people did not really want to bargain in stores. They wanted clarity on the price of goods. This is congruent with cultural patterns: bargaining implies a lack of order.

- Although the applications of e-commerce in the business-to-business (B2B) sector are increasing, use of business-to-consumer (B2C) is still not very widespread. This may have less to do with technology and more to do with the issue of trust and security. A tangible product not only has greater appeal than a picture and description on a PC screen, but many consumers still doubt the security of supplying credit card details on-line. The importance of giving German consumers a feeling of security in the product and the transaction should never be underestimated.

- The so-called *Erbgeneration* (inheritance generation), which is now inheriting the financial fruits of their parents' and grandparents' rebuilding efforts of the 1950s, 1960s and 1970s, is resulting in changes to consumer habits. Younger people now have far more money to spend than previous generations. In addition, they place a greater value on leisure time and activities. They are more readily influenced by the media and peer pressure to conform to new fashionable norms is greater than in the past. Brands, particularly in business and leisure clothing as well as brown goods, arguably play a far more significant role than in the past. Style also seems to be a more significant decision-making factor for buying clothing, brown goods and furniture than in the past. However, the traditional values pertaining to functionality – stability, reliability, sturdiness, longevity and high technical quality – are still very evident.

What the consumer wants and why

The German mindset is based around the concept of order. This applies as much to consumer as to work place behaviour. Precision engineering is expected in technical products, both function and finish. Quality is expected, not simply wanted, whereby quality means there should be almost no chance of a product breakdown. This expectation of quality is nowadays accompanied by an expectation of low prices. Business and leisure clothing should present an orderly appearance: not necessarily smart for young people's leisure clothes, but orderly in line with the fashion being worn. If a retailer aims to present a quality image, well-sorted and clearly identifiable displays are expected. Tables containing allsorts are for sales, cheap products and one-off offers.

These factors all meet the values of security, time as an important organisational factor and efficiency ('I know it will function when I need it to function'). Functionality is a key concept.

Additional factors and paradoxes

Technical innovation sells. German engineering universities are among the best in the world and people just love gadgets: they want the newest, latest technology and to be able to play with it.

Quality sells, but no longer at any price: consumers expect high quality at low prices. Premium brands are still able to command a premium price, but they do need to compete with increased quality in the mid range.

Mail order is still a significant market, despite consumer needs for security in knowing what they are buying. Established mail-order companies generally offer unconditional product return, overcoming this hurdle.

One of the success stories of post World War II food retailing is Aldi, a supermarket chain that displays its products in cardboard boxes, going completely against the idea of clean and orderly presentation. Initially, the stores were just cheap. Today, the products have a reputation for being cheap and good quality.

Environmental factors are clear also: not only do Germany's environmental laws require many products and almost all packaging to be recyclable, but consumers themselves also tend to be far more environmentally conscious than in many other European countries. Resource-saving product design and the ability to recycle are worthy selling points.

Conclusion

Technical product innovation is essential, as is presentation of the innovative, state-of-the-art features of the product. Technical specifications are probably explained to the German consumer in more detail than anywhere else in the world: they demand this, to the extent that features often outweigh function in product presentation. There exists a whole range of consumer product test magazines, the results of which frequently form the basis of purchasing decisions.

Manufacturers, retailers and consumers continuously call for relaxation of restrictive retailing legislation and regulations. New trends particularly from the United States and United Kingdom arrive far more quickly than in the past. Notwithstanding this focus on trend and innovation as essential selling features, fundamental consumer habits change far more slowly.

Eric Lynn is managing director and founder of LCT Consultants, which specialises in international integration management: integrating people for better results.

Eric Lynn, LCT Consultants, Adam-Kraft-Str. 45, D-90419 Nürnberg.

Telephone + 49 911 397702. Fax + 49 911 331477. E-mail ericlynn@lct-consultants.org; http://www.lct-consultants.org

CREDIT RISK MANAGEMENT

Keith Baxter, worldwide practice leader, credit and bonds, at Royal & SunAlliance ProFin on avoiding bad debts in Europe.

Any business entering Europe is unlikely to get very far before the issue of credit risk management emerges. Europe offers UK industry new markets, bigger markets and the opportunity for some counter cyclical risk spread across international frontiers, but also brings in its train a considerable measure of credit risk. The challenge is to find suitable partners and this often means being able to deal in foreign languages. Not everybody either wants to do it or can do it and consequently there is a significant opportunity for those companies with both appetite and a suitable credit management approach.

Cash transactions on a 'payment up front' basis carry the least possible risk for the exporter, but are not often commercially acceptable to customers. 'Payment by letter of credit', or by a 'documentary credit' as it is sometimes called, carries only limited risk for the exporter. Under this arrangement, payment for the goods is made as soon as the goods are available after shipment. This method of payment is popular, but is not always acceptable to the customer. Open account credit terms under which the customer pays the supplier after the elapse of a given number of days after invoice or delivery are a commonplace alternative to other payment methods and carry with them the potential for significant credit risk. It is essential

that any exporter who deals on payment terms other than cash up front has a credit risk management policy in order to prevent potentially serious losses to bad debts.

There are two phases to the credit risk management task: pre-delivery and post-delivery. The pre-delivery phase is essentially concerned with customer selection. This means making sure that customers are selected carefully in order to avoid the risk of a customer falling insolvent and leaving the supplier with unpaid bills. During this phase, the exporter assesses the customer's willingness and ability to pay. This is done using financial statements, bank reports, credit agency reports and personal contact in order to arrive at an informed judgement about how much credit to allow (the credit limit) and over what period of time (terms of payment). If it is at all possible to visit the prospective customer, a personal call is recommended, and if the order is significant, this becomes essential – and always having regard to language skills. Lack of customer knowledge at this stage can be highly dangerous and wherever possible personal relationships should be used to build trust.

To some extent, the pre-delivery phase can be short-circuited by purchasing an export credit insurance policy. Export credit insurance underwriters have extensive knowledge of European companies and can provide confirmed credit limits and terms of payment for customers. In addition, there is the benefit of insurance protection if the customer should fail to pay, as would be expected from this kind of risk transfer instrument. Many companies choose to insure their export risks as a way of managing the increased risk represented by exporting activities.

Whether you buy credit insurance or not, it is always preferable to avoid a bad debt than to try to mitigate the loss after insolvency has occurred and it is probably wise to be particularly careful about larger orders from companies with whom you have no trading experience. Companies that are known to have financial difficulties within their home markets will sometimes seek credit from abroad as one way of maintaining supplies. This means that it is important to develop the most extensive local knowledge and network that you possibly can in order to improve your chances of being aware that a prospective or current customer has difficulties.

Always make your payment policy clear. State your terms of payment boldly when you make your quotation and make sure that you discuss payment terms when discussing price. Seek a clear understanding and make sure that you state your payment terms again when confirming the order, making sure that your payment terms will prevail. It is also essential that you make contact with the person who will actually be making the payment to you and resolve any language difficulties that you might otherwise encounter.

Once credit has been granted, the second phase of the credit management exercise comes into play. This phase is sometimes referred to as collections or receivables management. The importance of personal contact has already been emphasised and it is better to have established a strong relationship with a customer before problems arise. Use the telephone the day before an invoice is due in order to establish that all is in order. Telephone again the day after due date for payment, requesting your money. Diary and follow up according to the response that you receive and at seven days past due date, send a fax or e-mail reminder. Seven days later send a stronger message requesting immediate payment. If that fails, send a message to a senior person at the customer's office stating that you must be paid. If that also fails, you have no alternative but to instruct your local legal representative to pursue the debt.

Some companies choose to outsource their credit collections or receivables management to a third-party ledger management service. This service comes at a price, but provided that the service provider has the right credentials it can be an excellent way of managing overseas collections without all the hassle of doing it yourself. The service can be either disclosed or undisclosed and the better service providers will use native language speakers in supported teams in order to manage your receivables.

Throughout the process you should be aware that insolvency procedures vary from country to country within the European Union and that some of those procedures appear to be easily invoked and long-term in nature. Most of the more protracted 'insolvency' procedures involve suspension of payments while a company is reconstructed with a view to continuing trade. Wherever you trade, it is important to understand what the various procedures are in the territory in which you are dealing before you encounter difficulty.

Royal & SunAlliance has recently launched 'Management Assurance', a packaged product providing specialist insurance protection with bespoke cover to suit the needs of each and every business, public or private. It covers risks such as Directors' & Officers' Liability insurance, Employment Practices Liability insurance, Crime, Kidnap Ransom & Extortion, Pension Scheme Liability insurance, Professional Indemnity insurance and Libel insurance. The product includes unique value-added services designed to help insureds avoid distracting and time-consuming losses and ultimately support the insureds in managing their future with confidence.

Contact: Keith Baxter, worldwide practice leader credit and bonds, Royal & SunAlliance ProFin.

Telephone +44 (0)20 7337 5952; http://www.profin. royalsun.com

Part 7

Sources of Funding

SMES AND THE EUROPEAN INVESTMENT BANK

Entrepreneurship and innovation are now at the core of the EIB's activities in the United Kingdom.

The European Investment Bank (EIB) is usually associated with major projects that are the economy's lifeblood: roads, rail, electricity and water. For the last three years, it has been pursuing an additional objective. 'We are actively promoting investment in a knowledge-based innovation-style economy,' says the EIB's director in London, Tom Barrett.

Smaller companies are likely to feel the benefits of that commitment in one of two ways: either as credits available through banking intermediaries on preferential terms or as new sources of venture capital designed to cover gaps in the equity market, particularly in areas of emerging technology. All told, the Bank's SME programme adds up to €600 million, one-fifth of the €3 billion that it spends in the United Kingdom each year.

Loans for SMEs

The EIB is an autonomous institution within the European Union, owned by the member states which subscribe to its capital. Its job is to contribute towards the balanced development of the European Union. For SMEs, it provides lines of credit via local banks for operations that comply with each country's particular policy needs.

'We provide funding that is longer-term through banks that SMEs already know,' says Barrett. 'It is a great strength of our system. They do not have to deal with an additional institution and the product is integrated to the service which high-street banks already provide.'

In the United Kingdom, the EIB deals with HSBC, Barclays and RBS, as well as regional or specialist institutions such as the Co-op Bank, Alliance & Leicester and Halifax. The definition of SMEs is generous: companies with up to 500 employees and a turnover of up to £75 million can apply.

The EIB's main facilities are for capital investment. Loans are usually £150,000–£250,000, although amounts as low as £5,000 are considered. 'It is very much the smaller end of the market that we want to reach,' says Barrett. 'Our loans are designed to add capacity to the market.' The EIB's involvement is fully transparent and, as it is a not-for-profit institution, the financial benefits are passed on in the form of lower interest rates and longer maturity.

'We have a broad objective of serving all SMEs that are making a capital investment, but we have sought to ensure that our banking partners are more open to the innovative side of what industry is doing, although they have got to fit the broad character of the book of the bank. If we can favour the more productive side of investment, we will.'

'There are also many standard SMEs out there, carrying out valuable activities, which also need support. Thus, the EIB aims to ensure that the general economy is supported. We want to ensure that there is an even geographical spread and we make funding available to a full range of small businesses at every stage of the company life cycle.'

Venture capital

The other critical element of the EIB's support for SME development is its involvement in venture capital. An initial commitment of €1 billion made three years ago was doubled after the European Union's Lisbon summit in 2000. To date, the EIB has committed to 45 venture capital funds in the European Union, of which 20 per cent by value are in the United Kingdom.

'We are often coming in at the lower end of the market, which is often less well served, particularly as an equity gap has developed as funds seek larger deals,' says Barrett. 'Some might say getting deals for less than £1 million was difficult. Others would say: if you think that is difficult, try less than £500,000 or £250,000. So there is a market gap in raising funds in different technology sectors.'

'The EIB is providing capital as a patient investor. We do not consider it to be soft finance. We see it as commercial, but strategic. It is policy driven, but we have every expectation of making a reasonable return. We have not chased the hot spots in the market. In some cases, such as biotechnology, we could reasonably say that we were ahead of the market. In areas, such as nano-technology, we are seeking to help new developments in the market. If others are happy to fund the second and third rounds of funding, we will withdraw and graduate to other sectors and regions. We want to be a catalytic influence. We are seeking areas where we can reinforce.'

The EIB was an early investor in Dr Chris Evans's Merlin Biotechnology Fund, for instance, taking a 30 per cent stake. It has also signed up to the UK high-technology fund set up by the Department of Trade and Industry (DTI) and to the Barings English Growth Fund, which has a strong regional structure.

'Senior debt is an excellent product for certain types of business, but it is less appropriate for innovative growth ventures. We wanted to make sure that the same range of financial instruments should be available nationally. Thus, in forming partnerships we wanted to ensure that the product could be delivered throughout the country. Let a thousand flowers bloom.'

'The Bank does not apply a quota approach in allocating funds, but follows good ideas,' says Barrett. 'We are particularly pleased with the range of firms we are working with.'

The EIB has been working on supporting regional venture capital funds ever since the idea was introduced. Support is now coming in from other commercial banks. 'The nine funds give an expression of regional identity, although they will not be a soft touch. It just means that companies will have access where there might have been no access at all before. It will also get a regional infrastructure going, opening the doors for other funds to come in. It is still an early stage, so it will take until next autumn to get all nine up and running.'

The EIB is also heavily involved in R&D. Barrett is particularly interested in creating synergy between science parks and incubator units. A programme is being launched shortly to complement existing sources of funding for research in universities. 'One of the purposes will be to encourage universities to transit from the stage of primary research to more commercial development through incubators. I would hope to see new funding going into technical and technological work in universities, creating a better flow of deals to venture capital. The aim is to allow the universities to develop their position commercially as well as academically, reinforcing research activities.'

Public private partnerships (PPP)

Within the broader framework of the EIB's activities, Barrett is a strong supporter of public private partnerships (PPPs) as a way of improving the quality of public services. He cites the recent modernisation and refurbishment of all 29 secondary schools in Glasgow as an example. Ten per cent of the upfront investment of £250 million was directed at improving IT skills in the belief that children should have an abacus of digital skills. 'In one go we have modernised the entire school population,' he says. 'Under a conventional procurement route it might have taken 30–40 years. It gives you an idea of what can be done.

'PPP vehicles have been very valuable in reforming public procurement, achieving value for money, better risk management and better quality service. EIB brings a capacity to work closely with capital markets and to take a long-term view.'

Even the experience of investing in Railtrack has not shaken Barrett's confidence. Although he regrets the company's demise, he does not see it as a PPP issue. It is a phase in the development of the industry's structure, he argues, when amendments can be made to deliver what the government and the travelling public want.

Up to now, the framework has allowed in a whole variety of new entrants, which has resulted in substantial growth in passenger and freight usage in the United Kingdom. 'It is difficult at the moment,' he says, 'but the industry has considerable prospects.'

http://www.eib.org

SOURCES OF FUNDING FOR SMALLER BUSINESSES IN EASTERN EUROPE

The European Bank for Reconstruction and Development (EBRD) is offering a range of financial facilities for enterprises in eastern Europe in the form of loans, private equity and leasing.

Support for the development of micro, small and medium-sized enterprises is a fundamental part of the European Bank for Reconstruction and Development's mandate and is one of its key operational priorities. Smaller businesses play a crucial role in strengthening private sector development and overall economic transition in the EBRD's countries of operation – 27 countries across central and eastern Europe and the Commonwealth of Independent States (CIS). They generate income and new employment opportunities, de-monopolise the industrial structure, improve the quality and quantity of production and services, and increase entrepreneurship and the movement to a market economy. By providing small-scale finance through local intermediaries, the EBRD is also supporting the development and diversification of financial sectors in the region.

The EBRD has disbursed over 100,000 loans in its small lending programmes, which operate in 13 countries. It has acquired considerable experience in structuring and implementing these projects and all are currently progressing well. In almost every country, arrears levels are below 3 per cent, and actual loss levels are less than 0.5 per cent. This demonstrates that small enterprises are extremely creditworthy borrowers who value the access to formal finance which the EBRD's programmes bring them. In many cases the EBRD's programmes are replacing the informal or grey credit market, which was previously the sole source of finance for small and micro borrowers.

The EBRD is grateful for the continuing donor support, which has been a crucial element in the success of these programmes.

Micro and small business loan programme

The EBRD has established loan programmes in Albania, Bosnia and Herzegovina, Bulgaria, Estonia,

Georgia, the Former Republic of Yugoslavia (Serbia and Kosovo), Kazakhstan, Moldova, Russia and the Ukraine to provide micro and small enterprises (MSEs) with finance to fit their particular requirements. Under the programmes, the EBRD works with banks to help strengthen their capacity to lend to micro and small businesses. At present, new programmes are being developed in Azerbaijan, Belarus, Poland, Uzbekistan, Romania and Slovenia.

Micro and small loan financing is provided through branches of banks and/or specialised micro-finance institutions. Loans are provided on a purely commercial basis. In order to be considered for financing, businesses must have adequate financial standing and cash flow, market demand for their products, and sound management.

Small loans are usually available in amounts of up to US$125,000 (depending on the particular programme), with maturities of a maximum of three years. These loans are provided to companies involved in trade, production or service industries. Potential borrowers must have sufficient cash flow from the project to repay the loan and good management skills to obtain credit.

Micro credits, of US$100–US$20,000, are generally available for 9–12 months initially. As companies build up a credit record, they are allowed longer and larger loans for a variety of purposes (trade, services and investment). The firm's debt capacity is analysed before loans are extended. Individual entrepreneurs and firms may apply for micro credits.

EU/EBRD SME finance facility

In April 1999, the EBRD and the European Commission launched the SME finance facility for enterprises operating in the 10 EU accession countries of central and eastern Europe (Bulgaria, Czech Republic, Estonia, Hungary, Latvia, Lithuania, Poland, Romania, Slovak Republic, Slovenia). The SME finance facility will make available funding of €450 million from EBRD and of €110 million from the European Union. The facility will consist of two 'windows' – one for loans to banks and one for equity investment through private equity funds.

Local banks may receive debt finance for on-lending to SMEs, with technical assistance and a performance fee provided through the EU grant to encourage them to enter this business. Equity finance will be available to SMEs through privately managed investment funds in the region. Financing will also be available for leasing companies from the end of 2001.

EBRD SME financing facility for south eastern Europe

In July 2000, the EBRD and the United States agreed to establish the EBRD SME financing facility for south eastern Europe with the objective of financing SMEs, and thereby assisting in the recovery of the region. The EBRD will provide US$100 million in loans to participating local banks and micro-finance institutions.

The United States has agreed to provide US$50 million over a five-year period, to be used for technical cooperation and investment (loan financing), together with the EBRD's funding for financial intermediaries. The US$150 million facility will concentrate on south eastern Europe initially, but may, subject to availability of donor funding, become available to assist SMEs and participating banks in the early transition countries (Armenia, Azerbaijan, Belarus, Georgia, Kazakhstan, Kyrgyzstan, Moldova, Russia, Tajikistan, Turkmenistan, Ukraine and Uzbekistan).

EBRD direct investment facility

The EBRD has created a direct investment facility (DIF) to demonstrate the viability of equity investments in SMEs in its countries of operation. The facility is primarily intended to provide equity and limited debt financing directly to attractive private sector businesses led by motivated and experienced local entrepreneurs. These may be existing enterprises that propose to expand their business or product lines, or start-ups that have an unusually strong business plan and sponsors with relevant business experience. The participation of foreign strategic investors or sponsors is not required, although it may increase the chances of a project being approved. Local equity participation in the investee companies is strongly preferred.

The investment range is generally US$500,000–US$2.5 million, although it is possible to finance up to US$3.5 million–US$4 million under exceptional circumstances. The EBRD's equity share target range is 25–30 per cent but up to 49 per cent is possible in the short term. The investment time span preferred is 3–5 years, but up to seven years is possible.

For detailed information on the EBRD's extensive programmes for smaller businesses in central and eastern Europe and the Commonwealth of Independent States, visit http://www.ebrd.com

OUTLOOK FOR PRIVATE EQUITY

Will Europe's buyout markets ride the wave or face the trough in 2002? asks Alex Cooper-Evans of Duke Street Capital.

It is tough to make predictions, particularly about the future, and particularly – which Yogi Berra failed to mention – when there is so much noise. These days, paradigms are regularly being made redundant (and usually then quietly employed again), the world changes by the day, and the rules are always being rewritten – or are they?

The fundamental drivers of markets are always the same: supply and demand. The buyout market shares these fundamentals. Moreover, the buyout market is less driven by herd instinct or gut reaction than the more visible and accessible public markets: the products in which it deals are heterogeneous; the number of participants is limited; the investment timeframe is uniformly years rather than hours or days; and the management of investee companies, often with an understandable eye to the value of its stake, also has a say in the timing of buyout exits.

Thus, fundamentals are the key to predicting the buyout market – and the fundamentals are pretty good.

Buyout firms are supplied with capital from a range of institutional investors and new funds – while more challenging to raise as a result of the impact of the high-tech and telecoms busts on investors' capital allocations – are still being raised. However, in any event, buyout firms are still sitting on the result of a boom in fundraising: in 2000 alone, European buyout funds raised some €24.3 billion of committed capital, yet invested only €14.4 billion,[1] creating an overhang of committed but non-invested capital of almost €10 billion. While data for 2001 are not yet available, the slowdown in the buyout market suggests that the overhang is unlikely to have shrunk.

Thus, buyout firms have the money, but can they spend it? They certainly want to: their customers – institutional investors – want to see their money invested and returned in short order. However, they also want to see a decent return on their money and for this the buyout firms need debt in their deal structures.

The leveraged lending market is currently extremely difficult for borrowers. In general, banks are reacting to the continuing deterioration in credit quality and earnings visibility (and no market is insulated from the United States in this) by constricting the supply of new credit.

[1] *Source:* ENN – EVCA Network News Supplement, *October 2001.*

Supply is further reduced by the exit of many bank and non-bank participants, particularly insurers, from the leveraged credit market. This gap in supply is only partly being filled by new participants, such as collateralised debt obligation funds,[2] for example Duke Street Capital's own Duchess-I CDO.

Thus, leverage multiples are declining while the cost of debt is increasing. So long as this trend continues, acquisition prices must come down if equity returns are to be maintained in buyouts. The machinations of banks' risk appetite and the leveraged syndication market mean that this will be a particular problem at the larger end of the market and less so in the mid-market (up to about £200 million of enterprise value).

Having noted the availability of bank debt as a real source of concern, however, deals are still being done: high-quality deals will always get done. But what makes a high-quality deal? Investment opportunities consist of a number of components. The most basic is a company that is for sale by a realistic vendor; there will always be companies for sale. Just how many will be affected by investment banks cutting back on M&A professionals; the number that actually get sold will be affected by sellers' price expectations: some asset values are permanently down but others may recover and some sellers may prefer to wait until then. Other sellers may not be able to.

Nonetheless, there will always be undervalued mid-cap companies languishing on the stock exchange, with no currency for acquisition or limited support from shareholders despondent at a stagnant or sinking share price; there will always be private equity portfolio companies for sale; and in these times there will probably be a number of distressed situations.

What else goes into a high-quality deal? Obviously, a decent business, but more important, to a buyout firm, are management and exit.

It is harder to create value in a difficult market than in a boom market. The availability of managers capable of managing in a difficult environment may scupper some buyouts. On the whole, buyout firms back managers to achieve agreed strategic and operational objectives; if buyout firms can invest more in proven managers, they will leap at this opportunity to de-risk their investments.

Exits are becoming ever harder to achieve. With the initial public offering (IPO) markets effectively closed and most strategic buyers either cautious or incapacitated, buyout firms are seeing the investment cost in their portfolios increase. In 1999 and 2000, private equity firms invested almost €26 billion yet realised only €4.6 billion; around 65 per cent of all private equity deals done between 1985 and 1997 have not yet exited.[3]

These two features point towards a real emphasis on acquisition-led strategies for investee companies – strategies known as 'buy-and-builds'. There will continue to be an appetite for taking public companies private, for investing in businesses, be they distressed or not. However, most buyout firms have realised that, if they buy platform businesses and then add on to them with further acquisitions, they hit several birds with the same stone.

First, they get to put more capital to work in a progressively lower risk investment. Second, they should be able to transform the businesses in which they invest by a step-change in scale, product, geography or technology; transformation is the key to a successful exit. Third, by standing behind what is effectively a trade buyer, they can afford to be more competitive on price. And fourth, by extracting cost synergies and benefiting from an improvement in the whole's strategic position, one plus one can often be made to equal three or four.

There are plenty of concrete examples of this strategy at work. Almost every company in which Duke Street Capital invests makes an acquisition at some stage. Many of these companies will change beyond recognition as a result. Russell Hoyle of Leisure Link and Bill Archer of Focus Do It All are great examples of managers, backed by Duke Street Capital, who have, through acquisition, transformed the businesses they run as well as the markets in which they operate.

---

[2] Collateralised debt obligation funds are funds which invest in a diverse portfolio of rated debt assets; this allows them to issue mainly rated securities to fund themselves.

[3] *Source:* BVCA.

Thus, buyout investors do face problems today, but uncertainty creates opportunity in addition to risk. Many buyout firms will probably fail to seize the opportunities for fear of the risks; others will have the confidence and ability to continue to build significant businesses.

Telephone +44 (0)20 7451 6600; e-mail cooper-evans@dukestreetcapital.com; http://www.dukestreetcapital.com

BUSINESS ANGELS

In 1999, only 62 business angel networks were operating in Europe, reports Christian Saublens of the European Business Angel Network. By mid-2001, numbers were up to 140, helping to make a reality of Europe's new entrepreneurship culture.

Business angels have always been active in Europe and other countries. What has been proved reasonably successful is the creation of business angel networks (BANs) to boost the number of serial angels, which means more support to newly created enterprises.

Sometimes known as informal private investors, business angels are individuals who invest their capital and, in addition, bring to an entrepreneur their know-how and experience in company management. They normally invest in a minority stake for a limited period of time.

Business angels finance companies in their early stage. They have an interesting leverage effect for other sources of funding for that company (eg loans from banks, formal venture capital).

Business angels invest mainly in local projects because they want to be in regular contact with the manager of the enterprise in which they have invested. Business angels are looking for innovative projects either in traditional sectors or in high-tech industries.

The personal relations and trust between the angel and the entrepreneur are key factors in a successful deal-making process.

In recent months, it would appear that some business angels are interested in participating in a team of angels (syndication), resulting in larger amounts being invested.

Business angels invest in newly created innovative companies.

Business angel networks are organisations (public or private) that act as intermediaries between business angels and entrepreneurs. Business angel networks act in order to create a marketplace.

The BAN's main function is to facilitate the alchemy process of the matching between an entrepreneur and a business angel. This can be named the 'enabling function' of a BAN and can be presented as illustrated in Figure 1. This function needs to serve both the entrepreneurs' and the business angels' interests.

Most BANs are created in a regional context. However, in some countries, BANs operate on a national basis.

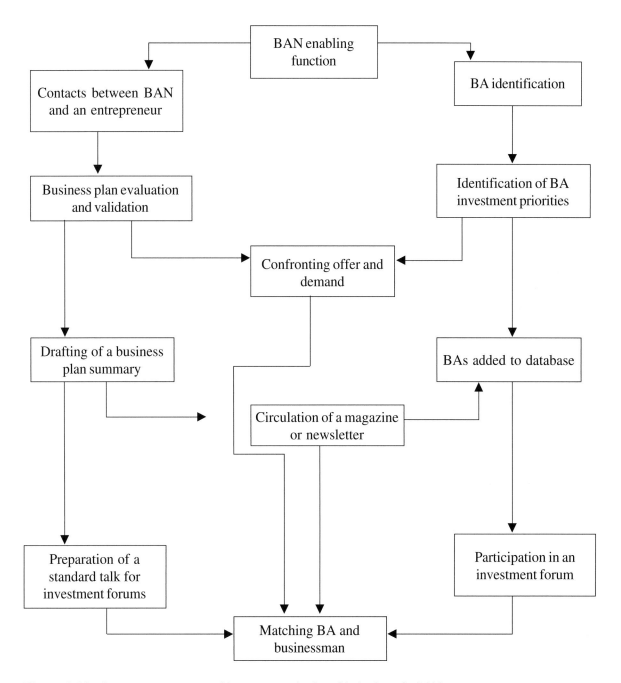

Figure 1 Matching entrepreneurs and business angels: the added value of a BAN

Source: EBAN Toolkit

It should be noted that business angels invest as individuals or sometimes by means of an investment company. These investment companies can be owned either by a single business angel or a syndicate of angels, and this makes the collection of statistics on business angel activities rather difficult. At this stage, data in Europe is only available about business angel activities conducted through BAN. This data is there-fore a small proportion of the activities carried on by business angels.

The private investor brings to the investee:

■ his knowledge of entrepreneur or enterprise management;

- a network of partners;
- equity capital.

Moreover, a private investor invests his money and entrepreneurial knowledge, while a venture capitalist invests someone else's money (mainly from banks, pension funds, insurance companies, corporate investors, individuals or government agencies).[1]

In Europe, the equity gap has to be considered while taking into account:

- the volume of equity required (entrepreneurs find it difficult to raise amounts ranging between €100,000 and €500,000 due to a lack of seed and start-up venture capital and a reluctance on the part of banks to lend at affordable rates to start-up SMEs);
- the type of enterprises (start-ups and small companies);
- the regional context (venture capital tends to be concentrated in capital or important cities).

In the future, the bank sector will be even more reluctant to offer credit to SMEs as a consequence of the Basle Committee regulation concerning the ranking and reinforcement of their prudential control. Venture capitalists tend to go for larger deals due to the cost of due diligence as well as their expectations for return on investment (ROI).

It should be noted that the average deals made in Europe by venture capitalists were multiplied by two between 1997 and 1999 as shown in Table 1:[2]

This context and its future development will need to stimulate business angels and BAN activities as

Table 1

	1997	1999	2000
Seed capital	€322,500	€776,000	€985,010
Start-up	€539,500	€770,000	€1,520,000
Venture capital (development and management buyout)	€1,853,000	€3,001,000	€4,914,000

one of the few solutions to help Europe partially close the equity gap.

By comparison, business angels invest between €25,000 and €250,000. If the formal investors increase the amount of finance they bring, the equity gap will become larger. That is why the practice of business angel syndicates starts to appear in the more mature informal venture markets such as Scotland and England.

In the future, Europe will need more business angels and business angels networks, due to following:

- Banks will see their prudential regulation become stronger.
- Venture capital companies will invest in second or third rounds of fundings in enterprises they already have in their portfolio instead of investing in new enterprises because of difficulties in finding exit ways of giving them good ROI.
- Business angel networks can bring much added value for both entrepreneurs and business angels. The added value of a business angel network can range from:
  i) extensive knowledge of the business angel's field of interest and management skills he can offer to the investees and the time he is ready to commit to the investees;
  ii) cooperation with banks, regional development agencies, universities, incubators and venture capital enterprises;
  iii) screening of the business plan and making the investment ready for a business angel;
  iv) supply of investment opportunities;
  v) opportunity to learn from other successful business angels.

At regional level, it is also interesting to support such networks. Business angel networks stimulate the endogenous potential and can best be compared to local collections of financial development agencies, specialising in supporting start-ups.

Since business angels operate in isolation, it is and will continue to be difficult to supply accurate

---

[1] *Source*: EVCA 2000 Yearbook.
[2] *Source:* EVCA and EBAN magazine No 1 – May 2001.

statistical data about the size of business angels' activities in Europe or elsewhere. In the United States, 80 per cent of business angels seem to operate outside any structure. Therefore, the only data that can be collected comes from operations conducted as part of BANs as well as the trends of the creation of such networks in the different countries. In 1999, only 62 BANs were operating in Europe (among them 49 were located in the United Kingdom). In mid-2001, EBAN identified 140 BANs operating in EU member states, Monaco, Switzerland and Norway. These figures are promising and show that a new entrepreneurship culture in Europe is on the move.

Further details of the European Business Angel Network tel: 00 32 2218 4313; e-mail: info@euraxa.org

NEW SOURCE OF VENTURE CAPITAL FOR SMALL BUSINESSES

The EU has given its blessing to the UK Government's scheme for regional venture capital funds. Alex McWhirter, head of business enterprise at Yorkshire's regional development agency, explains how its £25m fund is going to work.

A priority objective of the Regional Economic Strategy (RES) is to achieve double the rate of business start-ups that last so that we can create a radical improvement in the number of new, competitive businesses that endure and therefore can contribute to the long-term prosperity of Yorkshire and Humber.

Over 95 per cent of businesses in Yorkshire and Humber are actually SMEs of less than 250 employees, and as such meet the criteria outlined in Yorkshire Forward's Business Birthrate Strategy, which has the primary goals of creating a long-term culture change to value entrepreneurs, enterprise and creativity, to make the business support structure fit the purpose, develop entrepreneurial and business skills, improve access to finance, and generate and promote potential high-growth businesses. Identified as 'clusters', the strongest industries in the Yorkshire and Humber region include advanced engineering and metals,

bioscience, chemicals, digital industries, and food and drink.

Yorkshire Forward established an advisory panel comprising representatives from key regional organisations, including the northern office of the Bank of England, accountants Ernst & Young, solicitors Pinsent Curtis Biddle, the Small Business Service (SBS) and the Regional Assembly to examine the exact requirements of Yorkshire and Humber. This reaffirmed the importance of backing such high-growth potential small businesses, and following clearance by the European Commission after an eight-month review the regional development agency announced the establishment of a £25 million venture capital fund in June 2001, as part of the national initiative promoted by the chancellor of the Exchequer, Gordon Brown, and former trade and industry secretary, Stephen Byers.

The fund will definitely benefit entrepreneur-minded small companies across the region by plugging a gap in the marketplace. Historically, the venture capital community has been more concerned with bigger deals of £500,000 or more, rather than smaller deals of between £150,000 and £250,000. The new fund will therefore redress the balance in the region, by allowing more than 20 small businesses a year to access sums of up to £250,000, and if needed, follow-on funding up to a maximum of £500,000 per company.

After a tendering process organised by Yorkshire Forward in 2000, Leeds-based Yorkshire Fund Managers (YFM), the fund management subsidiary of Yorkshire Enterprise Group, was appointed fund manager. Yorkshire Fund Managers was selected on the grounds of the investment staff resources it can apply, its commercial track record and its knowledge of the local marketplace.

During the European Commission's review, a Yorkshire Forward/YFM bid for cornerstone funding put to the Department of Trade and Industry (DTI) proved successful with a conditional contract for the DTI to invest £10 million in the new fund. Discussions then took place with banking and other institutional investors to raise the balance to £25 million, with an agreement in principle to invest from four of the region's pension funds and one of the major clearing banks.

Once the official contractual arrangement is agreed with the DTI, the Yorkshire and Humber Regional Venture Capital Fund will be officially launched in early 2002. It will be run on a commercial basis with the clear objective of delivering an acceptable return to its institutional investor markets and will have a 10-year life, with the first five years being dedicated to investment work and the second five years to investee company development and realisation.

It is anticipated that the Fund's success will lead to the launch of further funds so that there is, on a continuing basis, a much more sophisticated small companies' investment infrastructure than in the past. It is also intended that the Fund will complement existing funding projects in the region, including that of the South Yorkshire Investment Fund (Objective One) and the work underway in Objective Two areas.

Yorkshire Forward is the driving force behind the economic regeneration of the region, delivering a programme of change that will make a positive difference to local people, business and the environment. http://www. yorkshire-forward.com

CIMA

the financial qualification for business

The ever-increasing pace of global business demands financial management skills and vision that keep individuals and companies ahead. CIMA enables forward-looking, strategically aware managers to meet those demands. We are internationally recognised as providing the leading qualification for management accounting. Members and students worldwide rely on CIMA's dedication to meeting both established and developing business needs.

CIMA students begin their studies at Foundation level with a thorough grounding in the fundamentals of accounting and business knowledge. These exams underpin the Intermediate level where focus is on the development of a broad range of managerial and technical skills, with particular emphasis on the key functions of management accounting. Expertise and skills developed through the lower levels provide sound preparation for the Final level exams where students must demonstrate their competence in strategic management techniques.

Within the Final level is a case study that tests higher level strategic skills. The case study integrates knowledge gained throughout the CIMA syllabus; students are required to use their skills and expertise to analyse data, communicate recommendations and solve 'real life' business problems.

In total students must complete 17 exams, although they may be awarded exemptions from some subjects if they already hold a relevant qualification. Commitments to work are acknowledged in the flexibility of our exam system. Students can choose how many exams they sit and how often. There is no time limit on completing the exams and each pass is permanently credited. Students can also choose how and when they study. A list of approved colleges and the types of course they offer is available to help make this decision.

CIMA places an equal amount of importance on practical experience – at least three years' relevant work experience is required before students can apply for membership. The diverse and wide-ranging skills used by Chartered Management Accountants are reflected in the broad practical experience requirements, so whatever your business environment, the requirements will be applicable to your organisation. Students are encouraged to gain their practical experience whilst studying for their exams so their real business experience will complement their studies. Our Training Through Partnership (TTP) scheme helps organisations supporting CIMA students develop an integrated training programme. Information is available on our website.

CIMA is committed to supporting students throughout their studies and training, and to developing a flexible and forward-looking qualification. Currently a new assessment method is being introduced which allows students to sit the Foundation level exams by computer. The benefits of computer based assessment are enormous - students can sit the assessments as and when they are ready and results are immediate with personal feedback on exam performance. The increased flexibility that will be generated by computer based assessment will allow students to progress at a fast pace through to the Intermediate level exams.

Once students are registered with CIMA they have unique access to a password-protected area of our website where key resources and information are at hand to help them through their exams and training.

To find out more about how CIMA can drive your business forward please visit our website at www.cimaglobal.com.

Part 8

Selecting a Location

WHAT MAKES EURO REGIONS PROSPER?

Anthony Light, senior economist at Business Strategies, discusses which factors are important in driving economic prosperity in Europe, and highlights which regions are likely to lead the way over the next decade.

The pattern of economic growth in Europe's regions is poised to change over the coming years and this has profound implications for decision-makers in both the public and private sectors. While there have been numerous studies that have tested growth theory across European countries, empirical studies of regional growth disparities are relatively rare. However, all this has recently changed. Business Strategies, a UK economic consultancy that specialises in modelling and forecasting regional economic indicators, in partnership with DRI WEFA, has recently completed a project that examines what makes euro regions prosper. The results identify the factors that determine regional economic performance and provide detailed industry specific long-term forecasts for employment and output for each EU region.

Thus, what are the main drivers of economic growth? At its most basic level, Business Strategies' European model is based on the premise that regional economic prosperity goes far beyond national economic policies and hence it is essential to look at the fundamental long-term drivers: productivity and the employment rate. In other words, GDP growth is dependent on the quantity and quality of labour and capital that is available to each local economy.

Business Strategies has found that the employment rate in any given region is dependent on a number of long-run factors:

- Existing employment rates – as it takes time for other variables to impact on current performance.
- Industrial structure – regions with more favourable industrial structures (a relatively high reliance on the faster growing sectors) are likely to enjoy higher employment rates.
- Infrastructure – regions with favourable infrastructure (particularly close proximity to international airports) tend to have high employment rates.
- Qualifications – a better-qualified workforce will improve employment rates.
- Consideration is also given to the role that Objective One funding plays in economic development.

The level of productivity in each region was found to be very dependent on the qualification mix of the workforce. Other intangible factors such as the level of technology, the flexibility of the labour market and worker morale are also likely to be important.

All very well for the theory, but how has this all come together to create a map of regional economic performance across Europe?

A central belt of prosperity (as measured by GDP per head) is evident, stretching from the Irish Republic, through the south of the United Kingdom to northern Italy. Either side, Scandinavia and France are notable for the majority of regions being close to the EU average. To the south and south west of this belt, in Spain, Portugal, southern Italy and Greece, prosperity is much less evident.

An important question to ask is whether this pattern of economic prosperity has changed over recent years, and more importantly whether the gap between the best and the less well performing regions has narrowed or widened. The evidence argues there has been little change in the variation in economic performance between 1996 and 2001, although given the short time period this is not entirely unexpected.

However, what about future expectations? In general terms, most of the regions that are currently doing well are expected to retain their favourable position in 2006. Likewise, those that currently perform less well will continue to do so. Indeed, the top four performing regions in 2001 are expected to retain their positions in 2006 – Luxembourg, Upper Bavaria, Hamburg and Darmstadt. The Irish Republic is expected[1] to join these regions in the top five.

A number of other general trends also emerge:

- Many of the regions in Scandinavia that have recorded above average growth rates over the past five years will continue to do so over the medium term.
- The majority of regions in Belgium and the Netherlands are expected to achieve above average growth.
- Across south and south western Europe, many regions of France, particularly in the west, will continue to experience above average growth, while those Spanish and Greek regions that performed well over the past five years are likely to see a moderation in growth.

In terms of individual regions, Table 1 highlights those regions that are expected to top, and prop up, the economic prosperity growth league in 2006.

Table 1 Hot and cold spots of the European Union, 2006*

Top five prosperous regions	
	Luxembourg
	Upper Bavaria
	Hamburg
	Darmstadt
	Irish Republic
Five least prosperous regions	
	Ipeiros
	Dessau
	Pelopponese
	Magdeburg
	Ionian Islands

*Note** the measure of economic prosperity used in this analysis is GDP per head of working-age population.

But what is driving this array of performances?

Most regions in south and south western Europe, particularly in Spain, Greece and Italy, are expected to suffer from both an unfavourable industrial structure and low workforce qualifications. They could improve their prospects by implementing measures designed to raise the qualification level of their workforce and would also benefit from improvements to their industrial structure, encouraging the development of business services in particular. Such firms often provide services to the manufacturing and construction sectors, and therefore the presence of more traditional industries can be used as a platform for development.

Most of Portugal's regions are expected to develop a favourable industrial structure, and the main drag on growth is thus expected to be workforce qualifications.

France is expected to be somewhat of a mixed bag. Many northern regions are expected to suffer from below average qualification levels, but in most cases their industrial structure is likely to be favourable. In contrast, relatively well-qualified regions to the south are expected to be comparatively worse off in terms of their industrial mix.

---

[1] For the purpose of this analysis, the Irish Republic is treated as one region. That said, detailed historical and forecast indicators are available for eight Irish regions as part of Business Strategies' European research.

Virtually all regions in north and north western Europe are expected to enjoy a relatively well-qualified workforce, with a number of regions in the Netherlands, Belgium, western Germany and Finland forecast to see their performance dragged down by a relatively unfavourable industrial structure.

Regions in the east of Germany, despite the forecast of a well-qualified workforce and a favourable industrial structure, are expected to produce below average GDP because of intangible factors that result in productivity being well below the EU average. These regions are in many ways a special case given the many years of insufficient investment prior to unification.

In Austria, the industry mix is generally expected to be good. Eastern regions, where GDP per head of working-age population (adjusted for commuting) is expected to be below average, might benefit from measures designed to raise workforce qualifications.

Business Strategies is one of the United Kingdom's leading economic consultancies. Established in 1988, Business Strategies supply a range of consultancy and forecasting services covering all aspects of economic and business activity. 'What Makes Euro Regions Prosper' is one of many consortium-led research projects carried out by Business Strategies and provides detailed forecasts and analysis for over 1,000 European regions.

DRI WEFA was created by the integration of DRI and WEFA, two of the most respected economic information companies in the world. DRI WEFA also provides a broad range of consulting capabilities covering market analysis, business planning, investment strategy, risk assessment, infrastructure analysis, policy evaluation, and economic development and impact.

Telephone +44 (0)20 7901 1300; e-mail anthonyl@ business-strategies.co.uk; http://www.business-strategies. co.uk

EUROPE'S LEADING CITIES

In 2000, five cities dominated Healey & Baker's ranking of Europe's cities. In 2001, it was six. Barcelona has now joined London, Paris, Frankfurt, Brussels and Amsterdam at the top. Martin Newman reviews the results.

How we see ourselves is not always the way others do. While Londoners may only see a city of dubious infrastructure, abortive attempts at a national stadium and crawling traffic, the businessmen of Europe have once again judged London as Europe's number one business location.

London's status as the first choice for business is confirmed in the 2001 European Cities Monitor, the annual survey by Healey & Baker, the international real estate consultants. Conducted for the firm by Taylor Nelson Sofres, the survey asks executives from 500 of Europe's top companies about their favourite business locations, their views of the main cities on a range of factors and their investment plans. With cities increasingly in competition for inward investment, the survey highlights a number of the issues they need to address and indicates how effectively they are being met, in addition to gathering opinion on wider, cross-continent business issues.

London's continuing success

London's continuing success is based on its ability to maintain a mixture of traditional strengths and an eye to the future. Its number one position is the result of high rankings in each of the key factors considered essential for locating a business. It remains first in the top four factors: easy access to markets, customers or clients; the availability of qualified staff; external transport links; and telecommunications. The increasingly cosmopolitan nature of the city is also reflected in its first place for languages spoken.

In an era when inter-city competition is fierce, London scores highly for self-promotion. The United Kingdom's capital also benefits from a positive government-created climate for business, second only to Dublin in ratings for this.

However, respondents also recognised London's shortcomings. It stands in 15th place for value for money office space and fell to 17th place in terms of cost of staff. While Londoners may raise an eyebrow at the UK capital's second place behind Paris for public transport, they will recognise all too quickly the 25th place for freedom from pollution.

The United Kingdom is also represented in the Cities Monitor by Manchester in 14th place and Glasgow in 19th. Both cities' strengths are recognised: Manchester is praised for its quality of telecommunications and makes the top three for value for money of office space. Respondents indicated that Glasgow's external transport links have improved, as has availability of office space.

However, neither city registered as one that has actively promoted itself over the last 12 months. The strong showing of cities at the top of the overall league table among those who are spreading awareness of themselves demonstrates the need for cities to do so effectively if they are to maintain, or preferably improve their positions.

Since the European Cities Monitor started in 1990, the competition from southern and from eastern and central Europe has increased and cities such as Prague and Warsaw have shown their keenness to address their relative unfamiliarity within the business world.

Big issues

The survey also asks broader business questions regarding the factors most likely to influence business over the next 10 years. Even before the events of September 11 and their aftermath, the performance of the US economy was widely regarded as the factor likely to have the most significant impact on business, followed by enlargement of the European Union. As a sign of the times – and how quickly things can change – the Internet (2000's most important factor) was rated only third in 2001.

London's – and the United Kingdom's – position as a financial centre was also put under the spotlight. Respondents to the survey were asked for their views on London staying out of monetary union. While a small majority said that the United Kingdom's position had not harmed London so far, a larger number felt that it would do so over the medium term. Nevertheless, London was seen to be extending its lead over Frankfurt as the perceived future financial capital of Europe.

From a political standpoint, Brussels is clearly seen as the future political capital of the continent, with Berlin and Paris lagging some way behind.

Big five to big six

The 2001 Cities Monitor has also seen significant change at the top of the league of 30 cities. London, Paris, Frankfurt, Brussels and Amsterdam have been the big five at the top of the list, but have now been joined by Barcelona to form a breakaway six with a substantial lead on the remaining cities.

Most noteworthy outside the top six is Berlin, which has maintained its steady progress up the table and has broken into the top ten for the first time. Along with Frankfurt and Munich, Berlin's rise means that

Table 1 The best cities in which to locate a business today

	2001 position	2000 position
London	1	1
Paris	2	2
Frankfurt	3	3
Brussels	4	5
Amsterdam	5	4
Barcelona	6	6
Zurich	7	9
Madrid	8	7
Berlin	9	11
Munich	10	10
Milan	11	8
Geneva	12	16
Dublin	13	12
Manchester	14	13
Stockholm	15	17
Lisbon	16	15
Dusseldorf	17	14
Hamburg	18	20
Glasgow	19	19
Lyon	20	18
Prague	21	21
Budapest	22	24
Vienna	23	26
Copenhagen	24	22
Rome	25	25
Helsinki	26	28
Warsaw	27	23
Oslo	28	27
Athens	29	29
Moscow	30	30

Source: European Cities Monitor 2001, Healey & Baker

Germany is the only country to have three cities within the top ten, an achievement built on the country's increasing lead as a manufacturing location.

Into the future

The Cities Monitor makes no claims for crystal ball gazing but its respondents' answers do provide a clue to the way in which they are viewing their companies' future plans. It certainly looks as if they are increasingly looking eastwards, with Moscow, Warsaw, Prague and Budapest judged as likely to see the greatest inflow of companies. Among the more established, western, cities it appears that Milan, Madrid and Paris have the most reason for optimism.

However, the indications were that global expansion plans had decreased compared with 2000. If companies did say that they intended to expand their existing presence beyond Europe, Beijing led the way as the most popular location, followed by Sao Paolo, Shanghai, Buenos Aires and New York.

What the 2001 European Cities Monitor makes evident is that cities win no points for being shy. Cities are brands and need to promote themselves accordingly – the most successful publicise their merits vigorously and continuously. This is a factor that London has recognised and will have to maintain as a priority if it is to remain competitive – and as Europe's number one.

Martin Newman is a marketing consultant at Healey & Baker.

Healey & Baker operates the European, Middle Eastern and African division of Cushman & Wakefield, the pre-eminent global real estate services provider, delivering a worldwide service through 147 offices in 49 countries. Founded in 1820, Healey & Baker provides all types of commercial property advice and acts for a range of prominent clients across the corporate, public and private sectors.

Telephone +44 (0)20 7629 9292. Fax +44 (0)20 7514 2398; http://www.healey-baker.com

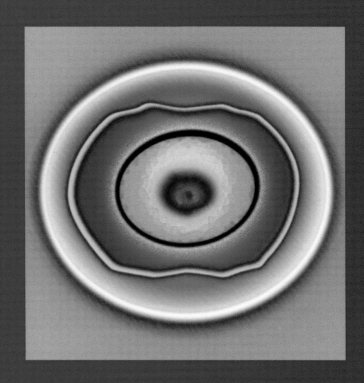

Nucleus for growth

fast growing
expanding faster than any town in Kent

natural selection
chosen for major growth by government

development potential
sites available for immediate development

opportunities multiplying
investment growth to be gained

ASHFORD
Borough of Opportunity

Economic Development Unit
Civic Centre Tannery Lane
Ashford Kent TN23 1PL

tel **+44 (0)1233 330310**
email **edu@ashford.gov.uk**
www.ashford.gov.uk

Keeping facilities profitable during economic change.

by Marc Bird, head of marketing, Kinnarps office furniture.

The task of refurbishing an office interior or keeping pace with the growth in staff numbers can be draining on the bottom line, particularly when budgets are tight and every penny must be well spent. A changing business needs to be able to adapt quickly but can often be held back during times of slowdown, economic uncertainty or the introduction of a new currency in the form of the Euro.

It's at times like this that the Facilities Team is often under pressure to produce real savings or to prove that the office environment is as cost effective as possible.

In modern business life, the creation of a truly inspirational working environment can have more effect on the bottom line than anyone imagined in the property development of the 60's and 70's. Today's office furniture is about creating value in a multitude of ways, both measurable and more ethereal. Working environments now have a recognised influence on staff retention, motivation, and productivity. At the end of the day it can make a difference to financial performance.

Lost in Space
Obvious savings come from space management. Choose a flexible desking system that can offer a variety of configurations and you are already able to limit the space required to function as a unit.

The ultimate saving is being able to cancel an expensive move – by installing new furniture for the whole team in the existing building (which has huge added values in itself), creatively adding more workspace without loss of comfort. The cost of the flexible furniture is small compared to the costs of a move.

Keep it Simple
When I speak of flexible furniture I mean truly flexible. This means being able to reconfigure quickly, easily and efficiently. Kinnarps success is built on simplicity and I urge you to think simple too. Why was Lego voted toy of the last century. Its simplicity created a versatility that no other could match. You could make what you wanted, and when you felt like a change it was easy to break down and rebuild in a new form. Furniture should offer this simplicity too.

Future proofing is becoming a buzzword . . . keep things simple and you hold the best cards when that unknown arrives.

Everybody's Moving
Churn – the movement of staff and furniture within the building – is now so common that some facilities teams are continually moving people . . . every weekend. There is an ever-increasing cost to just keep the teams functioning.

Use the most flexible and reconfigurable desking system you can. The long term benefits will be huge. Some of our clients have developed a flood-floor strategy, where furniture layouts remain static and uniform, so wherever you relocate a team, there are suitable desks waiting for them. You move very little furniture, reducing expensive weekend costs, and only move people.

Throw it all out and start again
As we move to a new Europe and even more potential to file lorry loads of paper, my recommendation regarding storage is to "throw it all out and start again". If you put everything in a few crates and leave them in your garage for a month you'll be surprised how infrequently you have to open the garage door. The knock-on effect is a cost saving . . . everybody needs less storage than they perceive.

Retention and Attraction
The attraction of a modern, exciting work environment is a real benefit that should not be overlooked when it comes to staff recruitment and retention.

Ask an HR manager for the true cost of replacing a customer service agent with five years experience and you may be surprised. Keeping valuable people owes as much to where they work and how they feel as to remuneration and status.

Being able to afford it all
In the uncertain world we live in, the opportunity to spread the cost of new furniture and to finance the office interior in a flexible way has great appeal.

Why not consider leasing?

It is possible to provide employees with a dynamic and inspiring office, incorporating the best in ergonomics and health & safety . . .keeping your finances healthy too, with a simple leasing plan that takes the strain out of the economics and takes value-for-money to the limit.

A great example of a Kinnarps leased package is a fully electronic, height-adjustable workstation with fully adjustable office chair for less than 65 pence a day !

You can contact Marc Bird via e-mail marc.bird@kinnarps.co.uk or telephone 01753 688874

PAY RISES CAN SERIOUSLY DAMAGE YOUR WEALTH

A comparatively high gross salary in an assignment location does not automatically mean that your standard of living will match what it was in your home country, says Andrew Payne of ECA International.

'Earning more money' and 'being better off' are not necessarily one and the same thing. For, in the often-complex world of international expatriation, a pay rise can actually add up to a fall in an expatriate's overall spending power. Such miscalculations do not only happen at salary review time; problems frequently arise at the beginning of an assignment, and stem from an inadequate initial remuneration package.

The trouble is, there is an inclination to assume that when sending an employee to a country where high gross salaries are the norm, simply paying them a local salary will be sufficient. Or, if the cost of living is noticeably cheaper than at home, it seems reasonable to believe that the current home salary will not only keep the employee in the manner to which they are accustomed, but will also constitute an improvement. If only life were so simple.

Tempting though it is, blind adherence to comparative gross salaries as a guide will not work. In fact, gross salaries are virtually worthless in this respect

unless local taxation and social security are also taken into account. Similarly, while cost of living figures play an essential role in salary calculations, they can prove extremely misleading if not used in tandem with exchange rate movements and inflation.

'Being better off' is all about having greater purchasing power at one's disposal. However benevolent your intentions, if the remuneration package accidentally reduces this then employee de-motivation will soon follow (if you can persuade them to take the assignment in the first place!). Raise it too much and quite simply your costs are too high. Either way, getting the salary wrong can have grave consequences for the assignment and business as a whole.

ECA International's Inter-Country Executive Remuneration Comparison, or ICC, illustrates these points well. Designed to ensure that the main aspects of pay calculation are fully considered, the ICC compares salaries at various executive levels around the world, and then analyses the impact that local tax and cost of living have on buying power. It works from a number of base countries, so that users can compare not only the movement of expatriates to various host locations, but also the implications of moving employees of different nationalities. Essentially, the ICC suggests the best approach to salary calculation for each set of circumstances.

Consider this scenario (figures are taken from ICC 2001): a company wishes to move a senior manager from Denmark to Greece. The typical Danish gross salary for this executive level is €96,377. The equivalent gross in Greece is considerably lower at €53,895 and the first impression is that paying a local Greek salary is not an option.

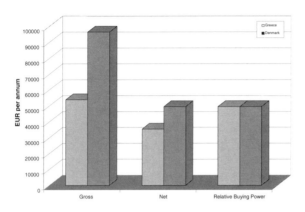

Figure 1 Senior manager: Denmark – Greece

However, as Figure 1 shows, when local taxation and social security are brought into the equation, the relatively heavy tax burden in Denmark means that at net level the two salaries compare more favourably. The net salary in Denmark is €49,392, while in Greece it is €35,417. Nevertheless, a local salary in Greece still appears to fall short of the mark.

At this point, the ICC applies a cost of living index to the Greek net salary. The index is derived from a comparison of prices in the home and host countries and incorporates inflation and exchange rate fluctuations. The resulting relative buying power shows that the Greek salary would go much further in Greece than it would in Denmark. Now things look rather different: the Greek net salary translates to €49,399 (remember the Danish net was €49,392) and the Danish senior manager going to Greece on a local salary actually receives a small increase in purchasing power. The difference is minimal, but a local salary is viable after all and would leave the expatriate no worse off than at home. A pay rise on top of this may well provide the incentive to move.

It is also worth looking at the situation in reverse, where a Greek manager is moving to Denmark. At first glance, the huge increase in gross salary that the

Greek national would receive on local Danish terms would appear to provide ample reward for taking the post. However, as the ICC has shown, this particular 'pay rise' would not equate to the expatriate being better off. In fact, the reverse would be true.

When a local salary is not viable, the ICC clearly shows this. In such a case, a build-up or balance sheet approach may be more suitable. This method is designed to maintain home purchasing power by adjusting the relevant 'spendable' portion of the home net salary for cost of living differences in the host location. While it is more scientific than simply paying a local salary, the build-up approach can have significant consequences for the expatriate in relation to their peers, some of whom will be local nationals and may be comparatively 'out of pocket'.

By producing league tables of relative purchasing power, the ICC allows for comparisons between both locations and nationalities. It reveals 'expensive' locations where it might be beneficial to consider employing a local national rather than sending an expatriate. It also indicates which nationalities would be more 'affordable' to send to certain locations. For instance, a New Zealander would become wealthier by being posted to Portugal on local terms, while a German would see their purchasing power greatly reduced.

The various approaches to calculating salary packages can produce very different results. Choosing the right one can mean the difference between a successful assignment and a costly failure. It can also result in a motivated and efficient expatriate workforce, instead of one that cannot understand why earning more money is making them miserable.

ECA International is the world's largest membership organisation for international human resources, serving a global network of over 4,000 HR professionals in 35 countries. The leading provider of on-line data, software solutions and advice for more than 1,500 international companies, ECA's innovative approach has been providing companies with cost-effective solutions to international HR management since 1971.

Telephone +44 (0)20 7351 5000; http://www.eca-international.com

FLEXIBILITY AND GROWTH IN THE NETHERLANDS

The Netherlands has achieved structural reform by consensus not polarisation, says Mirjam Schuit, executive director of the Netherlands Foreign Investment Agency in the United Kingdom and Ireland.

The Netherlands is expected to be the best place in the world to conduct business over the next five years according to a survey published in November 2001 by the Economist Intelligence Unit (EIU). The EIU has developed a global business rankings model, which is applied to the world's 60 largest countries, and seeks to measure the quality or attractiveness of the business environment and its key components. The model considers 70 factors which affect the opportunities for, and hindrances to, the conduct of business in each country.

The Netherlands topped the list of 60 places, followed by the United States, Canada, Britain, Switzerland, Finland, Singapore, Ireland and Sweden. 'The Netherlands scores particularly highly for its political environment, its policy towards foreign investment, its liberal foreign trade and exchange regime, the quality of the labour market and the availability of finance,' the EIU said.

Most EU countries move up the league table in 2002–2006, improving their position relative to other countries. This reflects improved macroeconomic stability (particularly a better fiscal position and inflation performance as part of the move to economic and monetary union), and a broad move towards deregulation. Improved competition policy, the beneficial impact of the single market and continued technological change are all making Europe a better place to do business.

The Netherlands ranks as the fifth most competitive nation in the world in the *World Competitiveness Yearbook 2001* by the International Institute for Management Development (IMD). Compared to other European countries, the Netherlands came third after Finland and Luxembourg. The report measures the 'competitiveness' of 49 countries by weighing nearly 300 criteria ranging from liberal trade policies to economic strength, and from venture capital raising to the number of Nobel Prize winners. According to the IMD, the Netherlands scored particularly well in openness to foreign influences and their positive attitude toward globalisation.

The success of the Dutch economy is credited in part to the government's political style which has become known around the world as the 'polder model', in which the political decision-making process focuses on consensus rather than polarisation. Structural reforms enacted since the 1980s have led to a strong, internationally oriented economy fostered by a tradition of intense negotiations between trade unions,

Table 1 Overall world competitiveness ranking according to the IMD

1	United States
2	Singapore
3	Finland
4	Luxembourg
5	The Netherlands
6	Hong Kong
7	Irish Republic
8	Sweden

the business community and the government. The gain in the Dutch position was also attributed to greater labour market flexibility, a lowering of corporate and income taxes and increased privatisation. The wide variety of public and private services available are consistently of a high quality. Sophisticated services that handle goods, money and information flows are important location factors not only for headquarters and offices such as support units, R&D and communications, but also for production and distribution facilities. The cumulative results of these policies have been a competitive Dutch economy and continued economic expansion.

Foreign trade has been the driving force of the Dutch economy for centuries and the international orientation of the Dutch has made the Netherlands one of the most open economies in the world. This experience and expertise continues to have a positive impact on the European Union. With just 4.2 per cent of the EU population, the Netherlands accounts for 9.4 per cent of EU exports. In addition, exports of goods and services account for more than 60 per cent of Dutch GDP and imports amount to almost 61 per cent. Dutch exports to EU and other European countries average 86 per cent (€113 billion) of all exports.

An open economy is favourable to international trade without national and/or regional barriers and wel-

comes foreign investments. Therefore, an indispensable feature of Dutch legislation is, among other things, that company law does not make a difference between Dutch nationals and foreigners. In addition, companies created under foreign law are free to operate in the Netherlands.

Dutch legal entities are internationally regarded as sound and generally respected. This reputation is ensured by Dutch business law, fine-tuned by case law, which governs the institution, running and liquidation of legal entities. For foreign investors, the most important entities include a private limited liability company (*Besloten Vennootschap (BV)*), a public limited liability company (*Naamloze Vennootschap (NV)*) and some forms of partnership. However, in case he does not choose to set up a separate legal entity in the Netherlands, a branch (*filiaal*) might be an option.

Last but not least, the Netherlands is well known for its flexible and multilingual workforce. Companies achieve flexibility through a mixture of arrangements, such as different kinds of labour contracts, flexible working hours, the use of various types of shift work, and the frequent employment of temporary workers.

The Netherlands is by far the most multilingual country in comparison with other European countries. The Dutch have a better working knowledge of English than any other nationality on the European continent. Most also speak German and French, while a growing number also speak Spanish and Italian.

Mirjam Schuit MA is the executive director for UK and Ireland for the Netherlands Foreign Investment Agency. Her responsibilities focus on locating British and American companies who are considering setting up or expanding their pan-European operations in continental Europe.

Meeting the demands of our business travellers

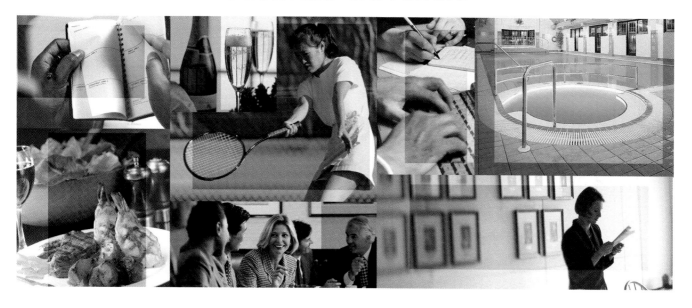

All the facilities you'll need to keep working while you're away on business.

With excellent accommodation and a wealth of business facilities on offer including: faxes, Internet access, ISDN lines and a range of reward programmes. When you stay with Best Western on business, everything is taken care of. What's more, with our choice of hotels near major motorway routes, award winning cuisine and health and beauty facilities, it's easy to see why we've become the preferred place to stay amongst business travellers.

For further information & reservations please call
Best Western Central Reservations
on 08457 73 73 73
quoting EB02

 Britain's widest range of individually owned hotels

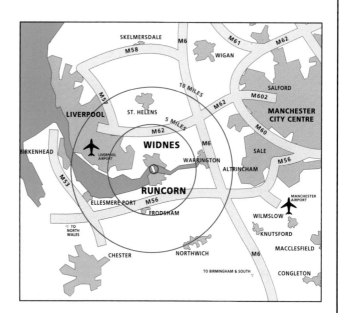

Halton Borough Council

Situated between the conurbations of Liverpool and Manchester, Halton has direct access to five million people within a 25 mile radius.

Widnes and Runcorn offer an impressive range and choice of land and premises in prime locations within the M62 and M56 corridors, within easy reach of Liverpool and Manchester International Airports and the Port of Liverpool. Halton is also served by the West Coast Mainline and Transpennine high speed rail links.

The area offers an unbeatable workforce which is skilled, productive, adaptable and committed – fully supported by customised education and training facilities.

'The council and its partners can help inward investing companies to access assistance from regional and national, public and private sector funding sources to support physical improvements to land and premises, to purchase new plant and to fund the acquisition of land and premises said Cllr Rob Polhill, Executive Board Member at Halton Borough Council with responsibility for Environment, Planning, Transportation and Development.

'We can also build an attractive employee development and training package.'

Halton boasts more than 2,500 individual companies trading successfully in a range of attractive, well serviced employment areas. Internationally renowned names such as Ineos Chlor, Guinness, YKK, Yokogawa, Origin, BT/Cellnet, Laporte and Eutech all have a significant presence in Widnes or Runcorn.

In the last five years Halton has attracted a further 150 new companies into the Borough, creating approximately 6,000 new jobs. Fine chemicals, pharmaceuticals, food and drink, plastics, engineering, telecommunications, distribution and financial services are all represented in Widnes and Runcorn, clearly demonstrating the diversity of the Borough's economy.

Halton has already has already taken full advantage of it's position between the M62 and M56.

In 1999 Martin Dawes Telecommunications Ltd rationalised their call centre operation at a new, purpose built, one site facility at Whitehouse in Runcorn. Martin Dawes were subsequently absorbed by BT/Cellnet and the facility continues to go from strength to strength, currently employing in excess of 1,100 people.

The Borough of Halton also boasts two high specification business parks with direct access to the M56 which are particularly suited to telecommunications, head office and financial or shared service type operations.

Daresbury Park is a new 222.3 acre landscaped office park immediately accessible from Junction 11 of the M 56.

Daresbury Park is about to welcome it's first major tenants. ABB, one of the UK's leading asset management and operations consultancies, have recently occupied their new corporate headquarters at the Borough's flagship business location.

ABB choose Daresbury Park because of it's excellent communications and it's proximity to the company's client base.

ABB have worked closely with the Economic Development Division of Halton Borough Council, Business Link Halton and developers De Vere Group Plc to secure an offer of Regional Selective Assistance from the DTI to support the creation of jobs.

Cllr Polhill commentead: 'This is a great example of the power of partnership working. The Economic Development Division and Business Link Halton have been in discussions with ABB for a long time to ensure that the move to Daresbury Park was the right move for the company'.

Cllr Polhill continued: 'Darebury Park is a brilliant location for companies like Eutech and we're confident that this announcement will be the first of many which will confirm Darebury Park's status as a top flight international business location'.

ABB employ around 1,000 people in the North West and North East of England and the new corporate headquarters at Daresbury Park will initially employ 300 staff.

Daresbury park also recently celebrated one of the largest property deals in the North West. Application service provider Vistorm (formerly ESOFT Global) have signed a twenty five year lease for new 3,670 sq.m. premises, which will have the capacity to accommodate 350 staff

Commented Andy Lavin, Director of Maple Grove, a joint partner in owner developer Limerica, 'Following closely on the heels of asset management company ABB this latest letting is another coup for the Borough of Halton. The arrival of Vistorm contributes to the high profile line up of occupiers and we are delighted that the new move will generate additional jobs in the area'.

Vistorm, the European application service provider of the year, is one of the world's leading providers of managed internet security and managed internet applications. Vistorm has recently secured £25 million funding from 3i , Europe's leading venture capital company, Compaq Computer Corporation, CSFB Private Equity and Granville Baird Capital Partners to accelerate its growth strategy across the UK and Europe.

Halton's second top flight business location is the Manor Park 3 development.

Manor Park 3 is a greenfield site of around 300 acres owned by English Partnerships. The site fronts the main A558 Expressway and is less than two miles from Junction 11 of the M56.

Manor Park 3 offers companies an opportunity to purchase land freehold and construct their own facilities without developer ties. Manor Park 3's existing tenants include Business Post who recently constructed a new 6,689 sq.m distribution centre, the new Learning and Skills Council (formerly North and Mid Cheshire TEC) and supermarket giants Lidl who recently completed their new northern distribution centre.

Manor Park 3 has the advantage of planning consent for employment uses under Section 7(1) of the New Towns Act 1981 for B1, B2 and B8 uses.

Immediately adjacent to Manor Park is the Daresbury Court development the first phase of which, known as Origin House, was sold recently by developers HBG properties to Charles Street Buildings (Leicester) Ltd.

Origin House is a three story self contained building of 39,000 ft, two which has been let to Origin UK, the international full service IT solutions integrator who are part of the Philips multinational group.

Clive Perrin, regional Director of HBG properties commented: 'There has been considerable competition for this development opportunity and we are now marketing the second phase at Daresbury Court for bespoke office buildings. The second phase can accommodate occupiers seeking offices from 929 sq.m to 3,715 sq.m.'

The economy of Halton has also benefited from the decision by computer giant ICL and defence contractor Lockheed Martin's to create Europe's largest data processing centre at Catalyst Industrial Estate in Widnes in order to process the 2001 Census on behalf of the Office for National Statistics (ONS).

Recruitment of over 1,000 temporary employees had already begun the and it is hoped that ICL will endeavour to consolidate their investment in the project of around £23 million and retain the facility after the completion of the Census Project.

ASHFORD HAS BEEN SYNONYMOUS with economic growth and development for many years – and now it's not just the local authority that is "talking up" the town.

The government, too, has realised that the former market town in the heart of Kent has the location, the infrastructure and the workforce to make it one of the country's top three areas of potential growth over the next 20 to 30 years.

The government's Regional Planning Guidance last year identified Ashford, Milton Keynes and the Kent Thames-side corridor as those areas that were best placed for new homes and economic expansion in the south east in the mid- to long-term.

Ashford Borough Council has responded to the challenge by leading a major study into how the town should grow, at what pace and how that growth can be accommodated, while protecting the environment and ensuring real, sustained benefits for the people living here.

The study – entitled "Ashford's Future" – is being carried out by a partnership which brings together the borough and county councils, English Partnerships, the Environment Agency, the Government Officer for the South East, housing corporations, the Learning Skills Council, the South East England Regional Assembly and the South East England Development Agency.

The government's endorsement of Ashford's leading role in the economy of south east England and the rest of the country has further established the town which already boasts significant locational advantages.

The town is as close to mainland Europe as it is to the national motorway network, and as the world continues to shrink, that fact is increasingly important for businesses with an eye on the future.

While politicians in this country argue for and against greater integration with Europe, the simple fact remains that whatever the rhetoric, businesses are less and less bothered by national boundaries as they seek to expand their market from a UK springboard.

Ashford's East Kent location, astride the M20 motorway and at the hub of the domestic and international rail network, gives Ashford advantages that other towns can only dream of.

The town's international passenger station puts Northern France within one hour by rail, Paris just two hours away and Brussels around 1 hour 30 minutes distant. Freight operators have similar swift access to European markets by taking advantage of the nearby channel ports or by using the Eurotunnel shuttle link which is just 10 minutes down the motorway on the outskirts of Folkestone.

These major locational advantages are behind the relocation to Ashford of numerous British, European and American companies in recent years. They also explain the number of international headquarters such as Quest International and Coty Manufacturing UK.

It's not just those who want a foothold in Europe who are moving to the town. French companies, also, are moving across the water to take advantage of Britain's better business environment.

Lower social costs mean greater profitability for French companies operating out of the UK, and many have followed the lead set by InfoElec's Olivier Cadic, whose Ashford operation has caught the eye of many, including an unimpressed French government.

A leading Japanese company was amongst the new arrivals which helped take the number of firms based in Ashford beyond the 4,000 mark over the past year.

The Maruwa Corporation, a world leader in the field of combining ceramics technology with electronics, moved onto a four acre site at Eurotunnel Developments' Orbital Park – and made history as the first Japanese company to have invested in Kent without the artificial sweetener of grant assistance.

Maruwa's 3,000 square metre complex will include research and development and production facilities for a new range of microchips designed for use by the communications industry.

"The demand in Europe for our microchips convinced us that Maruwa needed a European production base, and after two years' extensive research we selected Ashford as being the ideal location," explained company director Kazunari Kawabata.

The Orbital Park site itself provides a good example of why Ashford is best for business. The purpose-built site is served by a dual carriageway, minutes from Junction 10 of the M20. Both the Channel Tunnel and the Eurostar service from Ashford International are just minutes away.

Ashford's government-backed growth role is likely to see a major expansion of the town and its infrastructure, further increasing its pivotal role within the economic heartland of the south east.

And while the town enjoys close links with Europe, it is shortly to benefit from even better links with London and the rest of the country.

Already served by two junctions of the M20 and providing swift access to the M25 and beyond, Ashford is also central to the Channel Tunnel Rail Link. Passenger trains will – in just a few years – stop in the town, providing a swift and comfortable journey to the city and adding "35 minutes from London" to the growing list of Ashford advantages.

Ashford already has a good reputation for its educational facilities, broad mix of housing and surrounding "Garden of England" countryside. New leisure opportunities include a 12-screen cinema, nightclubs, state of the art fitness centres and more, making an attractive package for employees moving to the town. A pleasant, pedestrianised town centre has been boosted by new shopping opportunities provided by the striking McArthurGlen Designer Outlet on the edge of town.

Development has been so rapid on Ashford's Orbital Park site that more land is now being released at Orbital 2, on the opposite side of the dual carriageway which serves as a southern route around the town, while speculative industrial development has taken place at Beaver Industrial Estate.

Demand for luxury office accommodation is on the increase, and a £1 million refurbishment project carried out at International House – one of the town's landmark buildings close the international station – saw a substantial part of the building let to British and American companies soon afterwards.

Also close to the station is the Victoria Road redevelopment site, now cleared following compulsory purchase by Ashford Borough Council, which is looking for partners to take forward ambitious and exciting plans for the area. The proposals include a hotel and conference centre, restaurants, offices, leisure facilities and riverside housing plus a pedestrian link to the station.

Other development schemes will follow as Ashford assumes its position as the leading growth area in the south east.

Part 9

Buying and Selling European Companies

EUROPEAN RESTRUCTURING

Have European corporates overtaken the United States in terms of efficiency? asks Gary Dugan of JPMorgan Fleming Asset Management.

The efforts of European companies to restructure into leaner, meaner corporations have been put to the test in the last 12 months as the global economy has slipped towards recession. If restructuring is supposed to enhance the ability of companies to weather more difficult economic conditions, the coming months will prove decisive for the European corporate sector. Encouragingly, the early signs are good.

The global economic slowdown came at a particularly sensitive time for corporate Europe, which in recent years has striven to achieve greater levels of competitiveness and profitability. European companies have cut costs, built larger global businesses and reshaped their capital structures. The payoff for this effort should have come during times of strong global growth. Unfortunately, that payoff is now likely to come as global demand turns down. The best that can be hoped for is that European companies will be well positioned to weather the inevitable slowdown in the global economy and that they emerge in a stronger competitive position.

Some measures suggest that the European corporate sector has now overtaken the United States in terms of corporate efficiency. For example, when we compare the return on capital of the quoted European corporate sector with the comparable return on capital of US-listed companies, the European return surpasses the US. This increased return on capital in Europe is the result of strong efforts by European companies both to reduce costs and to improve the capital efficiency of their balance sheets. It is interesting to note that the return on capital for the US corporate sector peaked in 1998. Since then there has been a gentle deterioration, which is in part due to the high level of US wage growth sparked by very low unemployment levels.

One further factor behind Europe's ability to close the gap with the United States has been the reluctance of European companies to get so heavily involved in the technology boom that has since proved to be the Achilles heel of the US corporate sector. Two decades earlier, corporate Europe had been guilty of getting too heavily involved in the property market, which led to the development of a massive black hole in the balance sheets of many European companies as they wrote off huge amounts of injudicious investment spending. Perhaps put off by the lessons of the past, investment spending by European companies on high tech as a percentage of GDP never reached the dizzy heights seen in the United States.

With hindsight, Europe's reluctance to get too heavily involved in the technology boom has turned out to be a masterstroke. Too many commentators suggested that the only way for European companies to match US corporate productivity was to match their levels of high-tech investment. However, much of the technology investment by US companies has since proved, at least in part, to be fool's gold. This is not to say that all US technology investment was foolish, but that the level of investment and the nature of some of the investment was, with the benefit of hindsight, unwise.

Although we might pat the European corporate sector on the back for its restructuring efforts over the last few years, there is still room for improvement. The labour market, in particular, remains in need of major reform. Recent moves in France to reduce the working week seem to have taken us back to the Dark Ages and we hope that the French experiment is no more than an isolated incident in the greater scheme of things.

However, people remain Europe's biggest under-utilised resource. At least part of the reason why the US economy has been able to achieve higher growth than Europe is the high level of immigration and the high participation rate (percentage of the population available for work) that the United States has encouraged. Europe, for political reasons, may continue to struggle to increase its level of immigration. However, Europe could do a great deal more to improve the percentage of its eligible population available for work. In the United States, for example, the employment-to-population ratio for 16–64 year olds is around 77 per cent. In Europe, the ratio falls to a paltry 62 per cent, with hardly any improvement seen over the last 25 years.

There remains considerable scope for further consolidation within a number of industries in Europe. The current poor state of the global economy should inevitably lead to the demise of weaker companies, which may provide cheap opportunities for the stronger companies to acquire market share. Some industries, such as steel, have continued to see high levels of mergers partly as a consequence of tough market conditions. In the first quarter of 2001, for example, French steel producer, Usinor, bought both Arbed of Belgium and Aceralia of Spain. Similar consolidation is expected in other sectors.

The last significant industrial bastion remains the financial services industry where consolidation has been painfully slow. However, the very serious setback in financial markets over the last few years may well speed up the process. We can also expect European companies to expand their global reach by continuing to make acquisitions in the United States. Transatlantic transactions have made up a substantial part of M&A activity for European companies. Between 1988 and the first quarter of 2001, European transatlantic M&A volume was US$1.2 trillion, which was 2.5 times North American transatlantic volumes. European transatlantic volume was 19 per cent of the European firms' total US$6 trillion M&A expenditure over this period, while North American transatlantic volume was only 5 per cent of North America's US$8.8 trillion total M&A activity.

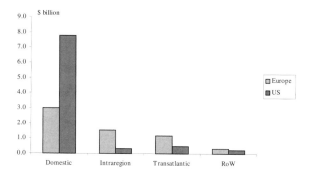

Figure 1 M&A volumes by type: Europe compared to the United States, 1998–Q1 2001

Source: JPMorgan M&A Research, Thomson Financial Securities Data

A final area that requires further hard work by European companies is capital efficiency. Although some work has already been done here, European balance sheets are still not efficient and they are generally too dependent on bank lending. The reason for this inefficient allocation of capital can be seen most starkly in the underdeveloped European corporate bond market, which remains relatively small with the par value outstanding for non-financial corporations at a little less than 4 per cent of GDP, as against 22 per cent of GDP in the United States. As the funding of European companies by marketable securities such as equities or corporate bonds increases, so the efficient allocation of capital in Europe is also likely to increase.

Email: gary.a.dugan:jpmorganfleming.com; tel: 0207 742 5289

EUROPEAN BUYOUTS

Prospects look promising in the German, French, Italian, Dutch and Scandinavian markets say Mike Wright, Andrew Burrows and Rod Ball of the Centre for Management Buyout Research.

The buyout market in continental Europe demonstrated strong growth in 2000, rising almost 15 per cent to a new record of €37.2 billion. Much of this growth was propelled by the emergence of the German market with an increase of over three and a half times the 1999 level to €15.2 billion. France slipped to second place with a fall of 13 per cent to €7.4 billion. Recent months have seen increasing concerns about the impact of recession and other factors on the continental European buyout market.

Divestments

Deals with a value of over €250 million contributed greatly to growth in Germany in 1999, accounting for nearly 90 per cent of the market; eight of these deals were divestments. Several of the large transactions of 2000 were backed by US private equity players that notably have yet to make a significant contribution in 2001. Kohlberg Kravis Roberts bought Robert Bosch Telecom and Blackstone Capital and Callahan Associates purchased the Deutsche Telekom cable divisions in North Rhine Westphalia and Baden-Wuerttemberg. In contrast to 2000, the German market in 2001 experienced consolidation with around €7 billion recorded in the first nine months. Local parent divestments continue to dominate with volume already ahead of the 28 completed in the whole of 2000.

In France, just over €6 billion has been invested in buyouts in the first three quarters of 2001 after €7.4 billion last year. Divestments from French groups accounted for almost a quarter of deals in 2000, including several large transactions. In 2001, Accor sold to Barclays Private Equity France and management its Serare subsidiary, which owns the restaurant chain Courtepaille, for FF830 million. Major French groups pursuing down-scoping strategies have now clearly identified buyout financiers as potential buyers of their unwanted subsidiaries.

Dutch buyout market value in 2000 fell sharply for the second year in succession to €1.8 billion. Domestic divestments continue as the most important source of transaction accounting for 45 per cent of deals. These deals reflect Dutch management teams' increasing recognition that MBO opportunities exist within large organisations not willing to invest in the growth of non-core businesses. Increasing concentration in Europe and greater focus on shareholder value has also led to growth in the divestment of non-core assets.

In Italy, the largest buyout in 2000 was Italtel from Telecom Italia for €1243 million. Buyouts from local and foreign parents accounted for nearly a third of buyouts in the last two years. Sweden was the largest Scandinavian contributor by value and number, as in 1999, accounting for about half of the Scandinavian total. In 2000, divestments accounted for a half or more of deals in each Scandinavian country. The largest source of buyouts in Spain in 2001 has been foreign divestments, notably the €76.8 million buyout of waste management group, Grupo TMA.

Private sales

The anticipated flow of Mittelstand buyouts in Germany has still to materialise. Concerns remain about whether this segment can become a market driver as current owners seek assurances that potential future owners will remain committed to the wellbeing of various local stakeholders. A recent pan-European study conducted by CMBOR suggests that the reluctance to deal with Anglo-Saxon-style private equity financiers by local entrepreneurs may be misplaced as buyouts can both increase employment and employee involvement.

Around two-fifths of buyouts in France in 2000 came from family businesses. Family buyout deals continue to involve the reorganisation of founders' wealth portfolios. The buy-in of Dietal was completed with its founder becoming president of the holding company while keeping a 40 per cent stake.

2001 was relatively quiet for Italy, although Itama, a Rome-based manufacturer of yachts, was bought out from the family for over €11 million. The Spanish buyout market has been led by family and private sales with around a third stemming from this source. In 2001, the privately owned Grupo Transcamer was sold to a management buy-in valued at €19.8 million.

Buyouts of listed companies

Taking companies private in Germany has not had the impact seen elsewhere in Europe, partly due to the complications arising from extensive crossownership of shares. However, Germany did see an increase in private-equity-backed de-listings in 2000. Of the four recorded, the largest was the €432 million

Kiekert, a car locking system manufacturer. At the time of writing, Grammer was the only public to private in 2001.

France saw several buyouts of listed firms in 2001 including Fives-Lille and Marc Orian, a distributor of jewels bought out in 1993 and introduced to the second marché in 1996. There was one public buyin the Netherlands in 2000 – Norit, a specialist in purification solutions – with public to privates expected to rise with venture capitalists targeting undervalued small listed companies.

Four buyouts of listed companies were completed in Scandinavia in 2000, with four by the time of writing in 2001. These are Dyno Nobel (Norway), Jamo (Denmark), Sanitec Corporation (Finland) and Lindab, a public buy-in in Sweden.

Secondary buyouts

Secondary buyouts are becoming an important source of deals as well as an attractive exit option. They have recently developed strongly, particularly in France with 18 in 2000. Secondary buyouts in 2001 include Astoria, 5 à Sec, Métaux Précieux, Germicopa and AOM-Air Liberté. In the Netherlands, seven secondary buyouts were completed in 2000 – those involving Heiploeg Shellfish and Welzorg being the largest and fourth largest deals of the year. In Italy in 2001, Wire Industries became a secondary buyout.

Exits

2000 saw a decline in the number of German buyout exits with just 11. At the time of writing, 2001 has so far been relatively quiet – the main exits being trade sales, such as MAP Medizintechnologie purchased by Resmed Inc.

France saw a total of 35 buyout exits in 2000 compared to 29 in 1999. Partial trade sales are an important exit route in France – major deals in 2000 including Tricoflex and Giraudy and Molinel. The number of buyouts coming to market has recently reduced, with only seven in 2000. In June 2001, the 1997 buyout Compagnie Générale de Santé was introduced on to the main market at a value of €810 million.

Exits rose to 14 in Italy in 2000, half of which were trade sales, while there were again four flotations. Reflecting the slowdown in deal activity, there have been only two trade sales so far in 2001 at the time of writing. 2000 saw eight trade sales in the Netherlands, the highest level for some time.

Scandinavian exits increased by 30 per cent in 2000, three-quarters of which were trade sales. So far in 2001, exits are at about half the level of last year. Exits in Spain in 2000 failed to maintain the level set in 1999. The three exits recorded in 2000 involved just one trade sale and two flotations.

Prospects

2001 looks to be one of consolidation in continental Europe. Figures for the first nine months show a combined buyout total of €24.6 billion compared to €37 billion for 2000 as a whole. The German market is unlikely to match 2000's extraordinary level, but seems poised to be the second highest ever in value terms. The abolition of capital gains tax on the sale of shares in subsidiaries may bring additional market impetus when these reforms are implemented in early 2002.

Several factors appear to favour future growth in the French buyout market: the good performance of buyouts; the development of secondary buyouts as an exit route; and the massive availability of funds raised by Anglo-Saxon players. The recent reduction in the number of flotations seems likely to mean that financiers are going to have to increase their investment horizons. There is a view that it will now be necessary to undertake two or three investment rounds to achieve an exit. This would contribute further to the recent increase in secondary buyouts.

Private equity continues to build in Italy with major private equity houses well represented. Despite the current slowdown, the Italian government's push for fiscal reform, improvement in capital gains tax, and cultural change to the family-owned businesses will provide future opportunities for buyouts. The new government continues to push for new corporate laws that would include a legal framework for buyout activity and which would address problems of transparency.

The outlook for the Dutch market seems generally positive in the context of considerable funding availability and pressures on corporations to restructure. Larger secondary buyouts are expected to become an increasingly important exit route. The future for the Scandinavian buyout market seems promising with some evidence of consolidation and internationalisation by local players.

The Iberian peninsular remains an immature area for buyouts, with provisional figures indicating that 2001 will be at best flat in relation to 2000. Nevertheless, there are signs of interest in the potential of the market with Spanish private equity firm Mercapital closing its second fund early in 2001 and the Carlyle Group recently opening an office in Madrid aiming to focus on investments in family-owned businesses.

The Centre for Management Buyout Research (CMBOR) was founded by Barclays Private Equity Limited and Deloitte & Touche at the Nottingham University Business School in March 1986 to monitor and analyse management buyouts in a comprehensive and objective way.

As an independent body, CMBOR has developed a wide-ranging and detailed database of over 17,000 companies which provides the only complete set of statistics on management buyouts and buy-ins in the UK and continental Europe.

CMBOR publishes regular reports on UK buyout trends in its Quarterly Review, as well as the results of specialist survey and case study research on relevant issues both in buyouts in the UK and Western Europe. The annual European Management Buyout Review is produced to complement this, providing an analysis and review of buyout trends throughout continental Europe.

Centre for Management Buyout Research (CMBOR), Nottingham University Business School, Jubilee Campus, Wollaton Road, Nottingham, NG8 1BB. Tel: +44 115 951 5493. Fax: +44 115 951 5204. Email: Andrew. Burrows@nottingham.ac.uk. Internet: www.cmbor.org

ACQUISITIONS: A NEVER-ENDING CYCLE

Why in the face of economic adversity are many European companies still bent on pursuing acquisition strategies? asks Andre Sawyer at mergermarket.

Given the collapse of the world's equity markets and growing fears of worldwide recession, it would be extremely easy to draw a conclusion and offer a less than sanguine view of mergers and acquisitions activity over the coming 12 months.

A prima facie look at M&A deal flows reveal that such transactions have indeed seen a marked fall of around 25–30 per cent in volume during the last year, according to mergermarket data. However, while many commentators have been quick to latch on to these figures – in some cases indirectly out of the need to goad those nasty, voracious investment bankers who earned vast sums of money during the M&A boom but now face the prospect of losing their jobs – very few have made any attempt at understanding the context.

The fall in M&A activity must be viewed as part of the backdrop to a five-year period that has seen corporate deal making reach unprecedented levels both in volume and value. When examined from this perspective, a 25 per cent fall does not constitute the need for alarm bells to start ringing. In addition, when presented with figures from mergermarket's

forward-looking data on companies currently looking to buy or sell businesses in Europe, the signs that M&A activity is set for a drastic contraction going forward become even less obvious.

Thus, why in the face of economic adversity are many companies still bent on pursuing acquisition strategies? For one thing, an economic contraction is not necessarily bad news in M&A terms. Downbeat markets tend to make strategic buys more enticing, owing to the relative valuations between those more successful businesses and their lagging counterparts. Companies such as Philips, while not being immune to the downturn, have still found the confidence to wrought out deals by pressurising their luckless rivals into selling at historically low prices. The Dutch technology group's recent acquisition of Marconi's medical systems division at a 50 per cent lower multiple than many in the analyst community expected illustrates this point.

A fall in consumer confidence, resulting in an equal fall in demand relative to industrial capacity, is also likely to precipitate consolidation. Companies faced with demand curves that are considerably more elastic than the industry as a whole, and confronted with the damaging prospect of price competition, will inevitably turn to M&A to bolster their chances.

The collapse in equity prices will also encourage companies to dispose of non-core assets as pressure builds up from their institutional investors to focus attention on key business lines. Germany in particular is likely to see a take-off in this type of M&A activity as the government finally repeals its capital gains tax on divestments that will make it easier for banks and companies to sell off assets that are not core to their corporate strategy. In the words of the Austrian economist, Joseph Schumpeter, German firms are poised to reap the rewards from the 'gales of creative deconstruction'.

That said, regardless of the above dynamics, it cannot be denied that the composition of M&A transactions in 2002 as a corollary of the current economic environment will be different to what we have become accustomed to.

We are almost certain to see fewer share-financed transactions and with that too the mega deals that splashed the front pages of newspapers little more than 18 months ago.

Cash will be used more readily to finance corporate purchases for those fortunate enough to have it in abundance. And while the high-yield markets remain closed as a financing avenue, some companies will nevertheless look towards the new types of private debt financing available.

From a sector perspective, old economy industries such as financial services, utilities, energy and manufacturing businesses are set to dominate the takeover scene in Europe in the short-to-medium term as the previous vanguards, namely telecoms, media and technology companies, show little signs of recovery from the fallout of the technology boom.

Private equity firms will also become more prevalent in M&A transactions this time round having sat back and amassed large stockpiles of cash during the boom years. In a throwback to the boot-strap deals of the early 1980s, buyout firms are now in a perfect position to acquire undervalued or poorly run businesses and divest all but the most promising units. One only needs to refer to the recent comments on the anxiety to do more deals made by that sage of public-to-private buyouts, Jon Moulton of Alchemy Partners fame, to realise the enthusiasm for many private equity firms to seek out M&A opportunities over the coming months.

Now it may be somewhat gauche to end this piece with a little rant at Europe's competition czar – it is always easy to find a scapegoat after all – but in a bid to sound fashionable, the tough stance taken by Mario Monti in recent months could have repercussions way beyond the M&A universe. The recent blocking of a number of high-profile deals by the commissioner may not only prompt a more drastic drop in M&A activity but, ultimately, may hamper Europe's economic recovery. In his defence, Monti did present a reasonable case on the bundling issue that arose from the GE/Honeywell deal. But another potential takeover in the shape of Swedbank's merger with Skandinaviska Enskilda Banken fell by the wayside because neither company was prepared to kowtow to the competition authorities' initial demands, despite the fact that Nordea, the other major banking authority in Scandinavia, has been allowed to carve up the surrounding region through a spate of smaller, lower-profile deals. This suggests that the competition commissioner ought to take a long hard look at his draconian, headline-making stance.

To conclude, it is clear from the arguments presented above that M&A, so long as it is not impeded, is a never-ending cycle. To that end, it can be argued that M&A is the best way to cope with capitalism's innate tendency to create over-capacity: in the 1930s, excess capacity was reduced by a protracted recession. Nowadays, corporate takeovers keep the extremes of depression and unsustainable growth in check. Europe's business leaders should take the initiative therefore when it comes to M&A. The more astute company executive ought be acutely aware that now, more than at any other point over the last five years, is the right time to buy. Those who remain skittish, aside from stymieing Europe's economic recovery, could find themselves ruing the day they allowed the prime opportunity to waltz by.

Andre Sawyer is an assistant editor at mergermarket, the M&A intelligence portal.

Mergermarket's forward-looking intelligence data is made up of over 26,000 intelligence reports of companies likely to buy or sell businesses in Europe. It is based on interviews with company executives, investor relations personnel, investment bankers, equity analysts as well as an extensive analysis of company earnings statements and the European business press.

Mergermarket, Old Truman Brewery, 91 Brick Lane, *Telephone +44 (0)20 7377 8940; Fax +44 (0)20 7426*
London E1 6QL *0159; e-mail abs@mergermarket.com*

HIDDEN LIABILITIES IN BUYING AND SELLING COMPANIES

Asset values should in theory be unambiguous, but in reality accounting practices in Europe mean that great caution must be employed, advises Keith Baxter, worldwide practice leader, credit and bonds, Royal & SunAlliance ProFin.

Most companies at some time or another will have the opportunity to buy or sell a company as part of their European strategy. Buyers may want to establish a presence in a new territory or might be looking to consolidate an existing presence and an acquisition offers the prospect of an immediate step increase in scale. Sellers may be looking to dispose of a non-core activity or may wish to release shareholder funds back to investors as part of an exit strategy. In either event, valuation issues are of great significance as the counter parties' wrestle with the issue of how much the company is worth. Both will of course employ competent professional advisers, but at some point the respective Boards will have to make the final call on price. This means resolving the question of what the company is worth – what does it actually owe, what does it own, what are its earnings, and setting that last ques-

tion in the context of the size and timing of future earnings.

Establishing the correct valuation of a company is no easy task and directors must take care to ensure that they use all reasonable care to determine the correct figure. The Board must guard against being on the receiving end of an action from disgruntled shareholders who, with the benefit of hindsight, allege negligence in paying over the odds for the acquired company (or alternatively, letting the sold company go too cheaply).

Asset values should in theory be unambiguous, but in reality accounting practices across Europe are such that great caution must be employed. For example, plant and equipment may be recorded in the company's accounts at book value, which means original purchase price less an amount for 'fair wear and tear' (depreciation). This means that it can be difficult to establish exactly what a piece of plant and equipment is worth. Of course, you could try to establish what the market price for the plant and equipment would be, but this is going to be a transitory value and remains somewhat subjective. The danger for the director lies in that subjective element, because it is open to future challenge if the investment or divestment appears to have been at an under- or overvalue in the judgement of an interested third party, such as a shareholder or indeed a liquidator. Similarly, the value of existing contracts post acquisition can be difficult to determine with real accuracy.

Stock valuations are probably even more difficult to determine. Most kinds of stock are not realisable at book value. You just have to think about the so-called 'fire sale effect' to realise that most kinds of stock are not worth much on a resale. Debtors on the other hand may be more valuable – provided of course that you can actually collect the debt, a valuation issue which again calls upon the subjective judgement of the buyer's directors. The human capital or value contained within the deal can often prove problematic. Recognised accounting procedures do not recognise the human contribution to the worth of a business venture, but this can be a pivotal factor in determining the future success or otherwise of a venture. Key players may need to be retained in order to ensure future revenue streams, and if this does not happen (possibly because it is not appreciated) then the buyer of the business may be disappointed in his investment.

A key point is that the value of a company may depend upon how much net cash flow its business will generate in the future, and this is a notoriously difficult thing to establish. For directors and officers who are involved in these kinds of transactions, the slightest error or oversight could leave them exposed to criticism and possibly even legal action. Their conduct and integrity could be scrutinised with considerable vigour and they could be held responsible for wrongful acts, errors or omissions, negligence, misstatement or improper disclosure if expected revenues fail to materialise.

Accounting practices are a particular minefield for the unwary. Some practices are clearly fraudulent, such as recording bogus revenues or failing to disclose liabilities, but some other areas can be more subjective. For example, costs may not have been amortised over the right time frame and establishing what the right time frame should be means accepting a subjective element within that judgement. Similarly, there might be a postponement of discretionary expense payments that can have a distorting affect

upon the disclosed financial position of the company. Failure to understand fully the implications of accounting practices could lead to significant valuation problems and this area clearly carries with it the potential for dispute. In addition, cultural differences and differences in business practice across Europe can magnify the scope for misunderstandings. Consequently, it is vital that proper financial advice is taken and it is also vital that any assumptions that have been made in the preparation of the financial presentation are explicitly stated. This approach will serve to mitigate the risks involved, but will not eliminate them.

It is also important to be aware of the changing environment within Europe. Not so long ago it was rare for directors in France to be held responsible in a personal capacity for corporate activities, but this is now changing as French law is brought closer into line with the Anglo-Saxon model, in part as a recognition of shareholders' rights and interests. In Germany, the collapse of Metallgesellschaft AG and the subsequent legal action against the company's former CEO mark a watershed that has heralded an increasingly litigious environment. In Spain, new corporate crimes legislation has recently been enacted to the effect that directors are now liable in criminal law for falsification of accounts and for failure to co-operate with the regulators.

This trend for increasing directors' accountability seems set to continue and directors and officers need to find new ways of meeting the threat. In addition to taking qualified financial and legal advice, directors' and officers' liability insurance can be a significant risk management. The insurance covers the liabilities of the director or officer of the company assumed while conducting the affairs of the company. The cover also provides protection against the costs of defending an action, which can be substantial, particularly in international cases. Establishing a relationship with an insurance company means that you can be sure of having access to lawyers who are best placed to defend your case – an important consideration when personal reputations are at stake.

Above all, business leaders need to have a realistic attitude toward international company acquisitions and disposals. These deals often represent very significant opportunities for the parties concerned, but as so often in life, the risks tend to be commensurate with the rewards. The vital issue is to ensure that the risks are comprehensively managed through a combination of qualified advisers, proper documentation and insurance protection.

Royal & SunAlliance has recently launched 'Management Assurance', a packaged product providing specialist insurance protection with bespoke cover to suit the needs of each and every business, public or private. It covers risks such as Directors' & Officers' Liability insurance, Employment Practices Liability insurance, Crime, *Kidnap Ransom & Extortion insurance, Pension Scheme Liability insurance, Professional Indemnity insurance and Libel insurance. The product includes unique value-added services designed to help insureds avoid distracting and time-consuming losses and ultimately support the insureds in managing their future with confidence.*

Keith Baxter, worldwide practice leader, credit and bonds, Royal & SunAlliance ProFin. Telephone +44 (0)20 7337 5952; http://www.profin.royalsun.com

REALISING THE VALUE OF EUROPEAN ACQUISITIONS

Jeremy Stanyard, Nick Chaffey and Alex Dowdalls, leaders of PA Consulting Group's European M&A integration team, on how deals in Europe do not come unstuck.

No organisation, even one set on a path of organic development, can ignore the opportunities for growth offered by mergers or acquisitions (particularly as the price of potential targets is now at a more realistic level!).

Despite the total amount of M&A activity halving in 2001, European companies have remained active in acquisitions, buying into the United States with deals such as Deutsche Telekom's acquisition of Voicesteam Wireless, with national deals such as Allianz's acquisition of Dresdner Bank, and with cross-border deals such as Philips' acquisition of Marconi Medical Systems.

However, the majority of deals still reportedly fail. PA Consulting Group's experience and extensive research indicates that by far the most common reason for failure is poor post-deal integration – advances in strategy and deal-making do not seem to have been reflected in the quality of integration planning and execution. While conventional wisdom is for the acquirer to act fast to integrate the target company, PA has developed a more considered approach that proves that firms that develop a tailored integration strategy and manage the integration rigorously enjoy greater shareholder returns.

In addition, acquirers are more likely to be successful if they follow a two-phase approach to integration. The first phase, transition, is focused on putting into place essentials such as a common business/operating model and basic integration of informational technology. This is followed by a longer period of transformation, when the fabric of the two firms is integrated to realise the full synergistic benefits. PA's approach to integration management is founded upon five key principles:

---

[1] PA Consulting Group, 'Realising the value of acquisitions: a comparative study or European post-acquisition integration practices', 2001. This survey looks at the similarities and differences in post-acquisition integration practices in continental northern Europe compared to the United States/United Kingdom. It then derives best-practice principles for post-acquisition strategies across the two commercial environments.

- Refine and communicate the integration strategy. Making and then communicating key decisions as soon as possible is vital to a successful acquisition. From PA's recent survey into European deals, 'Realising the value of acquisitions',[1] it was found that successful companies targeted as a priority their own shareholders and staff, media, target staff and customers. Unsuccessful companies tended to ignore communication. A French company acquiring a UK company suffered staff loss and disruption when it failed to communicate clearly. This was caused by a Board-level dispute on management roles that delayed communication by a full two months.

- Design the integration programme around the benefits case. It is imperative to understand the specific challenges in each deal and design the integration accordingly. Despite the increasing use of shareholder value measures to drive a company's performance, many studies have shown that the majority of acquisitions can lead to a loss of shareholder value. One apparently simple way to avoid this is to incorporate shareholder value measures into the planning and implementation stages. PA's survey 'Creating shareholder value from acquisition integration'[2] found that benefits models built around cash flows enabled the average acquirer to acquire better returns (+2.7 per cent) than those using accounting-based measures. It also found that successful companies are also very focused on the cost of achieving benefits – sometimes even preferring to avoid or delay operational integration as a result. One European bank has three payment systems inherited from acquisitions, but has delayed migrating to a single system for cost reasons. This bank performs in the top quartile in terms of returns.

- Deploy outstanding programme management. Planning and programme management are vital to successful integration. PA's research has reinforced the view that companies that plan ahead in detail will tend to have more successful acquisitions. Forecasting and tracking benefits, budgeting, cost control and resource management are the areas that deliver most value. UK companies tend to favour central programme management supported by a programme office, while European companies tend to decentralise control, preferring to drive the integration through the line management structure. Interestingly, while a programme-based approach correlates with success in the United States/United Kingdom, in continental Europe there was no evidence to prove that one approach was better than the other.

- Address the people issues. No two companies have identical cultures – even when this appears so on the surface – and cultural differences can exist at both national and company levels, making cross-border deals the most intriguing to manage. PA's research found some simple guidelines with universal success – such as engaging people from both companies in the integration team and incentivising the management of the new organisation, such that individual and corporate goals are aligned with success. There are also more specific guidelines that can be followed, such as the use of cultural surveys to understand in depth the differences in organisations (complemented by training on national culture differences for cross-border deals). The use of these techniques can highlight why Anglo-Dutch companies have been successful (Unilever, Shell) whereas there are few Anglo-German comparisons.

- Manage the risks for success. Even when a programme has been well planned and structured, it still faces risks that must be managed. The importance of risk management was confirmed by PA's survey 'Creating shareholder value from acquisition integration'. Companies that used detailed risk management planning achieved superior returns (+4.1 per cent). Interestingly, most continental European companies take a more informal approach to risk management than their UK counterparts. In this area, PA recommends increased management of risks during integration.

PA's analysis of mergers has highlighted a set of practices that can increase shareholder returns. If the strategy or pricing is poor and this is not trapped by due diligence, these measures will not work miracles.

---

[2] PA Consulting Group, 'Creating shareholder value from acquisition integration – A revised integration model supported by quantitative analysis', 2000. The aim of this survey was to establish objectively how corporate acquirers can maximise their chances of success and reduce the risks during post-deal integration.

If, however, the strategy and pricing are realistic, these measures give a higher chance of realising value from the deal.

PA Consulting Group is a leading management, systems and technology consulting firm, with a unique combination of these capabilities. Established almost 60 years ago, and operating worldwide from over 40 offices in more than 20 countries, PA draws on the knowledge and experience of some 3,700 people, whose skills span the initial generation of ideas and insights all the way through to detailed implementation.

Further details: Global Business Transformation Group, PA Consulting Group, 127 Buckingham Palace Road, London, SW1W 9SR; tel: +44 207 33 5277; website: www.paconsulting.com/restructuring

Part 10

The European Company

SOCIETAS EUROPAEA (SE)

After 30 years of negotiation, a European Company Statute was agreed in October 2001. Cost savings could be huge, but will companies want to take advantage of the new structure? ask Jonathan Branton and Sophie Lawton of the European Law Unit at Hammond Suddards Edge.

A 'Societas Europaea' is a company that is regulated under a supranational European law (the European Company Statute) rather than the law of a member state. The idea of creating such entities was first proposed by the European Commission in 1970. Finally, 31 years, three months and eight days later, the Regulation to establish a European Company Statute (which will govern SEs) was adopted on 8 October 2001. It will enter into force on 8 October 2004. This has been described by Frits Bolkestein, the European Commissioner for the Internal Market, as 'a practical step to encourage more companies to exploit cross-border opportunities and so boost Europe's competitiveness'.

The underlying motive behind the creation of SEs is to encourage the formation of large companies able to achieve economies of scale, which would in turn enable them to compete on a more even footing with companies in Japan and the United States. The intention is that by allowing a company to operate under one set of rules throughout the European Union,

such companies will be more efficient in both financial and administrative terms. An EU advisory group has suggested potential savings of €30 billion per year as a result of SEs, although the Commission has no idea to date of how many companies will take advantage of the new structure, and as such this figure can only be a rough estimate at this stage.

The 30-year delay in adopting the European Company Statute was primarily due to disagreements in relation to worker participation. German and Dutch company laws include mandatory worker participation in management, whereas countries such as the United Kingdom have no such provisions.

What is an SE?

The European Company Statute will give all companies operating in more than one member state the opportunity of becoming an SE, subject to certain formal requirements (ie a minimum capital of €120,000). If proceeding to become an SE, effectively companies will become incorporated under a single legal umbrella avoiding the current expensive and time-consuming red tape involved in setting up European subsidiaries. Once formed, the letters 'SE' will follow the company name in the same way as 'Limited' or 'Plc' might at present (in the United Kingdom).

SEs will come into existence initially under two pieces of legislation. First, there is the EU Council Regulation adopted on 8 October 2001,[1] which contains the majority of the rules that will apply to the SE. Second, there is the EU Council Directive[2] on worker involvement, which will need to be transposed by every member state (by 8 October 2004).

An SE will be capable of being established using one of four methods:

- the merger of two or more public limited companies from at least two different member states;
- the formation of a holding company by public or private companies from at least two member states;
- the formation of a subsidiary of companies from at least two member states; or
- the transformation of a public limited company which has for at least two years had a subsidiary in another member state.

SEs will be registered in the member state where they have their main administrative office. It will not be sufficient simply to have a mailbox address in a country in order to register in that country. This is aimed at preventing SEs from being used as a vehicle for tax fraud or money laundering. There will be no central register of SEs. However, when a new SE is registered, its details will need to be published in the EC *Official Journal* (available on the Internet at http://www.europa.eu.int). Groups of companies within different sectors in different member states will be able to create separate SEs – for example, for each product line or activity.

The position as regards taxation of SEs will be the same as that of any other multinational company. There will, however, be benefits for an SE that has its head office in one member state but operates in other member states, as it will be able to offset losses from some operations against profits in other member states.

Worker involvement

The compromise finally reached in relation to worker participation is contained in Article 12 of the Regulation and sets out the requirements pursuant to Article 4 of the Directive. Article 4 prohibits the registration of an SE unless there is an agreement on arrangements from employee involvement pursuant to the provision of Article 7 (3) of the Directive.

In certain circumstances, upon creation of an SE, where negotiations are unable to establish provisions for worker consultation, the company will be obliged to apply standard principles of worker consultation as set out in the Annex to the Directive. This only applies in relation to SEs which have been:

a) created by a holding company or joint venture where a majority of the workers had the right to participation prior to the establishing of the SE; or
b) created by a merger where at least 25 per cent of the workforce held the right to participate prior to the merger.

Point b) has caused most controversy over the last 30 years. The compromise reached allows a member state to not implement the Directive on worker participation where an SE was created by a merger or acquisition. In such a case the SE can only be registered in that member state if:

a) an agreement has been made to implement worker participation; or
b) none of the participating companies was covered by participation rules prior to the creation of the SE.

In addition, in relation to an SE set up by transformation of an undertaking, the rules of the member states that previously applied to it regarding worker participation will continue to apply.

The compromise reached provides something of a loophole, as the European Company Statute does not, in general, force worker participation requirements on undertakings in member states which do not, at present, impose worker participation.

---

[1] Council Regulation (EC) No. 2157/2001 of 8 October 2001.
[2] Council Directive 2001/86/EC of 8 October 2001.

Conclusion

The adoption of the European Company Statute and the resulting creation of SEs are seen as an excellent opportunity both for businesses operating from the European Union and those overseas companies wishing to operate with a base in the European Union. It is hoped that it will attain its original goal of helping the European Union become a more competitive and cohesive place in which to do business, but given the apparent lack of determination on the part of EU member states to agree on a final text, as evidenced by the 30 years of legislative process, one must wonder if business will show a different level of enthusiasm in utilising the new statute in the way it was intended.

Hammond Suddards Edge is one of the UK's leading commercial law firms with offices in London, Leeds, Manchester, Birmingham and Bradford, as well as a specialist EU practice in Brussels. In the last year the firm has also opened offices in France, Germany and Italy.

The European Law Unit in Brussels is a recognised leader in its field and houses two primary specialities, namely EC competition and state aid law on the one hand, and EC and WTO international trade law on the other. Other areas of expertise include public procurement, and general and sector-specific regulatory advice, e.g. telecommunications.

Jonathan Branton and Sophie Lawton, Hammond Suddards Edge, European Law Unit.

Telephone + 00 32 2 627 76 76. Fax + 00 32 2 627 76 86; e-mail jonathan.branton@hammondse.com

TAX AND THE EUROPEAN COMPANY

Rob Norris of KPMG asks what the European company (Societas Europaea 'SE') means for EU businesses and for tax advisers, ever keen to sharpen their pencils and provide innovative structures for their clients. Now that the EU Council of Ministers has formally adopted the Regulation to establish a European Company Statute, does the SE constitute a new opportunity or is it a potential new layer of corporate bureaucracy?

The European company (Societas Europaea) was first proposed over 30 years ago. Its adoption has been delayed by many factors, including the need to accommodate different member states' practices on employee consultation. These issues have now been resolved and it is anticipated that the SE will formally come into being in 2004. According to an EU press release, 'The SE will be a single company under (European) Community law and so be able to operate throughout the EU with one set of rules and a unified management and reporting system. . . . For companies active across the Internal Market, the European Company therefore offers the prospect of reduced administrative costs and a legal structure adapted to the Internal Market as a whole.'

An SE will, for tax purposes, be treated in the same way as existing multinational companies (ie in accord-ance with the corporate tax rules in each member state). SE taxation is very similar therefore to that of an EU-based company with branches in other member states. Indeed, this is perhaps the best way to view the SE – as a slightly neater version of a traditional parent/branch structure.

An SE has the ability to move its registered office to another member state without having to wind up the company. This will give welcome flexibility and may also call into question the sustainability of current exit charges that exist in the European Union.

This ability to move across member states should also help facilitate cross-border mergers. At present, UK company law does not permit mergers, only take-overs. Some UK companies, however, will be allowed to participate in mergers to create SEs. Specific rules and regulations on this have yet to be published, but this development is a welcome step forward. Indeed, for cross-border mergers the SE may well become the vehicle of choice.

European companies created by merger will be the first type of company to be able to benefit from the existing directive on eliminating double taxation of cross-frontier mergers (which can be found on-line at http://europa.eu.int/eur-lex/en/lif/dat/1990/en_390L0434.html). However, this will require a technical amendment to the directive to add SEs to the types of company eligible under the directive.

From a more basic perspective, why have a European company when there is no single European code of company law and there are no European taxes? Perhaps in anticipation of this question, on 23 October 2001 the European Commission announced a strategy for company taxation in the European Union. This document proposes a series of measures to reduce the impact of cross-border tax issues, proclaiming that 'company taxation must adapt to the changing environment'. These measures include an examination of the basis of calculating tax liabilities for pan-EU companies advocating a move to either 'home state taxation' or a 'common consolidated tax base'. While political realities are likely to ensure that these proposals remain, in the medium term, proposals, the document offers an interesting insight into the thought processes in the European Union on company taxation. The SE will undoubtedly have a part to play in any future harmonisation of EU company tax laws, but initially it will provide a useful vehicle in order to smooth over some of the 'rough edges' that face companies that wish to trade in different EU member states. In this sense, it builds upon other EU initiatives such as the Parent/Subsidiary Directive, which removed withholding taxes on dividends between parent and subsidiary companies established in different member states.

Many of the issues facing an SE will, however, be familiar. For example, the tax residency rules of the member state in which the registered office is situated would need to be examined carefully as part of the decision-making process of choosing a corporate location. Furthermore, separate VAT registration will still be required in each territory, and tax computations/returns will need to be made/submitted for each permanent establishment. Thus, from a tax point of view, an SE does not necessarily in itself mean a reduction in compliance costs and red tape.

Essentially, the foundation of European taxation is 15 independent member states with 15 different tax systems and in the short-to-medium term this is unlikely to change. There are always opportunities with any new development, however, and to quote a member of the European Commission, 'it may have taken 30 years to finalise the SE, but the glass of water is half full rather than half empty'.

Rob Norris is a tax director at KPMG, Birmingham, and has extensive experience on all aspects of international tax.

EXERCISE OF CORPORATE CONTROL

In continental Europe, an atmosphere of secrecy used to pervade decision-making among corporate entities: voting rights were unevenly distributed to preferred shareholders; board appointments were private affairs and executive salaries were not disclosed – but that is all changing now, says Pat Drinan of Royal & SunAlliance ProFin.

As a legal person, a corporation can act only through the agency of natural persons. Company law lays down the principles of corporate governance, defining how the decision-making functions of the corporation are divided among its owners (the shareholders) and their agents (the directors and managers).

Historically, in continental Europe, an atmosphere of secrecy pervaded decision-making among corporate entities, voting rights were unevenly distributed to preferred shareholders, Board appointments were private affairs and executive salaries were not disclosed.

There is now, however, a clear trend for the market to play a bigger role in the exercise of corporate control due, in part at least, to the increased globalisation of markets. The level of foreign investment in Europe has markedly increased in recent years with new investors seeing Europe as an attractive option compared to less stable markets. Institutional investors have increased their share of listed companies in several European countries and this trend is likely to continue due to developments in retirement, financing and healthcare, as the ageing of the European population will lead to increasing dependency on funded schemes in the financing of retirement provisions.

However, foreign institutional investors export the attitudes of their home markets and with US investment in particular has come a demand for improved corporate governance with greater accountability to shareholders, transparency through disclosure requirements and harmonisation of these higher standards throughout Europe, making companies more comparable across borders.

In recognition of the need to attract foreign institutional investment, many European countries realised the need to be more aware of the ideas of shareholder value and corporate governance, and made increased efforts to promote good governance throughout the 1990s. For example, in France (which has seen a great increase in foreign investment), the corporates took the initiative themselves by commissioning Marc Vienot to issue a report outlining the state of corporate governance in France and ways in which to improve it. In 1999, Vienot issued a second version of his report, making specific suggestions to improve corporate governance, including the division of the roles of chairman and CEO and the publication of pay and compensation packages for Board members.

In early May 2001, another significant reform was achieved when the French parliament adopted a long-delayed legislative proposal to make it compulsory for companies to disclose the salaries of their top management.

In Germany also, steps have been taken to promote better corporate governance. In July 2001, Theodore Baums, chairman of the German Government Panel on Corporate Governance, delivered a report to the government containing recommendations for reform of German company law. This report included proposals to update corporate governance structures, to improve transparency and to strengthen shareholder protection. A new Code of Corporate Governance is at the core of these proposals and it has been proposed that adoption of this Code should be voluntary, but that if companies choose not to adopt it they would be required to explain their decision in their annual report.

Even in the United Kingdom, where improving corporate governance was tackled in the early 1990s through such reports as Cadbury, Greenbury and Hampel (which together formed the Combined Code, which itself forms part of the UK Listing Rules, requiring every listed company to 'maintain a sound system of internal control to safeguard shareholders' investments and the company's assets'), there remains room for improvement. The Kingsmill Report, the result of a recent UK-government-commissioned enquiry, will propose that larger companies should be obliged to report on how they treat their staff, and that information on areas such as male and female recruitment, pay, promotion and training should become a compulsory feature of companies' annual reports.

Among the Kingsmill Report's other recommendations will be the creation of an independent body funded by government and the private sector, which would carry out research and advise organisations on how to manage and retain female employees, and seek to eradicate the gender gap in pay.

It has also been suggested that in the interests of better communications, UK companies be required to report their financial results quarterly rather than half-yearly as now. Quarterly reporting has long been standard in the United States and is spreading across continental Europe – indeed, the European Com-

mission has issued a discussion document suggesting that it becomes standard.

It is unlikely, however, that in the short term the European Union will produce a single code of corporate governance best practice. However, there have been efforts to establish international benchmarks of good governance through a wide variety of principles, recommendations and codes – for example, the CEPS Guidelines, the OECD Principles of Good Governance and the European Association of Securities Dealers Principles and Recommendations.

Guidelines set down by these various organisations cover basic shareholder rights, general principles for board structure and procedures, and rules on reporting and control. They include the following recommendations:

■ Deviations from 'one share one vote' should be avoided and where they exist should be disclosed.
■ Shareholders' basic rights should comprise the appointment and removal of Board members and auditors, approval of the dividend, approval of the by-laws and the creation of shares.
■ The Board of a corporation should include a sufficient number of outside or independent directors who are highly qualified and experienced for the position.
■ All information provided to the market must be provided in a way that respects equal treatment of all shareholders.
■ Shareholder voting should be encouraged. Apathy among shareholders is a recognised problem in the United Kingdom. Corporate governance consultancy Pirc reported in October 2001 that the average turnout in proxy votes at UK annual meetings during 2001 was little over 51 per cent. The UK government has agreed to legislate on a proposal that the United Kingdom should copy the United States and force fiduciaries to consider voting as part of their obligation to clients.

The current trend seems very much for European corporations to take the initiative in the area of better corporate governance and adopt self-regulatory guidelines without waiting for further national or EU legislation – the incentive being that in doing so they will be encouraging further foreign investment.

Royal & SunAlliance has recently launched 'Management Assurance', a packaged product providing specialist insurance protection with bespoke cover to suit the needs of each and every business, public or private. It covers risks such as Directors' & Officers' Liability insurance, Employment Practices Liability insurance, Crime, Kidnap Ransom & Extortion, Pension Scheme Liability insurance, Professional Indemnity insurance and Libel insurance. The product includes unique value-added services designed to help insureds avoid distracting and time-consuming losses and ultimately support the insureds in managing their future with confidence.

Pat Drinan, UK areas practice leader, Royal & SunAlliance ProFin. Telephone +44 (0)20 7337 5986; http://www.profin.royalsun.com

CORPORATE GOVERNANCE

Corporate governance standards in Europe vary dramatically from country to country and from company to company, making it exceedingly difficult and time-consuming for investors to compare companies within their portfolio, reports Jean-Nicolas Caprasse of Déminor International.

There is a growing consensus among institutional investors that corporate governance is a key parameter to be considered when making investment decisions and reviewing existing portfolios.

An increasing number of institutional investors tend to examine the corporate governance standards and practices adopted by the companies in which they invest as part of their overall investment strategy and as a means of protecting their interests and rights as owners.

These investors realise that the governance structures of the companies in which they invest may have a significant impact on their financial risk. This is particularly true in this period of difficult and volatile financial markets, as shown by a number of recent financial disasters due to poor governance structures.

Furthermore, as many investors are increasing their asset allocation in favour of foreign shares, so the need

for in-depth corporate governance research has reached a global scale.

In Europe, this trend has been reinforced by the launch of the euro, which is precipitating the globalisation of European financial markets, providing a strong incentive for a further step towards truly European rather than national investment strategies.

What is corporate governance?

In the business community, corporate governance is generally understood to be the system by which a company is managed and controlled. It rests on the two pillars of transparency and accountability towards shareholders, ultimately leading to maximum long-term shareholder value. Furthermore, it involves balancing stakeholders' powers and interests in order to ensure the sound and strong development of the company.

Corporate governance problems, however, differ from country to country. In Anglo-Saxon countries with a more dispersed shareholdership, corporate governance relates more to possible conflicts of interest between executive, non-executive directors and shareholders. In continental European countries, which have traditionally stronger reference shareholdings, agency problems occur more on the level between shareholders and shareholder representatives in the board of directors.

The ultimate purpose of corporate governance is to create a proper structure within a company that ensures a good balance between all these individual interests in order to attract capital, perform efficiently, achieve the corporate objective and meet both legal obligations and general societal expectations.

In other words, corporate governance is not a purpose in itself, but a means in order to achieve the purpose of the company and to create shareholder value. Companies that have implemented a good corporate governance structure entail a proper system of accountability and transparency towards the market. Simply stated, a company in which managers are held accountable is more likely in the long term to outperform one in which they are not.

Concept of the ratings

The Déminor Corporate Governance Rating Service provides independent, reliable and comparative research on corporate governance practices in European companies.

The governance of the companies covered is assessed using an extensive analysis grid combining over 300 corporate governance indicators. Since 1993, the grid has been developed and continuously updated by

Déminor in collaboration with large institutional investors who act as opinion leaders in this area. The indicators can be classified into four main categories:

- Rights and duties of shareholders. This includes criteria concerning the respect of the one share one vote one dividend principle, voting right restrictions, voting issues, shareholder proposals and voting procedures.
- Range of takeover defences. This examines the presence and strength of anti-takeover devices such as poison pills, golden parachutes, core shareholdings, extensive cross-shareholdings and co-option systems that could be used to protect the company from a hostile takeover and to disenfranchise shareholders. Further to this, the dilution effects and economic barriers of such instruments are examined.
- Disclosure on corporate governance. This analyses the transparency of a corporation as measured by the quantity and quality of non-financial information on its governance structure, such as the diversity and independence of Board members, Board committees, director remuneration, accounting standards, information on major shareholders of the company, environmental information, etc.

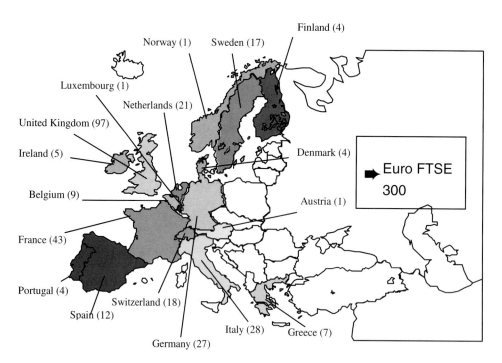

Figure I Euro FTSE 300 by country

- Board structure and functioning. This examines all issues relating to the governance of a Board, such as independent directors, division between the role of chairman and chief executive, election of the Board, director remuneration, the workings and authorities of Board committees etc.

The Rating Service covers the FTSE Eurotop 300 Index comprising companies from 17 European countries.

At the end of the consolidation process, a rating is allocated to each of the four corporate governance categories at both company level and country level. These categories are:

- Rights and duties of shareholders.
- Range of takeover defences.
- Disclosure on corporate governance.
- Board structure and functioning.

Each rating reflects the extent to which a company adopts and complies with 'Best Practice'. Each rating is measured on a scale of 5 to 1 Déminor, with 5 Déminor representing best practice and 1 Déminor representing the most questionable standard.

The ratings are updated annually to reflect changes relating to the corporate governance performance of companies.

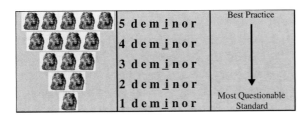

Figure 2 Ratings for corporate governance

A conclusive glance at the results

Rights and duties of shareholders

Investors are usually in favour of the one share one vote standard, which gives them the best understanding of the power structure in a company. Investors also appreciate being given enough time to cast an informed vote.

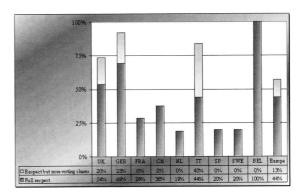

	UK	GER	FRA	CH	NL	IT	SP	SWE	BEL	Europe
☐ Respect but non-voting shares	20%	23%	0%	0%	0%	40%	0%	0%	0%	13%
☐ Full respect	54%	69%	29%	38%	19%	44%	20%	20%	100%	44%

Figure 3 Respect of the 'one share-one vote principle'

The companies analysed in the United Kingdom and Germany perform the best against these criteria. In fact, voting right restrictions are quite exceptional and shareholders have at least 20 days to cast an informed vote. The United Kingdom, however, is a touch below Germany when it comes to voting at general meetings, as it is customary in the United Kingdom to vote by a show of hands irrespective of the number of votes held by the person attending the general meeting.

The most questionable standard is displayed by the Dutch companies. Over 80 per cent of Dutch companies have shares with multiple voting rights, golden shares or list their ordinary shares as depository receipts that do not carry voting rights.

The second main criteria for assessing the rights and duties of shareholders are the voting issues, and in particular the election of directors by shareholders. In general, directors are elected by the general meeting; however, there are five categories of exceptions to this rule: directors elected by employees (50 per cent in Germany, also in France and Sweden); directors elected by owners of golden shares or by state representatives (all of the analysed countries except Belgium, Spain and Germany); directors elected by owners of special shares (United Kingdom); directors elected by core shareholders (Germany); and directors elected by co-option or by binding proposals (the Netherlands).

Institutional investors are also in favour of postal voting. However, this practice may be forbidden by law (in Switzerland and Sweden for example), and even if allowed by law, it is not taken up in the articles of association of companies (as in Belgium for example). Moreover, Internet voting is still not possible in any of the countries analysed. However, the United Kingdom is considering adapting its legislation to allow Internet voting.

A further issue is the attendance of shareholders at general meetings and particularly the attendance of the free float. In most countries, the attendance rate is not disclosed at all (Sweden, Belgium, United Kingdom, Spain), or just by a few companies (Switzerland, France, Germany, the Netherlands). However, in some countries the attendance rate is largely disclosed (80 per cent of the Italian companies disclosed the attendance rate, for example). In almost all countries, the percentage of free float represented at general meetings is generally quite low. Consequently, the voting power of core shareholders at general meetings is often considerably higher than their actual stake.

Range of takeover defences

In order to prevent hostile takeovers, the large majority of continental European companies provide some kind of takeover defence.

Figure 4 presents the level of obstruction against hostile takeovers (LOHT). The LOHT is computed as the probability that a company (its management, its majority or core shareholders) can resist a hostile takeover. For each country, it shows the LOHT for a company featuring the median of all protection mechanisms encountered. Spain, Belgium and the Netherlands show the highest LOHT. The only LOHT acceptable to the international shareholders is to be found in the United Kingdom.

Absolute takeover defences, consisting of the presence of a majority or core shareholder, the installation of ownership ceilings, the issue of golden shares and priority shares and the insulation of the management, can be found in all countries, although to a lesser extent in Sweden, Switzerland, Germany, and again in the United Kingdom, where there are no majority shareholders. On the other hand, Spain, France, Belgium, Italy and particularly the Netherlands are countries that are very well protected by absolute takeover defences.

The strength of absolute takeover defences is increased in some companies by a strong link between the issue of a golden share to the government and the installation of an ownership ceiling, in order to prevent the company (often a public utility company) falling into foreign hands. However, in other companies, the issue of multiple voting rights, in some cases to specific shareholders as in France for example, can preclude any possibility of the company being taken over. A similar effect is achieved in the Netherlands, where shareholders of several companies are deprived of their voting rights through the issue of non-voting depository receipts.

The use of relative takeover defences is applied in every country. The most common takeover defence, presenting the strongest relative defence, is to be found in the presence of important shareholders. The use of capital defences ('poison pills') is prohibited in some countries by law: the United Kingdom, Germany, Italy and Sweden. The granting of an authorisation to increase the share capital with the possibility to restrict pre-emptive rights is possible in the Netherlands, Belgium and Spain. Shares can be repurchased in France, Switzerland, the Netherlands and Belgium. The strategic placement of stocks is applied in both Belgium and the Netherlands. The installation of a voting right ceiling is the most important takeover defence in Switzerland and Spain.

Disclosure on corporate governance

Information to shareholders is one of the most important aspects of corporate governance, as it reflects the degree of transparency and accountability of the corporation towards its shareholders.

The basic documents required to make an analysis are the annual report, the articles of association and the agenda of the last AGM, preferably in English. In general, the disclosure of the above documents is good, although the annual report is the only piece of

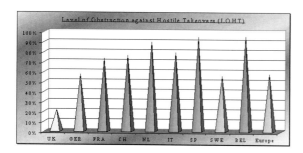

Figure 4 Levels of Obstruction against Hostile Takeovers (LOHT)

information widely available in English. The United Kingdom (for obvious reasons), Switzerland and Sweden are the best-performing countries concerning disclosure in English. The worst performers are French and Spanish companies.

Nearly all of the analysed companies run an English website, in most cases with a section dedicated to the shareholders. This is without a doubt a very positive development. However, still too few companies use their website as an active tool to communicate with shareholders. Apart from the annual report, none of the other basic documents is commonly available on the web.

The international investment community and Déminor advocate the use of an internationally recognised accounting standard, such as IAS or US GAAP. Analysis showed that still more then 40 per cent of companies use their own country's accounting principles. None of the Belgian companies makes reference to an internationally recognised accounting standard.

Figure 5 shows the existence of a statement of compliance with a Code of Best Practice.

UK companies have to 'comply or explain'. Although all Spanish companies make a statement, the value of these statements is questionable from a corporate governance point of view, because the Code of Best Practice may be adapted by the companies themselves. Dutch companies clearly lost interest in the Code of Best Practice drawn up by the 'Commissie Peters' in June 1997. In Sweden, no official code exists. A first German code was released in January 2000 and revised in July 2000.

Shareholders are interested in knowing who their fellow shareholders are. In most cases, the analysed companies disclose the general shareholder structure. However, more specific information (eg the breakdown of the shareholdings, the stake held by employees, existence of cross shareholdings etc) is rather rare and highly country-dependent.

A similar remark can be made for disclosure on the composition of the Boards. Although general identification of the members is available, in-depth information such as the academic background of Board members, the identification of independent Board members, the number of other executive and/ or supervisory functions held and the number of shares held, is often scarce.

With the exception of the United Kingdom, the disclosure on stock-option plans is often poor and does not cover aspects that are important to shareholders: volume of options granted; granting policy; exercise policy; vesting period; dilution for existing shareholders etc. Standardisation of disclosure on stock-option plans is totally lacking in this respect.

Board structure and functioning

In general, institutional investors consider the presence of non-executive directors, and particularly independent directors, as the most important corporate governance parameter. In order to promote constructive discussion between Board members, the Board should not be too large and should at least have an audit committee, a remuneration committee and a nomination committee.

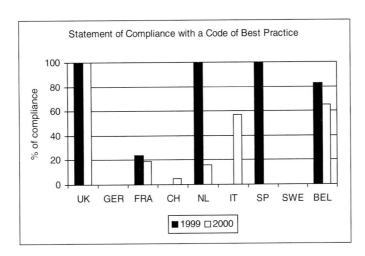

Figure 5 Statement of compliance with a code of best practice

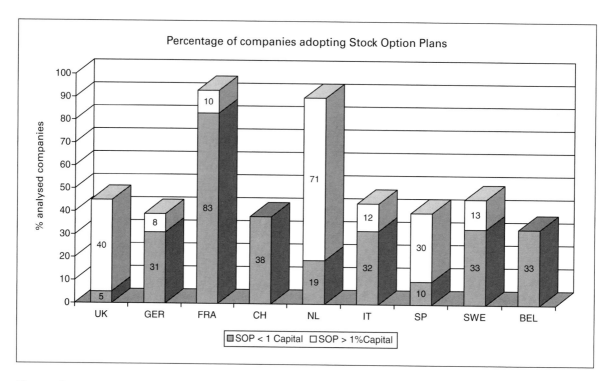

Figure 6 Percentage of companies adopting stock option plans

With regard to these criteria, most UK companies have set up a Board structure that can be regarded as best practice (5 Déminor). In fact, most non-executive directors are independent directors. Moreover, most of the analysed companies cannot be regarded as oversized or understaffed with between 9 and 16 directors. All companies have an audit committee, a remuneration committee and a nomination committee.

In the other countries, less than 25 per cent of the companies identify their independent directors, making it harder for investors to express an opinion on the necessary checks and balances at Board level.

Investors also like to see the interests of the executive aligned with their long-term interests as owners. This criterion can partly be met through the use of variable remuneration, as is the case in Italy, Sweden, France, the Netherlands, Belgium and Germany.

Figure 6 presents the use of stock-option plans by the analysed companies.

However, there are major differences in European countries concerning the beneficiaries of the incentive schemes. On the one hand, UK, German and Spanish companies allocate around 5 per cent of the

stock options to Board members, with the remaining 95 per cent being allocated to other executives. On the other hand, Italian and Swedish companies tend to allocate more than one-third of the stock options to Board members only. Companies in other countries fall in between these extremes.

There are huge differences in Europe concerning the operation of the Board. On the one hand, UK and Spanish companies are very sensitive towards the importance of audit, remuneration and nomination

Country ratings, 2000

Major countries	Rights and duties shareholders	Takeover defences	Disclosure	Board structure
United Kingdom	4	4	5	5
Germany	4	3	2	1
France	3	1	3	3
Switzerland	2	1	1	1
The Netherlands	1	1	3	2
Italy	4	1	3	2
Spain	2	1	2	3
Sweden	2	3	2	2
Belgium	3	1	3	3

Note: Country ratings are defined as the median of company ratings on each country level committees, while at the other extreme, more than two-thirds of German and Italian companies leave issues that might be very technical or where dramatic conflicts of interest could arise entirely to the Board.

Jean-Nicolas Caprasse is a partner at Déminor International, an independent consultancy that specialises in assisting institutional, private and corporate shareholders in managing their minority stakes.

Déminor Rating is a dedicated subsidiary of Déminor International, and is the first European Rating Agency to provide corporate governance research, ratings and advice to institutional investors and companies. Déminor Rating is composed of a multidisciplinary team of more than 15 professionals in corporate governance, corporate finance, law and communication.

www.deminor.com; tel: +32 2674 7110

CORPORATE STRUCTURES AND PRACTICES IN EUROPE

There are many different ways in which a corporation can be structured and operated in Europe, says Jeremy Cottle of Royal & SunAlliance ProFin.

Different vehicles exist for carrying on business in different countries in Europe. For example, in the United Kingdom it is possible for trade to be undertaken by someone as a sole trader, in a partnership (and it is possible to limit the liabilities of partners in certain circumstances), as a private limited company and as a public limited company. Moreover, there are many different ways in which a corporation, with its own legal entity, can be structured and operate. This Chapter considers the main vehicles for carrying on a business in the United Kingdom, Germany, France, Denmark and the Czech Republic.

In the United Kingdom, the two main forms of corporate structure are private companies with limited liability and public companies with limited liability. In both cases, the company will be a legal entity in its own right and the liability of the shareholders will be limited to the nominal value of the shares that they hold. A private company cannot list its shares on a stock exchange, although it does not need to maintain a statutory minimum share capital.

A public company must have a minimum share capital of £50,000. Only public companies can seek a listing on one of the UK stock exchanges.

Companies in the United Kingdom are run on a day-to-day basis by the directors who owe a fiduciary duty to act in the best interests of the company. This duty can attract personal liability if breached. There are a number of decisions that the board of directors cannot take without the approval of the company's shareholders – for example, an increase in the share capital of a company, the undertaking of specific transactions or the amendment of the company's articles of association. It is worth noting that companies incorporated in the United Kingdom will be jointly and severally liable for any civil wrong that has been committed by an employee while acting in the course of his employment (this would include negligence, for example).

In Germany, there are several forms of corporate structure, but the two most commonly used forms are the private (*Gesellschaft mit beschränkter Haftung, GmbH*) and public limited companies (*Aktien Gesellschaft, AG*). A limited company is similar to a UK company in a number of ways. The liability of the company is restricted to the company's assets following incorporation and registration, while the shareholders' liability is restricted to the shares that they hold. One or more directors who are appointed by the shareholders will represent a GmbH. The directors themselves, however, need not be shareholders.

The structure of a German public company is more complicated than that generally used for a German private company. An AG must have both a board of directors and a supervisory board that monitors the directors in order to protect the interests of the company's shareholders and employees. The directors and supervisory board of an AG can be held personally liable for problems occurring as a result of a violation of their respective duties.

France is similar in that there are various ways in which a company can be structured to achieve certain goals. The main two structures, however, are those of a private limited company (*Société à Responsabilité Limitée, SARL*) and a public limited company (*Société Anonyme, SA*). Although the formation and maintenance rules are not exactly the same, the end result is similar to the situation in the United Kingdom and Germany. Public companies are more closely monitored and have more complicated requirements than private companies.

In France, the company's articles will govern much of a private company's constitution and there is no standard term of office for a company's directors. A statutory auditor is only required in certain cases and there is no obligation for the directors to be shareholders. By comparison, a French public company must follow a specific timetable for the term of office of its first directors following incorporation, a statutory auditor is compulsory and members of the board of directors must hold at least one share each.

Denmark is another example of a country in which there is a split between public and private companies. A Danish public company (*Aktieselskab, AS*) must have a board of directors with at least three members. This can be contrasted with a private company (*Anpartsselskab, ApS*), which need not have a board of directors unless the number of employees exceeds a certain number. The legislation governing an AS is more complex than the rules applicable to an ApS, although the two types of company operate in a similar fashion.

Moving away from the European Union, it is worth looking at the Czech Republic. A joint-stock company (*akciova spolecnost*) is the Czech equivalent of a UK public limited company. There are also limited liability companies (*spolecnost s rucenim omezenym*), which equate roughly to UK private companies.

The differences between the two forms of corporate entity incorporated in the Czech Republic are in some ways similar to the differences outlined in respect of the jurisdictions above. The differences concern the share structure, capital requirements and governing structure of the two forms. Subject to the articles of association, the shares of a joint-stock company can be freely traded without registration in the companies register. A joint-stock company on the other hand must have a board of directors and a supervisory board. A limited liability company that has been incorporated in the Czech Republic may delegate decision-making powers to one or more designated 'executives' by the members of the company. It is important to note that there is no concept, however, of a separate board of directors.

Each of the jurisdictions above has a different procedure for the incorporation and operation of a corporate entity and the entities can operate in different ways in each country. The common theme, however, is the choice between public and private companies. Private companies are generally used by smaller businesses and tend to be less regulated than companies whose shares can be listed and traded on public exchanges. For example, in most jurisdictions a private company will have a smaller authorised capital requirement than a public company for registration and to commence business.

Jeremy Cottle is the Directors & Officers' Product leader for Royal & SunAlliance ProFin.

Royal & SunAlliance has recently launched 'Management Assurance', a packaged product providing specialist insurance protection with bespoke cover to suit the needs of each and every business, public or private. It covers risks such as Directors' & Officers Liability insurance, Employment Practices Liability insurance, Crime, Kidnap Ransom & Extortion, Pension Scheme Liability insurance, Professional Indemnity insurance and Libel insurance. The product includes unique value-added services designed to help insureds avoid distracting and time-consuming losses and ultimately support the insureds in managing their future with confidence.

Part 11

Employment

OUBS

Where the determined succeed

EQUIS

INVESTOR IN PEOPLE

Open University Business School
Walton Hall
Milton Keynes
MK7 6AA

www.oubs.open.ac.uk
information hotline:
+44 (0)8700 100311

The Open University

BUSINESS SCHOOL

Which MBA for your managers?

The biggest is among the best.

The Open University Business School is the largest business school in Europe. It is the only one that specialises exclusively in distance learning, the most convenient and relevant way for your managers to develop their skills and knowledge. Over 30,000 managers from around the world study for management or professional qualifications with OUBS every year.

The scale of the OUBS infrastructure – so important to successful distance learning – is underpinned by the quality of its programmes.

OUBS has been awarded the prestigious EQUIS kitemark by the European Foundation for Management Development (efmd). Only 39 of the very best business schools from around the world have earned this recognition.

OUBS was among the first distance learning programmes to be accredited by the Association of MBAs (AMBA). Currently a quarter of all managers graduating with an MBA from AMBA accredited business schools studied with OUBS.

If you want your managers to be among the best, support them on their way to an MBA with Europe's largest business school.

The Open
University

BUSINESS
SCHOOL

The Open University Business School – the largest provider of distance taught management education in Europe

Management education is a flourishing international business which has expanded massively over the last 10 years, not only across Europe, but also elsewhere in the industrialised and developing world.

In Europe alone there are some 250 business schools and if you include the United States that total doubles. These schools compete for an increasing number of students and managers, keen to acquire the skills and expertise of modern management techniques and to hold the most prestigious of business qualifications, an MBA.

The aim of the UK-based Open University Business School (OUBS) in this marketplace has been to provide management development courses and programmes of a high academic and professional quality taught by distance learning methods. This offers students a truly flexible way of learning where they do not have to give up their jobs to study full time. They can study in their own time at home or work and can continue to earn while they learn.

The Open University Business School

The Open University Business School has grown, since its foundation in 1983, to be the largest provider of distance taught management education in Europe. The School has grown considerably in the past decade, via collaborative partnerships with academic institutions or commercial organisations, and currently has an annual student base of around 25,000. Around 18,000 students a year study for the Certificate in Management or Diploma in Management with 7,000 taking the MBA programme. The OUBS has students in more than 40 countries around the world, including Western, Central and Eastern Europe (in Bulgaria, the Czech Republic, Romania, Russia and the former Soviet States, and Slovakia), as well as international programmes in Honk Hong, Singapore, India and South Africa.

OUBS flexibility suits managers and employers

Students do not have to give up work to take an OUBS course, they can fit their studies in around their work, their family, and other commitments.

OUBS students learn new skills and management techniques and put them into practice at work straight away.

Employers recognise the benefit of studying this way and support their employees – 60% of OUBS students are sponsored by their employer.

What the OUBS has to offer

The OUBS offers three modular programmes

- *The Professional Certificate in Management provides*
- *The Professional Diploma in Management*
- *Masters in Business Administration (MBA)*

In addition to these core management education programmes the OUBS offers a Certificate in Accounting and a range of courses leading to a BA in Business Studies.

The MBA programme

There are no short cuts to a good MBA. The OUBS MBA Programme is rewarding but demanding and is designed for practising managers in middle and senior positions. The programme is studied in English - a bonus to students based outside the UK who want a recognised management qualification in the universally accepted business language. A high standard of understanding, spoken and written English is necessary and OUBS can advise individuals on the level of English required.

An assurance of quality

OUBS is one of only 41 elite business schools world-wide to hold the prestigious EQUIS (European Quality Improvement System) quality kitemark from the European Foundation for Management Development (efmd). The award positions OUBS alongside IMD and UK leaders Cranfield, Warwick and Henley. The Association of MBAs (AMBA) has accredited the OUBS MBA, one of only 32 UK MBAs to be approved, since 1989.

Contact details

Open University Business School
Walton Hall, Milton Keynes MK7 6AA.
Tel. +44 (0) 8700 100311
E-mail: oubs-ilgen@open.ac.uk
web: www.oubs.open.ac.uk

Open University Business School
European Co-ordination Centre
Ave Emile Duray 38, B-1050 Brussels, Belgium.
Tel. +32 2 644 33 73
E-mail: oubs-cweenq@open.ac.uk

EMPLOYEE CONSULTATION AND RESTRUCTURING

Differences in employment relations between the United Kingdom and continental jurisdictions are most pronounced at the collective level, says James Davies at Lewis Silkin, as Marks & Spencer discovered in France. Will a new EU directive encourage practices to converge?

The appearance of the euro in 2002 highlights for business the gradual integration of the European market. Many small businesses in addition to major multinationals are finding little alternative but to expand their horizons beyond national boundaries.

In doing so, businesses invariably encounter the differences between the industrial relations cultures and employment law regimes of the various EU member states. Try as they might, it will prove impractical to harmonise employment terms throughout Europe or to adopt a uniform approach to human resource issues.

Nonetheless, a slow assimilation is taking place. In the United Kingdom, for example, the current government's 'family-friendly' initiatives are bringing it into line with its neighbours. German legislation,

by way of another example, recently gave employees the right to part-time work. Recent EC anti-discrimination directives will oblige all member states to introduce race and disability discrimination modelled on those in the United Kingdom.

There is little practical distinction between the requirement in the United Kingdom to show a fair reason and act reasonably in dismissals and the need in France to show *cause réelle et sérieuse*. Similarly, according to the German Protection against Dismissal Act, an employee can only be dismissed for specific reasons and after a specific procedure has been followed. However, in Germany, if the dismissal is considered unlawful, the employment relationship generally continues, which is in contrast to the more common awarding of compensation in the United Kingdom and France.

It is at a collective level, however, that the differences between the United Kingdom and a number of the continental jurisdictions have been most pronounced. This can be highlighted by Marks & Spencer's attempts in 2000 to close its French stores. In the United Kingdom, on the other hand, unions have had little opportunity to frustrate closures at Corus and others.

There are a variety of reasons for the different approaches. For one, in the United Kingdom, collective consultation failures result only in awards of compensation, whereas in France and other countries, the courts can annul decisions where consultation obligations have been ignored. Indeed, cynical employers often find when doing their sums that the compensation payments are unlikely to exceed the wages that would have to be paid out during the period of consultation. A further contrast between the United Kingdom and countries such as France and Germany is the importance attached in the latter jurisdictions to a social plan which must be developed by an employer making redundancies. This social plan sets out the employer's proposals for mitigating the consequences of the redundancies for the affected workers.

Moreover, in the United Kingdom, listed companies are generally more fearful of breaching stock exchange rules on delaying the disclosure of information than of infringing the arguably contradictory duties to inform employee representatives at an early stage.

The approach of UK companies is changing, however. The second half of 2001 witnessed a much-publicised spate of mass redundancies. Employers and their advisers are, often for the first time, establishing employee consultation bodies to be consulted. Businesses are coming to terms with the financial sanctions of ignoring their information and consultation duties – an award of up to three months' pay per affected employee. Workers and unions are becoming increasingly aware of their rights and claims are becoming much more commonplace.

Sometimes, employers will go through the motions of a carefully scripted consultation process with a closed mind, but on other occasions, employers will find the process beneficial and acknowledge the advantages of effective dialogue with their workforce.

The need throughout Europe to pay more than lip service to employee consultation will develop with the adoption of the EC directive establishing a general framework for informing and consulting employees in the European Community.

Currently, at a European level, the obligation to consult with worker representatives only arises where:

- mass redundancies are envisaged;
- part of the business will be transferred; or
- where the company or group is sufficiently large across Europe to be covered by the European Works Councils Directive.

The implementation of the new directive will impose significant new obligations on all employers with 50 or more workers. In the United Kingdom, for example, it is estimated that around 70 per cent of employees will be covered.

Representatives of employees will have a right to be told about the business's economic situation and informed and consulted about employment prospects and decisions likely to lead to substantial changes in work organisation or contractual relations.

In October 2001, the European Parliament agreed major amendments to the proposed directive. It will now be considered by the Council of Ministers.

Crucially, where a decision is taken in breach of the rules, the representatives would be able to delay any firm decision until further consultation has taken place. That sanction alone should mean an increasing attention to collective relations in countries such as the United Kingdom and an increased alignment throughout the European Union in employee relations culture and laws in the different member states.

James Davies is a partner at, and joint head of, Lewis Silkin's employment department. E-mail james.davies@ lewissilkin.com

'EMOTIONAL INTELLIGENCE': IS IT JUST A BUZZ WORD OR DOES IT REALLY MAKE A DIFFERENCE?

asks Chris Parker from Chameleon Training & Consulting

Can you think of the best boss you've ever had? What was it about them that motivated you, kept your loyalty and inspired you to deliver your best?

Emotional Intelligence expert Daniel Goleman would say that Emotional Intelligence (EI) differentiates great business leaders. Goleman defines EI as 'the capacity for recognising our own feelings and those of others, for motivating ourselves, for managing emotions well in ourselves and in our relationships'. Based on research with over 200 organisations around the world, he demonstrates that EI is twice as important as cognitive (IQ) or technical skills in differentiating high performance.

Furthermore, the higher you go in an organisation, the more important EI becomes, accounting for 85–90 per cent of the performance of top executives. In professional and technical fields the IQs of top executives are very similar, and IQ offers very little competitive advantage. So what does make the difference? With EI, executives develop the understanding and intelligence to develop competitive advantage over their peers by creating greater satisfaction levels and loyalty amongst customers, better staff morale and improved bottom line performance.

So how does it make a difference? Think back to that best boss again. Or in the words of Patrick O'Brien, formerly Vice President for North American sales at Johnson Wax – 'leadership agility, the ability to work with different styles and with people at all levels of the organisation, from the sales rep on the street to top management, demands empathy and emotional self management. You need agility in leadership and learning. We find an absence of this kind of agility is a top derailer for people we seek to develop'.

EI determines how we learn to be self aware, empathetic, adept and flexible in our relationships, to manage ourselves and motivate others. Goleman is a strong believer that these tools can be developed through the provision of expert training, ongoing assessment and individual development strategies. At Chameleon our experience shows that by using carefully tailored development activities targeted specifically at job-related competencies, individuals can break old behavioural habits and establish new ones which will bring them greater success.

At Chameleon we're committed to making managers the best leaders and we use EI to get them there. How do we do it? The first step is for individuals to complete the Hay Emotional Competency Inventory (ECI), the only EI assessment tool approved by Goleman. The 360-degree multi-rater tool provides accurate and sophisticated feedback, comparing individuals with world class leaders. Receipt of this data immediately increases an individual's level of self-awareness, itself a key component of emotional intelligence. Using Hay trained Consultants, Chameleon can then offer businesses a range of development options for developing levels of emotional competence. For senior executives, one-to-one coaching sessions have proved particularly successful and workshops designed to develop specific competencies are also popular. The ECI assessment also lends itself to self-development and self-directed learning.

EI is now being used as a central competency for management in some of the leading European businesses, and, as a result, realising improvements in both individual and organisation performance. The success of EI is not restricted to the leadership field. Numerous studies of the sales environment point to the impact that EI can have on the bottom line. In 1991, Lyle Spencer studied 44 Fortune 500 companies, including AT&T, IBM and Pepsico and found high EI sales people produced twice the revenue of average performers. At American Express, financial advisers increased sales by 20 per cent after EI training. In the service arena where the customer interface is the primary means of achieving customer loyalty the ability to empathise, understand and deliver exactly what the customer wants directly improves customer retention rates. At Chameleon we built EI into the customer service programme we designed for the British Airways London Eye, developing EI competencies for the business culture, which were reflected in the customer experience.

Chameleon's selection of bespoke EI programmes are helping to establish emotional competence within the fabric of British businesses, and developing the emotional intelligence of the next generation of successful industry leaders for increased performance and improved corporate profitability.

So is EI a buzz-word? Yes. And it is creating a step change in the leadership effectiveness and business results of those organisations that recognise its importance and invest in developing emotional competence amongst their leaders, sales and service teams.

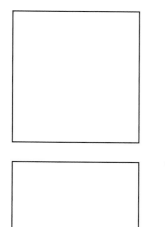

TALENT MANAGEMENT

What keeps Europe's chief executives awake at night is not operating efficiency or customer service levels, investment in IT or shareholder pressures, but the attraction and retention of talented employees. There are six essential ingredients to the effective management of talent in the years ahead, says Duncan Brown, principal at Towers Perrin.

According to a recent Conference Board survey in Europe, the number one issue that keeps chief executives awake at night is not operating efficiency or customer service levels, investment in IT or shareholder pressures, but the attraction and retention of talented employees in their organisation. This Chapter explains why this is the case and illustrates how Towers Perrin is seeing its clients successfully addressing their chief executives' concerns.

From an economist's perspective, there is both a supply-side and a demand-side explanation for the importance of the talent management issue.

Human capital economy

On the demand side, in our knowledge, information and service-based economy, not only are employees now the major operating cost for many organisations, but they have also genuinely become, as James Collins and Jerry Porras put it in their business bestseller *Built to Last*, 'the sources of sustained competitive advantage'. Their 50-year analysis of high-performing organisations highlights the criticality of the people factor.

However, it is not just any old people. What Professor Keith Bradley calls the professional sports model of competition is spreading to more and more sectors of the economy, in which key individual employees can have a massive impact on the overall performance of the organisation. The publishing executive at Bloomsbury who accepted the first book from an unknown author called J K Rowling contributed to the doubling of the company's revenue in 2001, which the Harry Potter phenomenon has produced. In terms of the downside impact, aside from Nick Leeson, what about the equivalent executive at a rival publishing house who had also read but rejected the script?

American academic Daniel Goleman studied the value added by the highest-performing individuals in a variety of occupations. In low-skill jobs they were contributing two to three times the value of the average employee. Interestingly, this is the typical difference between the pay increases of top-performing individuals and other staff in traditional performance-related pay schemes.

However, that was in the lowest-skilled work. In the increasing number of high-skill, professional jobs, the top performers were adding up to 10, even 20 times the value of their colleagues. And what do we do in most organisations? Say 'well done' and give them 3–6 per cent more on their base pay!

Sustained staff shortages

On the supply side, the declining levels of unemployment and evident skill shortages, in occupations ranging from IT workers and accountants, through teachers and police, to train and HGV drivers, have propelled the people and talent issue up the corporate agenda. The combination of demographic changes and increased competition has led Deutshe Bank to forecast a 33 per cent reduction in its traditional labour pool over the next decade. Meanwhile, the need simultaneously to retain a greying workforce, while attracting and motivating members of the street-wise and work-life balance-conscious 'Generation Y' poses huge challenges to most of our large employers.

Will the worsening economic climate evident in Europe at the time of writing alleviate the situation? Not if the experiences in the United States, who are further down this economic cycle, are anything to go by. According to a Towers Perrin study in North America in July, almost nine out of ten companies are finding it just as or more difficult to recruit and retain top employees compared with 12 months earlier. Moreover, three-quarters of them are continuing to hire in key areas despite general staff downsizing, and 42 per cent have targeted programmes to retain their top performers and key staff.

Indeed, in this new economy combination of circumstances, the traditional UK corporate-reflex response of pay freezes and last-in, first-out redundancies could prove disastrous. Even in the last major recession at the start of the 1990s, companies that cut more than 15 per cent of their workforce only succeeded in producing significantly lower shareholder returns than their competitors.

Effective talent management techniques

Thus, if recruiting and retaining talented employees is now so critical, what are some of the more enlightened responses that companies are making? Towers Perrin believes that there are six essential ingredients to the effective management of talent in the years ahead.

Towers Perrin is often asked to design incentive schemes or development programmes for talented employees, yet finds that the organisation is not clear about just who these critical members of staff are. The successful companies are those who address this 'who' question, asking themselves how many employees with what types of skills, values and needs are critical to the delivery of corporate strategy.

In one large investment bank, for example, it quickly became evident that the traditional labour sources would not meet their future demand. Thus, the work took the form of a diversity rather than an incentive or retention exercise, identifying non-traditional labour sources and developing recruitment strategies and reward programmes to suit these types of new employee.

Second, the companies that attract and retain the best employees are those with a very strong and distinctive employment brand. It is no coincidence that the names at the top of 2001's Universum league table of attractive employers for graduates in Europe – Microsoft, Coca Cola, Virgin and Nokia – have a powerful consumer brand and reputation, because this is matched by an equally strong employment offering and reputation: for being a great employer for training, or to have on your CV, or providing international work opportunities and so forth.

Third, this brand incorporates a total rewards offering in its broadest sense (see Figure 1), providing an appropriate and attractive package of pay and benefits, but often more importantly in respect of retention and motivation, learning and development opportunities and an appealing employment environment. Seventy per cent of companies in Towers Perrin's research among 460 European employers had increased their training and development spend in the past three years, with a focus on high achiever and high potential programmes.

Correspondingly, the provision of flexible working opportunities was a major differentiator between the opinions of highly satisfied and dissatisfied employees in recent research among 1,000 UK employers, commissioned by *Employee Benefits* magazine.

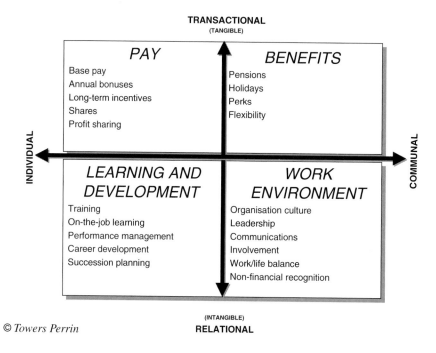

Figure 1 A total rewards approach

Taking this broad perspective on reward enables the successful companies to provide the fourth ingredient, personal choice and individual flexibility, in the make-up of the rewards package. The recessionary pressures will only increase the necessity for employers to maximise the perceived value of their package in employees' eyes at an equivalent, rather than providing expensive benefits whose value is neither understood nor appreciated by key sections of their workforce.

Generally poor communication on reward issues was a key finding of the Towers Perrin research, along with weak performance and rewards management. Yet as David Guest's research for the CIPD highlights, it is not the deal that you promise but the delivery of that deal in practice that characterises the attractive and high-performing employers. They therefore display the fifth requirement, a heavy attention to the processes of reward and performance management, evidenced by high levels of employee communication and involvement and extensive line management training.

In addition to having higher-quality management processes, the highest performing companies in terms of shareholder value and employee turnover in the Towers Perrin study were also differentiated by the final factor in effectively managing talent: they recognised and aggressively rewarded high individual performance, with a plethora of pay increase and fast-track promotion mechanisms, bonus schemes and recognition awards, all managed in a way that attracted genuine appreciation and recognition, rather than envy and criticism.

Succeeding in all six of the areas highlighted is a very tall order for any employer, and even then, the constant shifts in environments and markets means that the talent programmes need to be constantly reviewed and revisited. However, perhaps what distinguishes success in this area more than any other is the need for an organisation to take a strategic and 'joined-up' approach to the whole issue of attracting, retaining and motivating talented employees to deliver on the goals of the organisation (see Figure 2).

The traditional 'siloed' approaches to this issue in so many organisations, with uncoordinated and isolated initiatives in recruitment, pay and benefits, training and development and so forth, simply cannot address the scale of the challenges involved. However, they also demonstrate the potentially major competitive gains in employee attraction and business results that even minor improvements in this area can deliver for you.

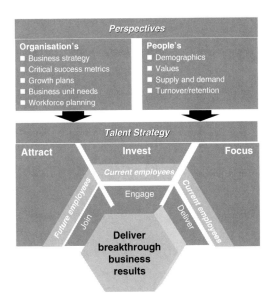

Figure 2 An integrated strategy for talent management

Duncan Brown is a partner in the London office of Towers Perrin, an international management consultancy that specialises in improving performance through people.

Towers Perrin, Swan Gardens, 10 Piccadilly, London W1V OAE. Telephone +44 (0)20 7806 6406; e-mail: brownd@towers.com

TEN WAYS TO ATTRACT YOUNG EUROPEAN PROFESSIONALS AND KEEP THEM HAPPY

How do you entice, satisfy and hold on to your best young people? Simply ask them to tell you about their deepest, most intimate career goals and desires – and then fulfil them.

So, you are a senior manager or human resource executive looking to hire a young European professional, age 30, with seven years' work experience and a business degree. You have lined up interviews with two candidates: an Italian woman from Rome and a Swedish man from Stockholm. Although both interviewees are strong candidates, they each have completely different national upbringings and work values.

Will you interview them differently because of their national differences? What kind of career goals and professional development programmes will you discuss with them? Are you prepared to offer a competitive salary and a tailored compensation package? Will the lucky candidate be working in an exciting international environment with inspiring colleagues? Will you offer flexible working hours so that the new employee can have a balanced personal life and career?

You may not be sure of all the answers to these questions, but one thing is certain: today's young European professionals have specific needs, wants and desires. Research company Universum Communications have recently launched the results of their first pan-European Young Professional Survey, in which more than 14,000 young professionals from 10 European countries voiced their opinions about work-related issues such as salary, compensation packages, career goals, recruitment, preferred industries and ideal employers.

'Human talent is today's most important resource,' says Ylva Johansson, director of business development at Universum, 'but it is also in short supply.'

So, how do companies become ideal employers and how can they meet the demands of today's young European professionals? According to the Young Professional Survey, there are 10 ways to attract these future employees and to keep them happy:

1. Be an ideal employer. According to Johan Carlberg, a Universum project manager, it all boils down to image. 'A company that makes the survey's Top 30 list of most ideal employers definitely has an attractive employer image.' When survey respondents from across Europe were asked to select the companies they would like to work for, they chose prestigious multinationals such as Coca Cola, Nokia, Ericsson and BMW. Almost half of the no.1 favourites on the Top Ideal Employers list are airline companies: Air France, Alitalia, Amsterdam Airport Schipol and British Airways.

Table 1 Companies ranked no. 1 in different countries

Denmark	A.P. Møller-Maersk
Finland	Nokia
France	Air France
Germany	BMW
Italy	Alitalia
Norway	Coca Cola International
Spain	Coca Cola International
Sweden	Ericsson
The Netherlands	Amsterdam Airport Schipol
United Kingdom	British Airways

2. Position yourself in a trendy industry. Certain industries are more appealing and exciting to young professionals than others. When asked which industry they would prefer to work for, the overwhelming majority of respondents chose 'IT consulting/data services', followed by 'media/public relations/information' and 'management consulting', respectively.

3. Present enticing career opportunities. 'Today's young professionals want it all,' says Johan Carlberg, 'an exciting career and a balanced life.' When asked about career goals, they prefer to 'work with increasingly challenging tasks', followed by 'a balanced personal life and career', and 'work internationally' respectively.

4. Offer attractive work characteristics. Respondents also want to work for companies that offer attractive characteristics such as 'flexible working hours', 'competitive compensation', and the opportunity to work with 'inspiring colleagues', respectively.

5. Build loyalty. Loyal employees tend to stay longer with an employer and work harder. When asked what factors are most important in building a sense of loyalty toward an employer, respondents say a company should first offer 'opportunities for professional training and development', second 'compensation and benefits', and third, a 'work environment'.

6. Do not make a 10-hour workday the norm. Today's young professionals are willing to work hard, but they also want a life after office hours. Most of the respondents say that they prefer to work '36–40 hours per week'.

7. Compensate well. Although money is not everything, more than half of the survey respondents said that they were not satisfied with their current compensation. The largest percentage of respondents said that they would like to earn 'between €30,001 and €40,000 per year'.

8. Offer extra incentives. Along with earning a competitive salary, young professionals would also like to receive an attractive compensation package. The top three items they would like to be offered are 'paid overtime', followed by 'extra holidays' and 'performance-related bonuses', respectively.

9. Recruit on-line. On-line recruitment appears to be one of the best ways to recruit these ambitious young professionals. When asked how they plan to find their next job, the respondents' top three choices were 'on-line recruitment service', followed by 'newspaper advertisement' and 'work-related activity', respectively.

10. Follow through and ask for feedback. A little follow-through goes a long way. Meet regularly with employees to find out what their individual needs are and frequently ask for feedback and suggestions. 'Employees want to be recognised. They want to feel that their work is important,' says Johansson. 'When they are not satisfied, they will quickly look elsewhere for other career opportunities. That is why it is important to find out what they want, satisfy their needs and keep them happy.'

Universum Young Professional Survey

The Universum Young Professional Survey is conducted annually in 10 European countries: Denmark, Finland, France, Germany, Italy, Norway, Spain, Sweden, the Netherlands and the United Kingdom. The survey participants are young professionals aged 25–35 with an education in business, engineering, IT or humanities/social sciences, and a maximum of eight years' work experience. Questionnaires are distributed through the Jobline career network website, now a monster.com company. Along with the pan-European results, companies can also purchase country-specific and company-specific reports that include both areas of study and gender comparisons.

Universum Communications is an international research and management consulting company that understands the career expectations of today's students and young professionals.

Telephone +46 8 5620 27 00; e-mail ylva.johansson@ universum.se; http://www.universum.se

Consultancy & Training

Experience the ripple effect of great training

MaST International has been a driving and motivating force in the training and skills development of individuals, teams and managers for over 30 years. From in-house solutions to public Open Courses we have successfully helped many national and international companies achieve proven results.

Building on Experience

As a market leader, we recruit only the best people with extensive experience and knowledge of their specialist areas. We have created a winning team that can actively help your organisation generate immediate gains and long-term success.

MaST offers a broad range of consultancy and training products covering four core areas; Leading & Managing Skills, Business Skills, Communication Skills & Personal Effectiveness.

We also offer a wide range of services including Graduate Training Programmes, Training Needs Analysis, Diagnostics, Mock Tribunals and MaST Theatre. **MaST Theatre** utilises a wide variety of specialist techniques and products, including role-play, interactive theatre, conferences and videos.

Your Business, *Your* Solution

At MaST we believe that the answer lies in fully understanding the overall business needs of our clients. Whether your aim is to improve individual or team performance or help senior management implement change across a whole organisation, our consultants have the objectivity, experience and skills to get to grips with the real issues you face.

Making the Best Choice

If you want to find out how MaST can help your business, or would like further information about our products, services and courses then please call The Training Team on freephone **0800 316 9090**, or e-mail us at: **trainingsolutions@mast.co.uk**. Alternatively you can visit our website **www.mast.co.uk**

MaST International Group plc
Hermitage House, Bath Road, Maidenhead, Berkshire SL6 0AR
Tel: +44 (0)1628 784062 Fax: +44 (0)1628 773061
E-mail: trainingsolutions@mast.co.uk

EMPLOYMENT PRACTICES LIABILITY

Discrimination, unfair dismissal and failure to comply with the rules on consultation are just three grounds for employment liability in Europe, says Paul Wells of Royal & SunAlliance ProFin.

European law

The past few years have seen an increase in the amount of employment legislation at European level which all EU member states must implement. When directives are passed at EU level, member states are under an obligation to implement them into national law usually within a period of two years.

As a result, a large amount of European employment law (and consequently the employment liabilities in member states) is becoming increasingly similar across Europe.

The European Union has legislated for the following areas among others:

- equal pay between male and female employees;
- protection for employees who are to be made redundant;
- equal treatment for men and women;
- protection for employees in the event that their employer restructures or sells its business;

- protection for employees in the event of insolvency of their employer;
- protection for employees against race and sex discrimination;
- health and safety of employees;
- employees' working time;
- consulting and informing employees on redundancy;
- maternity and parental leave rights;
- part-time and fixed-term workers' protection;
- burden of proof in sex discrimination cases.

A new directive is planned in relation to equal treatment in employment, which member states have until 2 December 2003 to implement. This will prohibit discrimination on the grounds of age, sexual orientation and religious belief.

Applicable law

The Rome Convention on the Law Applicable to Contractual Obligations of 1980 is a treaty between member states, which clarifies the law applicable to contractual disputes. Pursuant to the Rome Convention, the question of which law applies to contractual disputes depends broadly on which choice the parties have expressly or impliedly made. Where there is an absence of choice, if the employee usually works in a particular member state, that law will apply, or if he works in more than one member state, the law of the state through which he was engaged will apply.

Finally, if overall the contract is more closely connected with a state, it will be that law which applies.

It is worth noting that even where the contract expressly states the choice of law, it is not possible to override the mandatory employment law protections applicable to employees in national jurisdictions. Thus, for example, an employee based in France who works for an employer whose permanent place of business is situated in England may be afforded the protection of French mandatory employment law, notwithstanding that the contract says that it is governed by English law.

This is significant in the context of employment practices' liability insurance because employers insured in one state may also attract liability under the law of another member state.

National laws

EU legislation is by no means the only source of employment law and each EU member state has different employment laws. Despite this, the concepts across the states are increasingly similar.

Below are some of the most important areas of potential liability at European level.

Discrimination

All member states prohibit discrimination on various grounds – for example, race or sex – although the scope of the protection varies between states. For example, in the United Kingdom, employees are awarded compensation if they are successful with such claims, but in Germany compensation for such discrimination is unusual (but not unknown). This is because the German courts prefer to rectify the effect of the discrimination – for example, inclusion in a pension scheme from which the employee had previously been excluded.

While there is no corresponding EU directive, EU member states generally have legislation prohibiting discrimination on the grounds of disability pursuant to a Recommendation of the European Council.

Unfair dismissal

In the United Kingdom, employees must have at least one year's service in order to make a claim of unfair dismissal. This is in contrast to other member states, such as the Netherlands and France, where there are no length of service restrictions. If such a claim is successful, the differences between compensation available to these employees varies greatly between the different member states and in some states reinstatement is granted to employees instead of compensation.

Consultation

Different laws apply throughout Europe in relation to informing and consulting employees prior to redundancies. In the United Kingdom, an employer who proposes to make 20 or more employees redundant within a period of 90 days or less has statutory obligations to consult with the recognised trade union or employee representative and notify the Department of Trade and Industry (DTI). Failure to consult collectively and individually can lead to a protective award per employee. Failure to notify the DTI may lead to a criminal conviction for the directors involved and a fine. This is contrasted with countries such as France and Germany where failure to consult renders any dismissals void and leads to reinstatement.

Clearly, legislation from Europe is widening the scope for employees to make successful claims against their employers. Businesses therefore need to be able to manage risks throughout their European operations in relation to the core of potential employment liabilities.

Royal & SunAlliance has recently launched 'Management Assurance', a packaged product providing specialist insurance protection with bespoke cover to suit the needs of each and every business, public or private. It covers risks such as Directors' & Officers Liability insurance, Employment Practices Liability insurance, Crime, Kidnap Ransom & Extortion, Pension Scheme Liability insurance, Professional Indemnity insurance and Libel insurance. The product includes unique value-added services designed to help insureds avoid distracting and time-consuming losses and ultimately support the insureds in managing their future with confidence.

Paul Wells, assistant underwriting manager, London, Royal & SunAlliance ProFin. Telephone +44 (0)20 7337 5874; http://www.profin.royalsun.com

Part 12

Better Management Practice

It's as much a myth as a 'born leader'

For over 25 years, The Leadership Tru (Training) Limited has been dedicated to th enhancement and promotion of leadersh in all aspects of society. Our leadersh development programmes are targete specifically at directors and senior manage and are applicable to all sectors of industr commerce and society.

We create the environment ar circumstances for delegates to 'look themselves in the mirror', to understar their own behaviour and, in turn, how the behaviour affects others. In so doing, the are able to identify, understand and develo their leadership skills.

For information please contact us on:

+44 (0)1989 76766

E-mail: enquiries@leadership.co.uk

Web: www.leadership.co.uk

The LeadershipTrust

Excellence in Leadership Developn

The Leadership Trust

Excellence in Leadership Development

The Leadership Trust (Training) Limited –
The Effective Approach to Leadership
and Self-Development

Poor leadership has been shown to be the most common reason for the removal of chief executives in business, after financial or ethical malpractice (Korn/Ferry 1995). The Leadership Trust's own research has also shown that strong leadership skills are the most important factor for achieving optimum performance at board and senior management levels.

As the speed of change and complexity of business continue to increase, as mergers and acquisitions continue to be a feature of the business landscape and human relations become more challenging due to the need to communicate cross-nationally, cross-culturally and electronically, the importance of effective leadership has never been greater.

Yet, how do business managers become more effective leaders? Is it possible to become an effective leader, or is it something that one is born with?

The Leadership Trust

Founded in 1975, The Leadership Trust has grown to become a major force with an enviable reputation as one of the UK's premier leadership development establishments. We believe that the potential to lead is within us all. **The key to effective leadership is to know, control and understand ourselves as leaders.** Then and only then will we be able to lead and enable others.

The Leadership Trust's philosophy has been shown to have no boundaries. It is applicable to all organisations and effective for everyone. We are the first and only UK-based organisation to focus purely on the subject of leadership. **The backbone of everything we do is** *leadership*. We will work with you to develop effective leadership in your directors and middle-senior managers.

Our Programmes

The Leadership Trust (Training) Limited, which is the wholly owned subsidiary of The Leadership Trust Foundation

(an educational charitable trust), offers a range of services from open (public) leadership development programmes for Directors and Senior Managers, through customised leadership development programmes targeted at Board Level Directors, to presentations and seminars on leadership.

Our programmes are designed to be highly relevant to the working environment and the development of action plans forms an integral part of each programme to ensure that learning from each programme is implemented back in the workplace.

In addition to our open and customised leadership development programmes, we also offer an MBA with a specialism in Leadership Studies through our parent organisation The Leadership Trust Foundation in conjunction with The University of Strathclyde Graduate School of Business. The MBA with a specialism in Leadership Studies provides a unique integration of learning; the development of practical leadership skills at one of Europe's foremost leadership development organisations (The Leadership Trust) combined with the intellectual depth and rigour expected of a top university business school (The University of Strathclyde Graduate School of Business).

The Learning Environment

At The Leadership Trust, we have created a dynamic environment in which delegates are encouraged to practise and experiment. They will discover more about themselves and how best to apply their natural leadership talents and skills. The learning emphasis is placed firmly on encouraging and enhancing leadership qualities.

All Leadership Trust programmes are designed to be lasting experiences with profound personal effects.

Fellow delegates provide feedback on performance throughout the programmes. Reports on performance are never supplied to sponsoring organisations. This high level of confidentiality encourages delegates to be true to themselves – to share views and feelings, and to experiment with new ideas, without compromising their businesses or careers. **It allows them to make mistakes in a totally safe environment, and to learn deeply from their experiences.**

Leadership Trust Facilities

The Leadership Trust centre is based in its own peaceful grounds in the Herefordshire countryside. Most of our 'open' (public) programmes are delivered at these premises. Customised and in-company programmes are available at any location to suit the client's needs.

Our facilities are also available for use by customers for their own training, development and other needs. On some occasions, the centre is available for sole use by your company. For further information, please contact our marketing team.

Leadership Trust Clients

The Leadership Trust's current clients include some of the world's most successful organisations. We work with delegates from organisations throughout the UK and world-wide, and from all sectors of the economy.

Delegates are drawn from senior management, director and managing director/chief executive level.

For a full list of our current clients, please contact our marketing team.

Want to Find Out More?

If you would like to find out more about The Leadership Trust, our leadership development programmes and the services we can provide or to arrange an informal discussion or one-to-one meeting, please contact us at:

The Leadership Trust
FREEPOST HR448
ROSS-ON-WYE
HR9 7BF

Telephone: +44 (0)1989 767667
E-mail: enquiries@leadership.co.uk
Or visit our web site at:
Web: www.leadership.co.uk

Please quote Reference Number: EBH2002 in all communication.

INNOVATION

Bruce Ballantine, chairman of Business Decisions Limited, investigates the unconventional patterns of innovation within the European Union.

The latest edition of the 'Innobarometer',[1] prepared for the European Commission, challenges conventional wisdom about innovation performance in the European Union in a number of areas, but confirms it in others.

Mediterranean countries lead

It reports that five out of the top six most innovative countries in the European Union are 'Mediterranean' (measured in terms of the average percentage of turnover coming from new products introduced in the last two years). Only Denmark in fourth position breaks the run.

This is important for the European Union because innovation is the single most powerful long-term driver of economic growth, improvements in living standards and employment. As such, the good performance of the Mediterranean countries helps the convergence process.

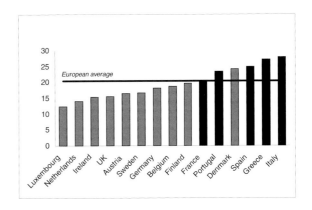

Figure 1 Percentage of turnover from new products introduced in the last two years

Lack of encouragement from customers

Equally surprising, however, is that these countries are among those that appear to obtain least encouragement from their customers. Measured in terms of their perception of the attitudes of their customers to their innovation efforts, companies in Italy, Portugal, Spain and Greece occupy four of the bottom five places in the league table.

However, taken overall, companies in all the countries of the European Union consider that support from customers is critical for their innovation efforts.

---

[1] 'Innobarometer: Results and Commentary', Flash Eurobarometer 100 prepared by Gallup Europe for the European Commission, 2001.

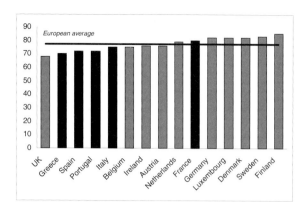

Figure 2 Drivers of innovation encouragement received from customers (index)

Importance of competitive pressure

However, the finding on competitive pressure is more conventional. Companies were asked to rate their innovation performance relative to their competitors. Companies based in Portugal, Spain and France occupy three of the bottom four places in the league table; they consider that their innovation performance is relatively poor compared with their national competitors.

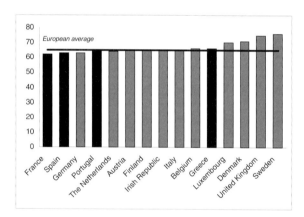

Figure 3 Performance relative to competitors (index)

Importance of the Single Market

Equally important for policy-makers is that companies in Portugal, Greece, Spain and Italy believe that their innovation performance would improve, if they were able to use the Single Market more effectively. Companies in these countries are at the top of the list of countries that believe that their innovation performance would improve if they were able to:

- attract highly-qualified personnel from other EU countries;
- improve networking with innovators in other countries;
- obtain access to finance on a pan-European basis;
- obtain better access to other EU markets more interested in their innovation.

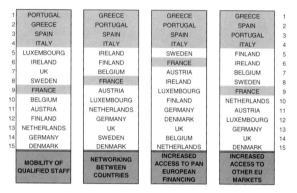

Figure 4 The importance of the Single Market

Importance of intangible as well as tangible investments

The finding that the two most important ways of accessing new technologies are through the acquisition of advanced equipment and cooperation with customers and suppliers (not R&D or licensing) would have been 'unconventional' a few years ago, but it is more in tune with conventional wisdom now.

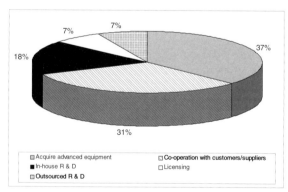

Figure 5 Access to new technologies

Interestingly, it is four of the Mediterranean countries – Greece, Portugal, Spain and Italy – that are the keenest to acquire advanced technologies from other countries.

228

Companies also consider that effective human resource policies are important for the innovation process, particularly the training and motivation of existing staff.

However, in this case, the five Mediterranean countries are at the bottom of the list, which presents another challenge to conventional wisdom.

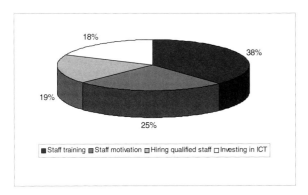

Figure 6 The importance of HR and knowledge management for innovation

Conclusion

The European Union is seeking to become the most competitive knowledge-based economy in the world. It is also seeking to achieve greater convergence between the different national and regional economies.

Innovation is key to both and there are signs that it is helping the less advanced economies of the Mediterranean to reduce the gap with the more advanced northern European countries. However, the jury is still out on the contribution of innovation to Europe's overall knowledge base.

Bruce Ballantine is chairman of Business Decisions Limited, a UK-based consultancy specialising in the impact of public policy on competitiveness. He is also a special adviser to the European Policy Centre, a leading Brussels-based think-tank. Telephone +44 (0)1892 822 156; e-mail bruce.ballantine@bdl-europe.com

BUILDING WORLD-CLASS COMPETITIVE ABILITY

Professor Mohamed Zairi, head of the European Centre for Total Quality Management, provides a blueprint for how European companies can measure performance in a way that achieves world-class results.

Introduction

The notion of 'world-class' is in many cases an elusive concept, unless there is clear emphasis on performance measurement. Indeed, many surveys have noted large gaps between organisations' perceptions on 'where they think they are' and the actual, impartial, objective assessment on 'where they really are' against world-class criteria. Performance measurement is the key trigger to achieving and retaining superior competitive positions. It is interesting to note that for as long as the total quality management (TQM) movement has continued to evolve, the significance of performance measurement did not really get highlighted until recent years. Whether it is as a result of the need to 'quantify' the benefits of TQM or to clearly demonstrate its credibility as a concept, the field of performance measurement remained a neglected topic of research until the early 1990s (Dale, 1992; Zairi, 1992).

Problems

It is perhaps relevant to point out at this stage that one of the basic problems associated with performance measurement is the lack of understanding and appreciation of its scope and pervasiveness. As Sink (1991) argued, '[Performance measurement is a] mystery . . . complex, frustrating, difficult, challenging, important, abused and misused.'

There are wide differences in the application of performance measurement terminologies. They are found in strategic management, human resources management, psychology, accounting and operations management, among other fields. In this regard, the American Productivity and Quality Centre (1999) has recently noted that 'performance measurement has experienced great scepticism. The problem is that there is no single recipe or methodology that will ensure success in implementing a performance measurement system. Organisations have piloted and used a wide variety of systems, both informal and formal, but struggle with selecting the system that works just right for them. Much of what is currently known about measurement is based on individual case studies, practitioner recollections, and anecdotal evidence.'

Overall, many agree that poorly designed measurement systems can seriously inhibit the ability of organisations to adapt successfully to changes in the competitive environment (Zairi and Sinclair, 1995). This is summed up by the phrase 'what gets measured gets done'. A recent benchmarking study by the American Productivity and Quality Centre (1999) highlighted that 'eighty percent of study participants have demonstrated financial and/or non-financial business successes as a result of implementing the performance measurement system. Hewlett-Packard, for example, shows the cause-and-effect relationship of its measures to bottom-line results through its business model for measurement.'

Measurement blueprint for sustainable competitiveness

What must be done at European level is to heed the advice provided in this Chapter, and to follow the proposed roadmap that is suggested and which is based on extensive research and the scrutiny of best practices worldwide. Organisations should now focus on the performance management system as a business management model on which to base business decisions. The most effective way to make measurement part and parcel of routine regular organisational activity is to address all the areas of business operations in a consistent and objective manner.

The proposed roadmap is based on the analysis of 15 world-class organisations. The resulting proposed model was in turn validated by the results from a postal survey of performance measurement systems in 115 companies. It is important to note that in most organisations there is no separate 'performance measurement system'. The model therefore integrates measurement within the overall management process. The model consists of five levels (as shown below) that are meant to bring together, in an encompassing approach, all aspects of business excellence.

- Element 1. Strategy development and goal deployment (including mission/vision, critical success factors and key performance indicators).
- Element 2. Process management and measurement (including impact, in-process and output measures, management of internal and external customer-supplier relationship, and the use of management control systems).
- Element 3. Performance appraisal and management (including performance appraisal and performance management).
- Element 4. 'Break-point' performance assessment (including internal and external benchmarking, self-assessment against business excellence criteria, and quality costing).
- Element 5. Reward and recognition (of individuals, teams and external suppliers).

The model is deployable at four distinct levels (Zairi & Sinclair, 1995) as demonstrated in the following figures.

Figure 1 illustrates the first 'level' of the performance measurement system model, concerned with the development of organisational strategy and the consequent deployment of goals throughout the organisation. Strategy development and goal deployment is the responsibility of senior management within the organisation, although there should be as much input into the process as possible by experts in this area and employees.

Figure 2 illustrates 'level' two, concerned mainly with aspects of process management and measurement. This process should be managed by the process owner with inputs from sub-process owners. The process outlined should be used whether an organisation is organised and managed on a process or functional basis. If the organisation is functionally organised, the key task is to identify the customer-supplier relationships between functions, and for functions to see themselves as part of a customer-supplier chain.

Figure 3 shows the third 'level' concerning the management of individuals and further explained by steps relating to performance appraisal and management. These activities should be undertaken by the individual whose performance is being managed, together with their immediate superior. The organisations examined in this study attempted to measure a combination of process/task performance (effort and achievement) and personal development. The frequency of formal performance appraisal is defined by the frequency of the appraisal process (generally within a minimum of six months). Most organisations recognised that this period was probably too long, but none suggested that they would increase the frequency. Between formal performance reviews, organisations rely on performance management techniques to manage individuals.

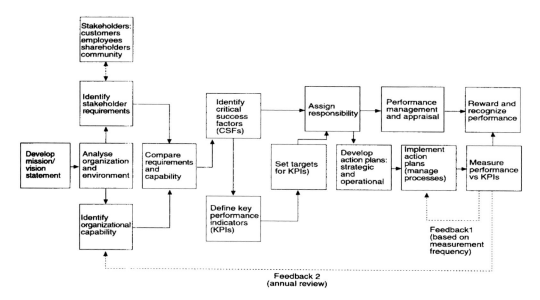

Figure 1 Strategy development and goal deployment

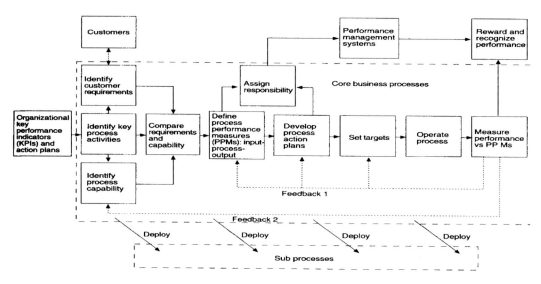

Figure 2 Process management and measurement

Figure 4 indicates the fourth 'level' concerned with gap analysis and internal/external performance assessment through benchmarking. The techniques identified for break-point assessment at the organisations examined in this study include: quality costing, self-assessment (against MBNQA or EQA criteria), customer satisfaction surveys, quality function deployment, and activity-based costing.

Finally, the fifth 'level' is concerned with reward and recognition from an output of performance measurement at the organisational process (including suppliers) and performance appraisal and management

(including performance-related pay and performance management). The proposed model considers reward and recognition as an integral element rather than one that gets 'bolted on' as found in most literatures.

Overall, the performance measurement system can be shown as a series of complementary PDCA cycles as shown in Figure 5. It should be remembered that each cycle operates at a different frequency, and within each cycle there will be individual cycles for each measurement. The frequency of the cycle is dependent on organisational level, process cycle time and criticality of the measurement.

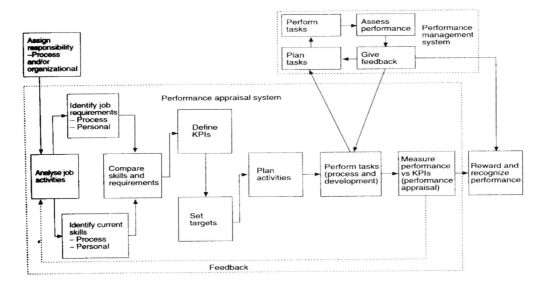

Figure 3 Individual performance measurement

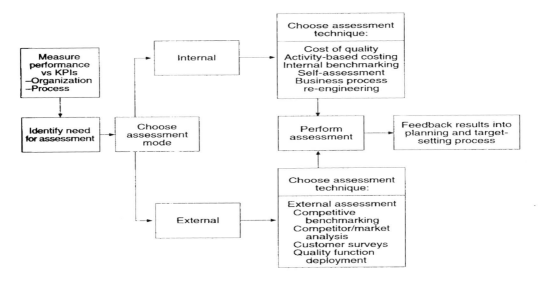

Figure 4 Benchmarking and gap analysis

Making your measurement efforts count: how to learn from the best

The following list of best practices has been compiled from various novel and model organisations (American Productivity and Quality Centre, 1997, 1999; Zairi, 1994; Drtina, 1999). These include:

1. Top management's full involvement (starting with initial system design meetings), and measurement training are key for successful implementation.

2. Performance management systems must be integrated and aligned with the annual strategic planning process. Organisations must ensure a close and direct correspondence between corporate performance measures and the vision/strategies/plans of the organisation.

3. Performance management systems must describe cause and effect through clear and direct links to organisational assessment and compensation processes.

4. Ensuring buy-in and gaining commitment from the people who will eventually implement the system is vital. In this respect, communication and training are two of the most critical success factors for performance management.

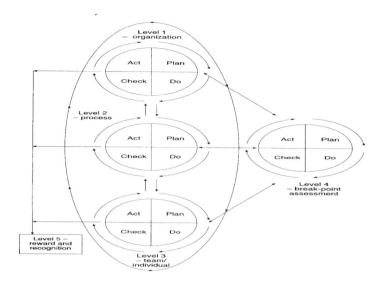

Figure 5 Performance measurement system model

5. The use of routinely generated, real-time, on-line performance information makes measures actionable and drives change throughout the organisation.

6. Continuous assessment and review of the measures and goals is essential to keep them current and effective.

References

American Productivity and Quality Centre (1999), *Achieving Organisational Excellence through the Performance Measurement System*, APQC, Houston.

American Productivity and Quality Centre (1997), *Enabling Success in Corporate Performance Measurement*, APQC, Houston.

Dale, B G (1992), 'Total Quality Management: What are the Research Challenges?', pp369–78 in R H Hollier et al, *International Opportunities: Cross Boarders in Manufacturing and Service*, Elsevier Science Publishers, BV.

Drtina, R (1999), *No Joke – Performance Measures can deliver*. Strategic Finance, Vol 81, No 2, pp 46–50.

Sink (1991), 'The role of measurement in achieving World Class Quality and Productivity Management', *Industrial Engineering*, June, pp 2–28, 70.

Zairi, M (1992), *TQM-Based Performance Measurement: Practical Guidelines*, Technical Communications (Publishing) Ltd, Letchworth, Herts.

Zairi, M (1994), *Measuring Performance for Business Results*, Chapman & Hall, London.

Zairi, M and Sinclair, D (1995), 'Performance measurement as an obstacle to TQM', *The TQM Magazine*, Vol 7, No 2.

Professor Mohamed Zairi is head of the European Centre for Total Quality Management and holds the SABIC CHAIR in Best Practice Management at the University of Bradford's School of Management.

E-mail m.zairi@bradford.ac.uk

REGULATED GROWTH: ZAHNARZTPRAXIS

A Swiss dentist used excellence to differentiate itself in a tightly regulated market.

Zahnarztpraxis, Switzerland's largest sole ownership dental practice, was founded in 1984 by Roger Harr. It is located approximately 15 kilometres from Basel in the Swiss canton of Baselland, where Harr grew up. In 2000, the practice became the first Swiss prizewinner in the European Quality Awards, and the first from the health sector to appear in the finals. The Zahnarztpraxis team's far-sighted and focused dedication to business excellence has seen the practice take further strides forward during 2001.

Zahnarztpraxis has grown in size and reputation despite the restrictive regulations of the Swiss Dentists Association (SSO)'s professional regulations, which severely limit the employment of additional dentists and do not allow advertising nor operating the practice as a legal entity or a branch establishment. Harr now leads a team of 18 staff, including four dentists and five hygienists, working in five treatment rooms in a single premises covering 180 square metres. Its quality award credentials are impressive – the only medical practice to appear in the European Quality Award finals when it became a prize winner last year, Zahnarztpraxis also won the Swiss Esprix Award 2000.

A typical country practice, the Zahnarztpraxis team is required to be generalist, covering the entire treatment spectrum to the maximum extent possible. Services cover the whole range from preventive dentistry and periodontics (gum care) through oral surgery to specialist interventions such as acupuncture. The catchment population of around 10,700 has little prospect for growth, given the narrow geographical boundaries of the Swiss side of the Jura mountains. With most of the population working in the agricultural sector, or in small mechanical engineering businesses, the average income of the district is 36 per cent lower than the cantonal average.

Zahnarztpraxis thus has an important social responsibility and cannot be solely profit-focused. Even so, the Swiss are sophisticated buyers of dental services – most treatment is paid for directly by the patients themselves – and are used to behaving like true customers in one of the world's most efficient dental systems. Harr has based his highly professional, quality-focused and proactive practice management system on a keen appreciation of likely market developments. One key trend is that dental practices will be called upon 'to distinguish between need dentistry and want dentistry, ie between objectively identifiable medical requirements on the one hand, and individual, subjective needs on the other', states the Zahnarztpraxis European Quality Award submission document. Competition is likely to stiffen once the SSO's regulations, which clash with other aspects of Swiss commercial law, are relaxed to allow advertising and the setting up of clinic centres. Despite the success of preventive care, demand will increase thanks to an ageing and more health-conscious population, which will bring its own special challenges. Technical advances and rising patient expectations will put further pressure on costs, while the prospect of Swiss integration into the European Union – resisted at present but thought by many to be inevitable – may see an influx of foreign dentists into the country (Harr points out that there are 2,000 dentists currently unemployed in Germany alone).

Faced with these possible coming challenges and changes, Harr decided that a progressive and preventative approach to business excellence was a better response than a retrospective crisis cure.

Taking a classical approach to quality processes in the medical sphere is problematic. Zahnarztpraxis points out that it would be wrong to deploy a complex approach – simplicity is the key, particularly as there are so many subjective variables affecting the output of a dental service. For example, the quality of treatment outcome cannot be guaranteed with the same level of certainty as for an industrial product, due to the complex nature of the diseases, the impossibility of calculating the course of illnesses, and the variety of solutions available (which, in turn, depend on the needs of the patient).

Standard treatments are not possible, as no two practitioners have exactly the same knowledge or preferred approach. Patient cooperation is a vital factor – even the best dental treatment will fall down if the patient does not heed advice on oral hygiene. Zahnarztpraxis points out that:

- The success of the work undertaken always depends on the post-operative behaviour of the patient.
- It can try to influence that behaviour, but can never control it totally.
- However hard it strives to achieve a perfect result, it may fail simply because of negative factors in the biological environment in which it is working. It is wrong to consider processes in a purely mechanistic light.
- It is not able to develop new materials within its practice as this would require enormous resources, well beyond its reach.

These caveats to one side, Zahnarztpraxis has plenty to smile about. Its professionals play a pioneering role in dentistry worldwide in the form of research papers and speaking engagements, and are actively involved in communicating the experience of the practice across all areas. 'We are years ahead of the sector as a whole in terms of TQM' is no idle boast. While many Swiss dentists have yet to wake up to the benefits of quality management, it is a hot topic in Germany where Harr is in demand as a speaker on management issues; at home most interest is shown by hospitals and non-medical service and industrial concerns.

Benchmarks and results

Harr has been extremely active in finding best practice benchmarks. This is no easy task in the health sector, but the problem was solved as follows:

- Since 1998, announcements and direct mail-outs were sent to many ISO-certified dental practices in Germany (37), Austria (2), Liechtenstein and Switzerland (3). Comparing this data with non-certified practices, Harr came to the conclusion that the certified practices gave him a best practice benchmark.
- Integrated in the best practice benchmarking pool are the toughest competitor in the market, the next largest practice in the north west of Switzerland, as well as other practices which prove themselves with special performance (innovation, technical competence etc).
- In relation to patient satisfaction, the practice compares itself to GPs among others, which according to the SWICS (Swiss Index of Customer Satisfaction) study have the most satisfied customers in all sectors in Switzerland
- Comparisons in the financial area are difficult to organise, and despite newspaper announcements, Zahnarztpraxis has been unable to find any benchmarking partners with a similar size and structure. For best practice values, Harr therefore took the German practices in the former West Germany, which show the best results in Germany.
- For quality of dental care, the practice worked with benchmarks from specialist clinics for each specialist field.

According to these and other measures, Zahnarztpraxis is clearly a high-performing concern. On all relevant financial criteria, it has outperformed German best practice measures by a considerable margin consistently in each of the past five years. The holistic nature of Harr's approach to practice management has resulted in high levels of staff motivation, satisfaction and trust in leadership. This is partly due to policies such as a 40-hour week (rather than the normal 42), full salary transparency and benchmarking, and a comprehensive bonus scheme to recognise special achievement. Absenteeism is low; staff retention levels are high. Most significantly, measures of clinical effectiveness across all major areas of the practice tell a similar success story – in preventative and restorative areas.

Looking forward, Harr and his team are determined to continue their proactive approach to practice management. Spreading the word about dental hygiene and business excellence is a passion for Zahnarztpraxis, and an increased programme of school visits and business networking events is planned for the coming months.

Further details on European business excellence: European Quality Publications Ltd, 39–41 New Oxford Street, London, WC1A 1BH. Tel: +44 20 7240 7474; website: www.european-quality.co.uk

COCO-MAT: EXCELLENCE IN ALL ITS FORMS

Technocrat or idealist? Paul Efmorfidis, founder of COCO-MAT, is both. He made a rousing and impassioned presentation at a conference for Greek winners of European Foundation for Quality Management awards.

Paul Efmorfitis of COCO-MAT, the Greek manufacturer of ecologically friendly mattresses and bedding – 'natural sleep products' in the company's terminology – has an important message for anyone thinking about taking a total quality management (TQM) approach. 'Unless you believe firmly that the purpose of being in business is to make better products, contribute positively to society and create a work place where your people can be happy and proud, don't bother to start.'

Striding between the aisles, shunning the microphone and wearing casual clothes in sharp contrast to the suits and ties of the delegates, Paul Efmorfidis emphasised that, for COCO-MAT and all its workers, the most important measure of success was playing a part in 'the formation of a sustainable culture, which included all types of human activity'. He threw out a challenge to everyone present, saying that he was convinced that they could all make more money if they took a New Age approach to the way in which they did business.

A fundamental pillar of operations is to encourage a spirit of solidarity and cooperation among employees. 'Moral support and encouragement of employees, assigning initiatives and developing teamwork to achieve this is the most important role that management can play,' says Efmorfidis. 'When people ask why bother to go to all this effort, I say why not? If you can make money, have fun and help people improve their lives, then the question answers itself.'

If COCO-MAT sounds like a hippy venture, then nothing could be further from the truth. It is a big business, market leader in its segment, has 31 retail outlets and exports 20 per cent of its products. It is one of the top 10 fastest growing Greek companies. Turnover increased by 4,000 per cent over 10 years and stood at over €8 million in 2000. COCO-MAT was formed in 1989 in Athens. It moved to Xanthi, a beautiful and under-developed region in Thrace (on the Greek border with Turkey and Bulgaria) in 1992, where it is located in an industrial region of 125,000 square metres. It employs 196 people and has a deliberate policy of positive discrimination for people with special skills – the term the company uses for special needs. It also employs a large number of refugees from former Eastern bloc countries and Russia, which comprise 70 per cent of the workforce. The cultural variations and multilingual patterns in the workforce are quite evident. Most of the employees do not speak the Greek language fluently. 'No problem if you enjoy rather than fear diversity,' says Efmorfidis.

While he acknowledges that this policy might be viewed as a way to obtain cheap labour, Efmorfidis denies that this is the case. His employees are paid at least as well as the average for the region and the industry. On the other hand, their desire to work hard and better their conditions, allied to high levels of education and skills, makes it obvious why COCO-MAT employs so many of the same people that normal society often marginalises. It is another example of thinking outside the box, something Efmorfidis and his team try hard to do as often as possible.

According to its founders, COCO-MAT operates like a large family, giving its employees the opportunity to get involved in the decision-making process, on issues of strategic importance, using the 'variety and freedom of opinion as motivation tools for growth and development'. COCO-MAT workers do not view their occupation simply as a means of securing an income, but also as an opportunity for personal achievement and fulfilment.

Employees receive a number of benefits such as continuous training, recognition and reward of personal achievements in the form of salary bonuses, promotions, gifts and recreation including Sunday excursions, football games and other leisure activities. Motivating its employees is consistent with the formation of a common company vision, 'by everyone, for everyone', for the creation of development prospects, perfect working conditions and a reduction of hours in the working week.

Continuous training and further education are encouraged, together with the cultivation of a positive view on the part of the employees of the social aspect of their work. Every two months, the best performances are rewarded and published in the COCO-MAT newspaper.

In addition, procedures such as 'human resources management' and 'criteria and factors for employee annual financial reward' are formalised and codified. Employee productivity is reviewed by means of the relevant productivity indices. COCO-MAT stands favourable scrutiny with the most rigorous of traditional employers in this regard, and pays attention to each and every EC directive regarding work place practice, according to its founder. For example,

COCO-MAT supports its personnel by providing continuous training, and medical insurance in excess of requirements set down by the national standard employment agreement. It provides flexible working hours and special leaves of absence for the pursuit of personal interests and activities.

This combination of an unusually open management culture combined with highly systematised processes is mirrored in the company's manufacturing activities. Advanced TQM principles such as the EFQM Excellence Model sit alongside conventional audit and inspection processes including ISO 9001:2000 and the ISO 14001 (environmental audit standard). Its mattresses, many of which are destined for hospitals and, because of their anti-allergic properties, asthma sufferers, are manufactured and inspected according to rigorous standards. It is quite literally a matter of life and death as to whether they are fit for purpose, and COCO-MAT's reputation, moreover, rests on their excellence.

The company is an avid proponent of environmentally friendly manufacturing using sustainable resources. All raw materials used for COCO-MAT products are natural, and environmentally friendly manufacturing is a matter of principle and ethics. Coco fibres, which come from the outer shell of the coconut, are taken from sustainable groves. Natural rubber from the Hevea tree is likewise culled from plantations with ethical work practices and sustainable policies. Raw wool and cotton comes from unspoiled regions of Thrace. Seaweed is used as a component of mattresses, owing to its high iodine content, said to benefit and comfort asthma sufferers. This is used to advantage in markets such as Scandinavia, Germany and Spain – where there are COCO-MAT retail outlets – which have significant numbers of green consumers. The COCO-MAT catalogue itself reflects these green credentials, produced on environmentally friendly paper using vegetable inks and to a modern but New Age design.

However, COCO-MAT has become a success by combining New Age eco-warrior practices with state-of-the-art business. It uses the most modern machinery to manufacture rubber layers to 96 per cent purity using the Tatalay method, which gives it best-in-class performance. It conducts regular and systematic customer surveys, continually updating its offering in line with feedback.

In an industry where its competitors have largely stagnated, COCO-MAT has seen consistent and pronounced growth. Its target is 45 per cent national market share for 2001. It also believes that sales will grow by a further 500 per cent over the next five years.

Among its many accolades, Maxi COCO-MAT won recognition from the Greek Ministry of Development in 1995 for its pioneering production methods and environmentally friendly products. In 1998, the Cambridge University Business and Environment Programme listed COCO-MAT as number one for ethical value. In the same year, it was awarded the SAFE Award by the European Union for its safety and hygiene in production processes.

In 2000, COCO-MAT was a finalist in the European Quality Awards for SMEs. In 2001, it went one better and become a prizewinner. Given its current rate of growth, it may outgrow the category before 2002. If it does, it will be a tribute to the unusual yet highly effective and ethically impeccable credentials of Efmorfidis, his team and his wonderfully diverse ethnic workforce, making natural sleep products in the hills of Thrace.

Further details on European business excellence: European Quality Publications Ltd, 39–41 New Oxford Street, London, WC1A 1BH. Tel: +44 20 7240 7478; website: european-quality.co.uk

INDEX OF ADVERTISERS

U.W.E.L. LEARNING RESOURCES

The Volvo S80 is the flagship model of the Volvo range and combines innovative styling, 'club class' levels of comfort and an impressive engine line-up to offer a rewarding all round driving experience.

Among the line-up are the powerful six or five-cylinder engines delivering a seamless blend of driving comfort, performance and environmental concern. You have access to the full power of the engine without pressing it – with immediate response.

The 2001 launch of the state-of-the-art, lightweight 'D5' aluminium diesel engine has enhanced the range further. The new D5 2.4 litre direct-injection five-cylinder turbodiesel is available with 163 bhp. The latest diesel engine technology utilising common rail direct injection gives excellent performance, smooth running, cleaner emissions and – not least – superior fuel economy. The engine's low weight contributes to well-balanced ride and roadholding.

Completing the line-up is the 2.4 litre five-cylinder 140 bhp Bi-fuel engine, which benefits both the environment and your wallet – without compromising driving pleasure or load capacity. It runs on gas (Natural Gas or LPG), with petrol as the reserve fuel.

From February 2002, Volvo adds 200 bhp 2.4T engine to the S80 executive saloon model. A top speed of 143 mph and 0-62 mph in 7.9 seconds, combined with low CO2 emissions and excellent fuel economy make it an attractive proposition for company car drivers, when the new company car tax rules come into place this April.

Complimenting this line-up of engines is a range of automatic and manual gearboxes. The responsive adaptive automatic adjusts the shifts to your driving style. The Geartronic transmission for the six-cylinder engines is two gearboxes in one: an adaptive automatic for relaxed driving and a manual for when you prefer more active driving. However, if you prefer to change gear yourself, then you can choose the five-cylinder engine and enjoy the smooth and distinct five-speed manual transmission.

Space and comfort were the two key parameters applied to the interior of the Volvo S80, where not just the driver, but all of the passengers enjoy a 'club class' experience. Air conditioning as standard, individual rear seat ventilation, ergonomically designed seats and excellent head and legroom for all occupants ensure that the S80 is as relaxing to ride in as it is to drive.

Combined with this interior comfort a torsionally stiff body and one of the most advanced chassis in the automotvie world make the S80 an outstanding drive. Front-wheel drive and independent suspension have been combined with a sophisticated multi-link rear wheel suspension. The result is first-class ride comfort and excellent handling.

As would be expected, the Volvo S80 confirms Volvo's position as a world leader in the field of automotive safety. The range of safety features offered includes head restraints and three-point seatbelts with pretensioners on all five seats, less aggressive front airbag inflation rates, standard anti-lock brakes and side marker lamps which make the car three times more visible from the side.

It also provides class-leading technology such as WHIPS (the Volvo Whiplash Protection System), SIPS (Side Impact Protection System) and an inflatable curtain that is concealed inside the headliner from the A-pillar to the C-pillar and increases passenger protection from head and neck injuries.

The S80 range starts from £20,640 otr. The diesel and Bi-fuel ranges start from £22,335 otr and £22,835 otr respectively.

And each car is as individual as its owner. With Volvo's 'built to order' policy the Volvo S80 offers packs, individual options and Volvo Life accessories to create and tailor the car to each driver's specific needs, thus offering real value for those looking for a comfortable five seat executive saloon.

for life